Philosophy and Everyday Life

Edited by
Laura Duhan Kaplan
University of North Carolina, Charlotte

SEVEN BRIDGES PRESS, LLC
CHATHAM HOUSE PUBLISHERS
NEW YORK · LONDON

Seven Bridges Press, LLC
135 Fifth Avenue, New York, NY 10010-7101

Executive Editor: Jehanne Anabtawi
Managing Editor: Katharine Miller
Composition: Bytheway Publishing Services
Cover design: Stefan Killen Design
Cover art: 2001 Photonica
Printing and Binding: Victor Graphics, Inc.

Library of Congress Cataloging-in-Publication Data
Philosophy and everyday life / edited by Laura Duhan Kaplan.
    p. cm.
  ISBN 1-889119-67-9 (pbk.)
    1. Life. I. Kaplan, Laura Duhan.

BD431 .P533 2002
100—dc21
                                00-012509
                                CIP

Manufactured in the United States of America
10 9 8 7 6 5 4 3 2 1

Philosophy and Everyday Life

For friends and family
who keep us firmly rooted
in everyday life

Contents

Acknowledgments

THE IDEA FOR this volume was sparked by the Society for Philosophy in the Contemporary World's (SPCW) 1996 annual meeting theme, "Philosophy and Everyday Life." Although ultimately only seven papers from the conference were included in this volume, my thanks go to SPCW members for their on-going support.

Many of the thoughtful and hardworking individuals who helped shape this book receive acknowledgment in the table of contents—they are the authors who have written the various chapters out of the raw materials of their own lives and their own philosophical education. All put up cheerfully with my heavy-handed editing of their initial submissions. I wish to thank a few additional colleagues and teachers for their inspiration and support: Laurence F. Bove, Diane P. Freedman, Clay Glad, Diana Taylor, Father Eleutherius Winance, and the anonymous reviewers chosen by Seven Bridges Press.

I particularly thank my editor at Seven Bridges, Jehanne Anabtawi, for her enthusiasm and her vision of the final product.

At the University of North Carolina at Charlotte, discussions with research assistant Brad Champion provided the basis for introductory sections. My colleagues Reginald Raymer and Donna Harding reviewed drafts of the introductory sections. UNC Charlotte secretaries Vicki Griffith and Debbra Lockett provided computer support for correspondence and PC-to-Mac translation. The University of North Carolina Foundation provided summer research funds for developing an anthology on autobiographical scholarship. And my partner, Charles Kaplan, was helpful in ways too numerous to name.

Many thanks to the staff of the following journals and press for permission to reprint articles and chapters or parts thereof. Luna Nàjera's essay "Engendering Ethnicity: The Economy of Female Virginity and Guatemalan Nationalism" originally appeared in *Radical Philosophy Review* 2:2 (fall 1999). Charlie Harvey's essay "The Malice of Inanimates" originally appeared in *Phenomenological Inquiry* 19 (October 1995).

Laura Duhan Kaplan
Charlotte, NC

Philosophy and Everyday Life

Preface:
From Reflection to Theory

WHY READ A BOOK of essays about philosophy and everyday life? After all, isn't philosophy an attempt to soar above everyday life, to think on a higher plane and spin sophisticated theories about the world? Perhaps it is, but it begins in everyday life.

Most thoughtful adults, as well as many children, have a philosophy of life—even if they cannot or do not want to express it in words. This philosophy might take the form of a set of ethical rules a person follows, or it might find expression in the quality of feeling they bring to all of their activities. A person's philosophy, and the way it is expressed, change according to experiences over his or her own life cycle.

For example, when I was sixteen years old, I invested a lot of energy in feeling independent of my parents. My guiding philosophy in all things was to figure out my *own* ways of making a life for myself. Since I liked to write, I wrote about this in my journal.

> At some point in his existence, a person begins to question the world around him. How does it fit together? Who influences my life? Who if anyone runs it? The people who think they control my life—are they any better than me? If I do what they tell me to do, where will it get me? Once I'm there, what will I have accomplished? Is that really anything? My answer: THE RELIGION OF EGOTISM!!! Its first principle: Love Thyself.

In retrospect it sounds pretty appalling. Fortunately, reflection came fairly quickly. Soon enough, I was a parent myself. My guiding philosophy became the pursuit of connections with others, hoping to find a way to wrap my life around the lives of others, neither too tightly nor too loosely. I wrote:

> You see, I now have children. In my free time, I once joked, I [get to] enjoy taking showers. Daily I am immersed in the practical problems of intelligently and enthusiastically loving others without time to replenish my energy. My attention is directed outwards from the self. The self is no longer a starting point. Others are simply placed before myself. I satisfy their needs before I satisfy my own. And their presence makes me who I am.[1]

At each stage I had different concerns and made different decisions. But, at each stage I devoted some energy to figuring out what my concerns were and how I should address them. I was "philosophizing!" In these two cases, I was concerned with the practical implications of my philosophy: figuring out how to live with family members. In coming to practical answers, I thought hard about many important but less practical questions. What are the ethical rules of life? Who makes them? Are ethical mistakes dangerous? If I make one, will I be letting anyone down besides myself? What is a "self"? Is it always connected to the other people it shares a life with, or can it take responsibility for itself and itself alone? Had my concern been opening a philosophical discussion or writing a philosophical paper, instead of solving a practical problem, *these* are the questions on which I would have focused.

Many professional philosophers start their philosophizing in precisely this way: trying to figure out how to cope with the circumstances of their lives. Obviously, their need to cope is no different from anyone else's. What makes them philosophers is their continuing interest in the questions they raise along the way. Long after the practical problems have been solved, these questions remain important to philosophical thinkers. Perhaps the questions connect what at first looks like a personal problem to a problem that is common to many people; perhaps the questions seem likely to be helpful in thinking through other challenges; or perhaps they are interesting in and of themselves because they seem to touch on enormous, exciting, or enduring issues.

Most published professional philosophy focuses on the questions rather than on the situations that provoked them. The essays in this book, however, explicitly show the connections between life situations that call for philosophical thinking and the philosophical questions that flow from them. Each of the authors, of course, has had different experiences, raises different (although related) questions, and answers them by coming to a unique philosophy of life. Each author also connects the questions and answers with the published work of other classical or contemporary philosophers, thereby making at least some use of the accepted style of contemporary philosophical writing. Most of the essays were written specifically for this book.

This book can be read on its own or in conjunction with more traditional philosophical works that stress abstract discussion. Either way, it can help readers to construct a bridge between thought-provoking questions that come up in the course of living and the more abstract discussions of philosophical questions. Some of this book's readers may be students taking a first formal course in philosophy. For these readers, who are likely to be familiar with philosophical questioning in everyday life, the book can lead to a greater appreciation of more abstract philosophical discussion. Other readers of this book may be advanced students or teachers of philosophy, comfortably immersed in technical and abstract discussions. This book can take these more experienced readers back to their roots, reminding them of the challenges that made philosophy interesting to them in the first place. It can serve them as a resource for teaching philosophy through everyday life situations and help them to share their appreciation of philosophy with others.

In order to highlight the connection between everyday philosophical thinking and the more formally organized discipline of academic philosophy, the essays in this book are organized into four sections. Each section bears the name of one of the recognized and highly developed subfields within academic philosophy: Ethics, Social and Political Philosophy, Epistemology, and Metaphysics. The essays within each section revolve around a selected theme. The themes were not chosen arbitrarily, but emerged from the essays themselves. It seems that certain themes more easily showcase the connections between philosophy and everyday life. For example, coming to a sense of self seems to inspire reflection on one's ethical commitments; becoming aware of one's social location sparks a re-evaluation of political commitments; butting up against the limits of knowledge prompts questions about epistemology; and surprising encounters with the unexpected lead to metaphysical speculation.

Readers can turn to the section introductions for more information about the philosophical subfield, the theme explored, and the individual essays included. The introductions are designed to inform novice readers of philosophy about each of philosophy's subfields and to offer all readers a brief glimpse of the themes explored in the section. The thought-provoking questions that follow the introduction invite novice readers into philosophical reflection. In every case, the introductions emphasize the philosophical questions asked and answered in the essays, rather than the philosophers cited. However, experienced readers of academic philosophy may want to know that within the pages of this book they will encounter Aristotle, Plato, David Hume, John Locke, Karl Marx, Simone Weil, Iris Murdoch, Martin Heidegger, Jean-Paul Sartre, Emmanuel Levinas, and many other "big names" from the contemporary philosophical canon.

NOTE

1. Laura Duhan Kaplan. *Family Pictures: A Philosopher Explores the Familiar* (Chicago: Open Court, 1998), 103.

PART I

Ethics: Virtuous Persons, Virtuous Principles

Introduction

OF ALL OF philosophy's subfields, ethics is the one that spins off most obviously from everyday deliberations about how we should live. Therefore, this book about philosophy and everyday life begins with essays on ethics.

Ethical deliberations take place when a person tries to figure out what to do and why. "What to do" is the practical part of the equation. But "the person trying to figure out" and the "why" are often topics for philosophical discussion.

Discussions about the why may aim to identify the most generally helpful principles for making good decisions. These discussions focus on principle-based ethics. Some principles favored by philosophers are versions of "Do unto others as you would have them do unto you," or "Always do the greatest good for the greatest number of people." A few philosophers even favor a version of "Look out for Number One—yourself." Typically, philosophers take the discussion to a deeper level and try to give reasons why their favorite principles are the best principles.

Philosophical discussions may also focus on the character of the person trying to figure things out. After all, some philosophers argue, no two situations are alike. A truly ethical person will move flexibly between different kinds of decisions—without becoming wedded to a particular ultimate moral principle. The real question is how a person develops a virtuous character. Discussions that flow from this question are considered perspectives in "virtue ethics" or "character ethics." Does developing a virtuous character involve the right upbringing, an experience of coming to maturity, a willingness to take responsibility or to honor the demands of others on our bodies and minds?

This section begins with essays that discuss virtue ethics, and concludes with essays that identify moral principles. Joe Frank Jones III, in his essay "Reluctant Soldier, Grateful Philosophy Teacher," speaks about his character both before and after his participation in the Vietnam war. Although he was determined not to repeat his father's life as a warrior, he found that without specific attention to his growth as a person, he would unwittingly do exactly that. In order to become a person in his own right, Jones had to undertake a long and difficult journey, both literal and psychological.

In his essay "To Thine Own Self Be True: Self-Appropriation and Human Authenticity," Mark J. Doorley gives a detailed analysis of his own journey to what he calls "self-appropriation"—taking control of one's own life. Self-appropriation, he argues, is a prerequisite for becoming a person who cares about ethical commitments. Doorley's journey began with his hard-won willingness to speak the truth about his failures, in his case, his alcoholism. It continued with the aid of a supportive community of friends, with the term "friends" understood as people who support one another in achieving ethical excellence.

Tabor Fisher, in her essay "The Birth of Personhood," gives a detailed analysis of the impact that supportive community can have on the experience of personhood. Speaking from her experience as a pregnant mother, she compares her first, easy pregnancy with her second, difficult one. In her first pregnancy, she felt supported emotionally and economically by family and friends. She felt as though her personhood was enhanced by her pregnancy and imagined the fetus inside her as a future person in her or his own right. During her second pregnancy, emotionally and physically draining, all her energy went into claiming her own personhood; she had little left to relate to her fetus as a person. Making connections with the contemporary debate about the morality of abortion, Fisher notes the impact that being considered a person has on the moral status of both mothers and fetuses.

In "Discipline or Domination: An Ethical Dilemma in Childrearing," Charles Kaplan builds a bridge between philosophical discussions of virtuous character and ethical principles. Speaking as a father trying to socialize his young children to be virtuous characters, he tries to find the right principles for making decisions about his parenting style. Once he articulates his goal, creating children who can be responsible and rational members of a community, he is able to choose an authoritative parenting style with confidence.

James B. Sauer, author of the dialogue "What's Wrong with Bribery?" also straddles the border between the two philosophical approaches to ethics. He argues for the ethical principle "Place the needs of society above the needs of the individual." His argument, however, depends on the ethics of character: A just society provides the context in which ethical behavior can flourish. Sauer explores his argument using the example of bribery. In the dialogue, a group of friends discuss the way in which bribery is an accepted practice in each of their professions. By the end of the dialogue, however, the friends teach each other that bribery eventually undermines systems that are built on trust and goodwill, replacing them with systems based on greed, favoritism, and economic inequality—systems that will produce individuals of corresponding character.

QUESTIONS TO GET YOU STARTED

1. When you find yourself trying to make a moral decision, what facts and principles do you take into consideration?
2. What consideration would you show a person that you would not show an object?
3. How have your ethics changed as you have grown and changed?
4. How do people learn to be ethical? Since ethics are learned in a particular social setting, are they relative to social contexts?

SUGGESTED READINGS

Aristotle. *Nicomachean Ethics*. Trans. Roger Crisp. New York: Cambridge University Press, 2000. Aristotle (384–322 B.C.E.) describes in detail the virtues of a person of good character.

Freud, Sigmund. *Civilization and Its Discontents*. New York: W.W. Norton, 1989. Freud (1856–1939) discusses the tensions between individual fulfillment and self-restraint that haunts individuals living in a society.

Gilligan, Carol. *In a Different Voice*. Cambridge, MA: Harvard University Press, 1993. Gilligan (1936–present) describes two different approaches to making moral decisions, one which honors principles and one which honors relationships.

Kant, Immanuel. *Groundwork of the Metaphysics of Morals*. Trans. James W. Ellington. Indianapolis: Hackett, 1993. Kant (1724–1804) articulates a principle that underlies all ethical behavior.

Kaplan, Laura Duhan. *Family Pictures: A Philosopher Explores the Familiar*. Chicago: Open Court, 1998. Kaplan (1959–present) describes her moral growth as she takes increasing responsibility for the care of family members.

Mill, John Stuart. *Utilitarianism and Other Essays*. New York: Viking, 1987. Mill (1806–1873) argues that ethical actions result in the greatest good for the greatest number of people.

Nietzsche, Friedrich Wilhelm. *Beyond Good and Evil: Prelude to a Philosophy of the Future*. Trans. Walter Kaufmann. New York: Vintage Books, 1989. Nietzsche (1844–1900) turns ethics on its head, arguing that moral virtue is really a sign of weakness.

Sartre, Jean Paul. *Existentialism and Humanism*. New York: Haskell House, 1977. Sartre (1905–1980) argues that we are free to choose our actions, which make us who we are.

Reluctant Soldier, Grateful Philosophy Teacher

Joe Frank Jones III

Joe Frank Jones III is a professor of philosophy and religion at Barton College in Wilson, North Carolina. In the essay below, he learns about who he is through many avenues, including philosophy. His journey continues with his current writing project, a book that connects ethics with metaphysics.

A KIND PERSON privy to the inner workings of the draft board in Fairfax, South Carolina, in September of 1968, told my grandmother my name was coming up. In 1968, young men nineteen and 1-A were being drafted into the Marine Corps and Army for duty in Vietnam. There was no lottery. I had personally achieved the 1-A draft classification by flunking out of Clemson University the year before. Shortly after my grandmother called, I mentioned to my father the possibility of going to Canada to avoid a war I thought worthy of less than my life. He told me he would find me and kill me if I did such a shameful thing.

My father, Joe Jr., had grown up in Fairfax, the son of an alcoholic father and an inattentive mother. His mother had married his father on a dare, the story went, because her girlfriends didn't believe this charming, handsome, talented Lothario could be tamed. Although Joe Sr. had a good job with the railroad, he could not get home with a paycheck sober, and was finally fired. They divorced when my father was ten. In a tiny, Southern Baptist town in the thirties, this was hard on my father. He flunked out of Clemson University in 1943, and enlisted in the Army Air Corps at seventeen.

Joe Jr. went to basic training, then was ordered to attend West Point on the basis of aptitude tests. He stubbornly refused, saying he wanted to be a pilot and didn't like college anyway. He was ordered to pick up cigarette butts on the parade ground until he changed his mind. Two weeks later a new commanding officer wanted to know who the hell that was policing the parade ground. A spirited conversation had Joe Jr. headed for Florida and pilot training. In Florida, it was quickly discovered that his eyes did not work in tandem to produce normal depth perception. I thought about this later and often, as he tended to tailgate and drive too fast. He was relegated to tail gunner's school, then assigned to a B-17 crew headed for England. A year later, he was the only one of that crew alive.

The crew flew twenty-two and one-half missions over Germany. During the twenty-third mission, in March of 1945, they collided with another B-17 in foul weather. The tail section was cut away from the fuselage with Joe Jr. in it. He could not get out through the twisted metal, and fell 13,500 feet into a plowed field near Ostende, Belgium. The field was owned by Mr. Henri Rijkeboer (whom we met later) and was only two weeks liberated from Nazi control. The rest of the crew perished. My younger brother is named for the pilot. Joe Jr. was nineteen.

Mr. Gilbert Deschepper watched the tail section fall. He had been an active member of the Belgian underground during the occupation. His bicycle carried him to the wreckage, where he reached inside and discovered someone breathing, barely. He called Mr. Rijkeboer over and they cut the survivor out. They deposited him in a farmhouse bedroom, and Mr. Deschepper rode off to get the nearest physician. The physician had been a Nazi sympathizer and came to examine the American flyboy only at gunpoint. Mr. Deschepper was a large man and could be very forceful. The doctor said my father would die and refused to administer morphine until again forced. Mr. Rijkeboer and Mr. Deschepper then carried Joe Jr. in a farm truck to an English mobile tent hospital in the vicinity of Ostende. Joe Jr. underwent surgery and remained unconscious for eight days. Mr. Deschepper rode his bicycle to the hospital every morning to check on him.

When they met, my father found a surrogate father. It was a good trade. Joe Sr. died in 1945, having fallen into a tub with the hot water running in the days before regulated hot water heaters. He was scalded to death. The newspaper said he was knocked unconscious in the fall. I was told he was drunk.

My family spent a lot of time with Gilbert and his wife, Rachel, during a tour of duty in Wiesbaden, Germany, from 1961 to 1964, when I was twelve to sixteen. I remember Gilbert (pronounced Jo-bear) vividly. He was large, quiet, and seemed strong. We were told by others he had accounted for the deaths of perhaps a hundred Germans during the war. Since the war, he had become head chef for a ferry line crossing the English Channel. He had also gathered around him a magical army of intensely loyal younger men, including my father. Most were abandoned teenagers he had picked up around the waterfronts on both shores. He worked them hard in the hot kitchens of his ships, and "made men of them." It seemed they would all die for him on a moment's notice.

By then Joe Jr. was considered a minor hero himself. His plane wreck and survival were the subject of a "Ripley's Believe It or Not" cartoon, and the story was recounted in a book titled *Silver Wings*. Visits with Gilbert and Rachel were covered by European newspapers. It was heady for a small town boy. The air war itself was enough to change a person. I recommend the movie *Memphis Belle* if you want a feel for it. Joe Jr. dedicated himself completely to his country. Perhaps it was the only source of positive reinforcement he had ever found.

He attached himself to a fledgling outfit called the Office of Special Investigations (OSI), part of the new air force. The whole idea of the OSI appealed to his ego and sense of romance. He wore civilian clothes, had no rank designation on his military ID save "S/A" for "Special Agent." Later, he carried a gun and a cyanide capsule and would be gone for periods of time. We would receive phone calls at exactly five o'clock every afternoon. A voice would say, "Mrs. Jones, your husband is fine. Have a good evening." I discovered as an adult that he smoked his cigarettes exactly like Humphrey Bogart in *Casablanca*.

He never talked about what he did. I caught him in an unusually relaxed and open mood long after his retirement and said, "As a teenager, I always thought you were a government assassin or something." He protested that it wasn't like that at all, just routine business mostly, "only once or twice did anything like that. . . ." He ground to a halt, and with unfocused eyes moved away to other things. He knew I knew. I knew he knew I knew. We both thought of the time I threatened to kill him, but that was after my war. I am ahead of myself.

Not having the weight to oppose my father at nineteen, I enlisted in the Air Force, at least avoiding the Army or Marine Corps. I was sent to the longest technical school they had, Electronic Counter-measures (ECM). After basic, I discovered many kindred spirits: reluctant enlistees who made an art form of being alienated from the socio-politico-economic machine of war which was, for us, our environment. Part of it was simple shame. We took refuge in drugs, sex, and underground political posturing. An incident from the ECM shop at Udorn, Thailand, may give you a bit of the flavor.

A fellow in the shop discovered a wire in a huge bundle behind the pilot's seat of an F-4 fighter/bomber that, if cut, would prevent the plane from dropping any ordnance. There would be no warning indication in either cockpit that the wire had been cut. The younger troops met in the back room of the shop to discuss how to handle this information. The division between alienated draft dodgers and career military "lifers" was so clear and deep that we knew who should and should not be there. It was noted in the meeting that F-4s cannot land loaded, which meant the plane would be sacrificed at the very least. It was further noted that a loaded F-4 cannot outrun a Russian MIG-23, which crews were reporting seeing over Hanoi lately. So the sabotage would, in all likelihood, sacrifice the crew as well. It made us feel good to decide not to cut the wires, even though stopping the death machines would have been to us a positive. It seemed we were refusing to play by the rules our country was observing. Killing would not be our reaction to a vulnerable target.

My personal experience diverged from that of my peers when I openly insulted a pilot. This young major, with the assistance of two other higher-ranking officers who had suffered the same treatment, arranged for me to attend an impromptu Marine survival school, then spend thirty days with the Marines guarding the perimeter of the base. I believed that these high-ranking men wanted me dead. I almost did die of fright when we met our "trainers." These men had just walked from Vietnam, through Cambodia, to Thailand. The smell of the killing fields was as fresh as the ears on the neck of a young man who stared contemptuously at us through eyes from somewhere I never wanted to go. I was grateful when he snorted in contempt and walked away with most of his group of twenty-five or so, leaving three to show us how to use the tools of the trade: M-16s, M-60 machine guns, grenades and grenade launchers, field radios, and slap flares.

There were large numbers of troops from at least three separate armies moving sporadically through northeastern Thailand in 1971. I listened in focused fear for four days to these three battle-hard men, knowing I may need what they were teaching me. With all channels open, I learned not only how to use the weapons, but I learned something about them. Among men at war, there are both hopeless killers and professional fighting men. Oliver Stone contrasted the two in the movie *Platoon*. If our teachers frightened me, I am still grateful they were the latter.

"Guard duty" turned out to be a euphemism for serving as an early warning system in case of attack. We were far enough away from the runway for the planes to take off if we radioed in that we were being overrun. While we did not have the firepower to withstand an assault of any strength, it was yet suicide for a lone "sapper" to be noticed by us. It was lonely and cold, staring into the otherwise beautiful countryside, wondering how many VC, Pathet Lao, or Khmer Rouge soldiers had your head crosshaired with starlight scopes out there in the dark.

My ostensible post was just beyond a heap of electromechanical carrion that had once been a couple of dozen F-4s. Wrecked or shot-up beyond repair, they had been hastily picked up by helicopter or bulldozed out toward the perimeter, not even stripped of classified gear in the haste of war. About two A.M. one cold December night, an American K-9 Corps soldier, with his dog, walked silently up behind me. He failed to offer the usual small noise considered polite, not to mention safe, in such situations.

I was sitting on a turned-up concrete block when I first heard him. He was close. It did not help that a sapper had been killed a couple of nights earlier not far from my post. Spinning, M-16 on full automatic, blood suddenly full of adrenaline, I searched desperately for some clue who was there. Finally, interpreting the soldier as this particular poor bastard, completely stoned, probably being led from cache to cache of drugs by his dog, I pleaded with the fates that the gun not go off though my finger was heavy on it. The silence of the night was blessedly welcome as ammunition clips, slap flares, and fieldjacket/flak vest buckles and straps finally stopped clanking or sizzling around. We never spoke.

My blood became ice as he ambled slowly away. Minutes later I shook as hot tears ran over cold cheeks. For the next several hours I went through a fundamental change. I have said since that I experienced a negative conversion. Piece by piece, I unloaded the tradition and upbringing I had received from my father, my church, my teachers, and my country. By morning I was naked. The conscious thought ran through my mind that it would be fine to be executed for the most heinous crime imaginable, so long as I had made my own decision to commit that crime. Having avoided turning the M-16 on myself, an incredible lightness of being coursed through my veins. I felt great. I could kill, and survive killing, even in an unjust cause. I would not realize for eight years just how alone and dangerous I became at that moment.

In May of 1972, I volunteered to assist in dismantling the ECM shop at DaNang, Vietnam, in preparation for giving the base to the ARVN (South Vietnamese Army). I volunteered in exchange for an early out to attend college that fall. Rocket attacks were frequent at night. I saw my first dead American. Loading the shop into a cargo plane, we hung on the side nets, retreating to Takh Li, Thailand. I had been in the military three years, nine months at that point and cashed in the early out. Two weeks later, I was standing in the living room of my parent's house in Savannah, Georgia, already registered for fall classes at Armstrong State College.

It was a quiet, humid morning. Children played in the wide streets in an elite subdivision called Wilmington Park. Mothers chatted in large yards, coffee cups in hand, smiling watchfully at their boys and girls. A 340 Dodge Duster suddenly squalled around a corner and blasted through at very high speed, a seemingly drunk teenager at the wheel. He turned and headed back through. Mothers rushed to gather their young. One young woman, incensed by the rude invader, stood in the street to wave him down. She was forced to leap aside as he recklessly blew through again, ignoring the distinction between grass and road surfaces. I walked quickly out through the garage, reaching under the seat of my brother's Volkswagen for his .357 handgun on the way, and walked into the street.

As I approached, several housewives had run to assist the stalwart but vanquished one. They dropped into staring silence. I noted their unease and reflected on it as I primarily listened to the car, which moved further and further away. Where I had lived for twenty-two months, my behavior would have been expected. Someone needed to kill that driver. I seemed in good position. But these women had not been with me for those twenty-two months. They were frightened—by the driver and by me. "I am in their world," I said to myself, "they are not in mine, and I am wrong in their world." I am grateful the car did not return, but this quickly became the less significant turning away from killing that morning.

My father, probably humiliated at the sight of his son standing in the street armed, rushed out of the house yelling, "Put the G_____n gun down!" I was calm as he ran toward me. I took a step toward him, slightly raising my left arm, protecting the gun in my right, quite ready to handle him physically. The move caught him completely by surprise. He skidded to a stop. Our eyes locked. He realized something about me he had apparently never imagined. He knew what I thought of my war as opposed to what he thought of his. He remembered his threat, which pushed me into my war. We both remembered our admiration for Gilbert Deschepper and the deadly violence of which Deschepper was capable. He saw it in me and turned white as a sheet. I thought he was going to faint. Then he stood straight, his eyes now blazing, and tucked his chin to signal the next move was mine. I walked to the garage and put the gun away. We both understood that I would never live at home again.

SOME REFLECTION

A week after the incident in Wilmington Park, I began an introduction to philosophy course. I wanted nothing from school but power. I saw degrees as a way to keep myself from being exploited again, as I had felt in the military. But as the professor spoke on that first day, I discovered brand new feelings and possibilities. This man, this philosophy teacher, seemed dedicated to no higher cause, obedient to no intellectual or emotional authority, and spoke of ideas subversive of tradition casually, clearly, and without apology. They were simply important issues: God's existence, civil disobedience, rational autonomy, etc. I couldn't believe it.

And he seemed an acceptable person in America, a hope I had nearly given up. He paid taxes, voted, and had a wife and children. It was a seed planted that flowered later, as it dawned on me that power need not be my only issue There might be an actual place for me in the culture. In my mind I have always contrasted my own reaction with that of a woman who sat beside me during that first class. As I sat afterward, ecstatic, she turned to me and said, "This class hurts my head," and I never saw her again. Philosophy doesn't seem to be for everyone.

My brother's friends told me that for the first year I was home, they were convinced I was addicted to a narcotic. My silence and physical presence were eerie, they said, as I never had my back to people and watched my environment too closely. That I never turned up dead from an overdose, or went mad, was a surprise. One admitted he was frightened to be around me. For a while it did seem I spent a lot of time talking myself out of hurting someone.

As luck would have it, I was encouraged by a next-door neighbor to read for a part in a play. The Little Theater in Savannah turned out to be an impressive thing. The director had acted for years with the Royal Shakespearean Academy's Traveling Troupe. I read. The director called, saying my look was perfect for the lead role, but my voice, though promising, would have to have its patterns modified significantly. He seemed to think I was worth the investment, but he warned it would be very hard work. He wanted my assurance that I was willing to work hard. If I knew I needed the theater, I didn't know I knew. The work forced me to think about how I was relating to other people, how to communicate my motives and desires through my body and my voice. It probably saved my life, because I began to realize how lonely and separate I felt.

After three years of intense study and four plays, I was headed for graduate school. Part of me was always trying to work through my loneliness and sense of shame, while another part was becoming intellectual. I explained myself now by saying that literary criticism seemed inadequate, therefore I would seek method in philosophy. Writing a master's thesis on the rationality of science, I described myself as realizing that understanding science required going deeper into its historical roots in the Greeks. A year or so before finishing a dissertation on Aristotle's view of geometry, and being awarded a doctoral degree, I realized I not only knew nothing but was still miserable as well.

I was technically competent, but my projects hung by sky hooks, with nothing but my own ambition connecting them into any whole. I was profoundly lonely and disturbed. Slowly, I realized that my guard duty epiphany and concomitant rejection of authority, seemingly reinforced so often and deeply by my philosophy teachers, was a form of ideological slavery. Just as children who try to establish their identity by doing nothing of which their parents might approve are controlled by those parents, I was controlled by my rejection of all things that smacked of the status quo. Even at this point, I tried to describe what was happening intellectually. I said that the assertions of science have no more epistemological respectability than the assertions of religion.

This was my way of moving closer to something I had dismissed as weak, useless, and evil in its institutional support of stupid government policies and decisions. I looked more openly into the history of not just the white church but the liberating black church in America. This caused me to think about the actual dynamics of personal and societal transformation and the embrace given tradition on the part of most successful reformers: Martin Luther King Jr., Jesus, and even Socrates, just to name a few.

This puzzling new identity caused me to look for a woman in whom I had been interested but left behind because she was religious. Incredibly, she was still single. We married and now have a wonderful child, Jesse Leandra. Her name means "God's graceful lioness." Even after this marriage, I struggled with a deep and arrogant prejudice against religious persons. A year of seminary allowed me to both work away from the prejudice and reintegrate my education. I began teaching part time at a liberal arts college close by. In a few years, a position opened up and I was hired full time. As I enter the sixth year of full-time teaching, I still look out at my students wondering what they see in me, remembering myself at the beginning.

Of course, few students have military experience these days, though there are some. It is more likely that today's students left home waving good-bye to a father with his arm around his third wife, his fourth martini of the day in his other hand. As they walk away, he says "Be true to yourself, kid." When they arrive here, they immediately transfer all of their cynicism and hostility to me. I must not only entertain, excite, challenge, and offer first-rate material, but must console and manufacture trust at the same time. I fail frequently, but it is honorable failure in an honorable task. Philosophy can be a mere intellectual exercise or can promote useful emotional and intellectual maturity. I succeed enough for it to be fulfilling.

If I had not come to consider my technical training in philosophy personally useless, and my power desires to have failed, I would never have discovered the riches philosophy offers. If I had never threatened to kill my father, I would never have understood how meaningful fathers are in their children's lives. I would also have never appreciated the stories of shame and redemption that inform my own religious heritage. It is these transformational moments that are our growth and development. I offer my students an entrance into a conversation rich enough to provide transformational moments for them. And, I am so pleased when they begin to accomplish this task of remaking themselves. It is their only real strength as they face an uncertain future.

In conclusion, we are all like the stream in a Sufi story. The stream has become a bog at the edge of a desert, lamenting its inability to cross. The wind whispers that the stream must let go of being a stream, and evaporate into the air, in order to cross. The stream is loathe to part with its identity, but the wind points out it has already become something other than a stream. It is a bog. Giving up, the stream discovers after being borne across the desert and falling as rain on the other side that it becomes a real stream again. Though in the same state as once before, the stream is transformed by knowing its own capacity for transformation. It is this dynamic that philosophy illuminates for me and that I wish to pass on to my students. It is a way to know ourselves better and to offer better parts of ourselves to others.

STUDY QUESTIONS
1. What issues of personal growth did Jones seem to be facing?
2. Jones says he experienced a life-changing event as he stood on guard duty one night. What was the nature of that event?
3. How did philosophy help Jones understand himself and create his own adult life?

To Thine Own Self Be True: Self-Appropriation and Human Authenticity

Mark J. Doorley

Mark J. Doorley teaches on the Ethics Faculty at Villanova University outside Philadelphia, Pennsylvania. His teaching builds upon his conviction that learning happens most effectively when the "place" of learning is one's own life. This conviction was forged in the fire of his own struggle with addiction.

THE MOST DIFFICULT words I have ever uttered had just escaped my mouth: My name is Mark and I am an alcoholic. My face and neck flushed red; the hair on the back of my neck stood up; my pulse was racing; I broke out into a cold sweat. I thought I was going to have a heart attack, yet I had only declared myself an alcoholic. Such a declaration was the end result of a long process during which I resisted such a claim. I fought against the truth of the statement and it was only after a process involving friends, family, self-honesty, and the grace of something beyond me, that I was able to utter those words, albeit under some physical duress. With the utterance of those simple, yet profound words, I spoke from my heart, from my depths, for perhaps the first time in my life.

Speaking from one's depths, uttering the truth about oneself, acting from the heart, are various ways of articulating the goal of ethics. The study of ethics is not a passing on of the ten commandments of human living. It is not the process by which the teacher gives the student a list of activities that are sanctioned as human and good, guaranteeing the student a happy life if only she or he would abide by this list. On the contrary, ethics is a journey of self-exploration leading to the discovery of one's heart, the center of authenticity in word and deed. It is a search for truth, one's own truth. It is not a solipsistic search that ends with one staring into a mirror at one's reflection, the sum total of all that is. It is a search that is accomplished only in community, only in conversation. It is the propaedeutic to human fulfillment and happiness. It is a continual search; it is an unfinished platonic dialogue, constantly striving for the "heart" of things.

My search began many years ago when I was first introduced to philosophy. It was not introduced as another subject whose answers must be memorized for the exam. It was introduced as a way of life. It is a way of life that enables the individual to uncover who and what she or he is. It enables the individual to utter the truth about herself or himself and then act in accord with that truth. What began those many years ago under the tutelage of my "Socrates" came to a defining point that Sunday afternoon over 12 years ago when I opened my mouth and declared myself an alcoholic.

This essay is an exploration of the process by which an individual appropriates herself or himself as an ethical being. We are ethical beings, whether we appropriate ourselves as such or not, because we are actors in the world. We make decisions and abide by them many times a day. The philosopher reflects on our character as ethical beings in order to facilitate a more regular attainment of authentic human action. If we can become more intelligent, more reasonable, and more responsible in our actions, perhaps we can overcome the personal and social ills that beset our time. It is self-appropriation that conditions the possibility of intelligent, reasonable, and responsible action.[1]

In order to explore this process adequately we will need to discuss several components of the process. These components include the role of questions, the role of the multileveled community of which one is a member, the affective dimension of human experience and the world-constitutive character of human action. By drawing these components into the light of analysis, I hope to extend an invitation to the reader to enter into the process of self-appropriation, which alone can supply the method by which one can achieve authenticity. First, though, I must say a word about the task of self-appropriation.

SELF-APPROPRIATION

There is a kind of person in our midst who is a drifter. The drifter follows the leanings of the crowd, a crowd whose identity changes as often as the direction of the wind. This person does not appreciate that she or he is the originator of action in her or his life. The drifter does not know that one's life is their own, and it will be what she or he decides to make of it. The drifter is not a bad person or one who is actively seeking a life of inauthenticity. However, because she or he is drifting, without an anchor sunk deep in her or his own truth, she or he is pulled this way and that by the current of a passing fad.

My high school and college years were those of a drifter. I wore the clothes that other kids wore. I listened to the music that others liked. I learned to like the drinks that others thought were "cool." I remember deciding to learn how to drink Scotch because a man I admired drank it. I was so unable to identify myself as an individual with my own tastes and dreams that I lived off the tastes and dreams of those around me. I drifted through life without an anchor.

Beside the drifter, there are also people in our midst who are engaged in the process of self-appropriation. Their actions and words manifest an ongoing reflective process that anchors them in a sense of identity. They have understood that who they are and who they can become result largely from actions taken and actions not taken. They know that they are the originators of their own identity and responsible action. They judge as valuable the fact that intelligent, reasonable, and responsible action is the normative path to human fulfillment and human authenticity.

Today I have a sense of who I am. My identity supplies me with a starting point for reflecting on the way in which I can meet the various demands of a particular day. I no longer depend on the opinions of others as to what my mood and direction ought to be. I can make decisions that reflect who I am and who I want to become. For most of my life I looked to the expectations of my parents, of my faith community, and of my friends for hints as to the kind of life I ought to be living. The realization dawned slowly that no one else is responsible for my life. I alone am the one who must live in my own skin. I understood that I have to participate in the difficult process of asking questions, seeking answers, asking for advice, and standing on my own two feet in the making of decisions that are constitutive of who and what I am.

The fruit of self-appropriation is twofold. First, there is a sober assessment of who one is as a human being in general and as this particular human being. This sober assessment includes an acknowledgment of one's past and a clear recognition of the value of that past. The successes and the failures of one's past are beneficial to the ongoing responsible performance of one's humanity. A second fruit of self-appropriation is a clearer sense of where one is headed. An aspect of authentic human existence is a sense of purpose and meaning in one's life. Life is more than a random collection of experiences in which identity is simply that which suffers through this collection. Self-appropriation reveals that human existence is fundamentally open to the future. This future includes not only that which is beyond one's control, but also, and more importantly, that which is in one's control. The self-appropriated individual knows, for the first time, that she or he is responsible for who she or he becomes in the journey of life.

As a drifter, I thought that my life was the sum total of all the expectations of the people around me: my parents, my church, my teachers, and my friends. I lived my life on the basis of those expectations, never questioning whether or not those expectations met with my own sense of what I wanted to do with my life. I did not have a sense of what I wanted to do! It was not until I was at the bottom of my struggle with alcohol that it occurred to me that my "problems" were primarily of my own making.

A few weeks before I was able to call myself an alcoholic, I was with some friends in a shopping center. We enjoyed a wonderful lunch at a popular eatery. During the lunch I had a few drinks. I did not think I was intoxicated, but I did begin to make rather rude comments to people at other tables. I commented on their clothes, the food they were eating, and the topics of their conversations. My friends were embarrassed and actually got up from the table and left me there, by myself! I was mortified! Then it occurred to me that I would not be in this predicament if I had not acted in the way I had acted. I was the one responsible for this state of affairs. Never so clearly did I understand how responsible I was for my life and its many difficulties. It also occurred to me that I was responsible for changing the direction in which my life was moving.

The process of self-appropriation begins before one is able to participate reflectively in it. My experience at the shopping center was the dawning of my own reflective participation. However, the process began in and through the experiences of my life to that point. Until that moment of insight, sitting alone at the eatery table, I was not aware of the process. This lack of awareness had limited my ability to participate actively in the constitution of my own life. Only with the benefit of a healthy after-the-fact viewpoint did I realize that the changes wrought in my life began long before I actively participated in the process. As a nonparticipant in my own life, I was a drifter. I held onto the opinions of those around me. In my own opinion I was an empty shell of a human being. There was nothing of value in my life, so I looked to those around me to give me value. This was my situation as a drifter.

Not every drifter thinks of herself or himself as valueless, but every drifter does not think to look within herself or himself for direction and purpose. Some people are not given the opportunity to enter into their own darkness in order to find the light. Others are not interested, which is to say that they have not met a person whose identity is strong enough to attract them into the walk within. Some drifters, like the one I had been, have learned to hate themselves, or to consider themselves beyond redemption, beyond salvage. The reality of the drifter's noncommittal, chameleon-like character is not an abnormal reality. Each human person must begin as a drifter and be invited by those who have gone before to enter into the journey toward self-appropriation.

Although the process of my own self-discovery or self-appropriation began before my alcoholic admission, it was not until I made the decision to accept and act upon my alcoholism that I took a fully active part in the process. My alcoholic admission centered me in an identity. Until that admission I had no sense of identity or purpose. With a center, with an identity, I answered the invitation to walk deep within my self, finding there resources of which I had never dreamed. I responded to the challenges of those others in my life who were engaged in their own processes of self-discovery. I awoke to my own resources for the first time. The possibility of a life lived from within my own center was presented as a real possibility. I had not known that such a thing was possible. The truth about who and what I am began to be revealed to me in and through the process of self-appropriation.

Self-appropriation is a process. It is a process to which one can only be invited. It cannot be commanded or mandated. It is a highly personal process, but its results are highly public. While the work of self-discovery occurs within the confines of intimate relationships, the result of the work affects all the people in one's life, from one's significant other to the driver of the local bus. Self-appropriation is a way of life. It is the way by which one can reach an authentic human existence. It has completely changed my life. I am no longer a drifter. I am a man who knows who he is, and I am willing to take responsibility for the person that I am today. This is a first step toward a life lived well.

THE ROLE OF QUESTIONS

The goal of the process of self-appropriation is to understand, judge, and choose ourselves as actors in the world. The process begins with a simple question: Who am I? It is a simple question, but like all questions it has the power to disturb the one to whom the question is addressed. To have the power to disturb and to actually disturb the recipient of the question are two different things. A question only disturbs a person if she or he intuitively knows that the question is a challenge to something or someone that she or he holds as a value in life. The question which most disturbed me was asked by a friend: "Do you have a problem with alcohol?" It disturbed me because I had a sense, a vague sense, that I was drinking too much, but I was at that moment not willing to deal with my drinking problem. I had succeeded in convincing myself that a drinking problem was not the issue in my life. My friend's question threatened to unravel my carefully spun rationalizations.

Even more significant is how people deal with the questions. Some people may be so ignorant of their own value conflicts that the question does not even register as a challenge to their way of living. Some people recognize the challenge and yet are unwilling to accept it and so react with anger or derision. Other people recognize the challenge and attempt to answer it with a sophistic twisting of words such that the questioner achieves more confusion than clarity. Lastly, some people recognize the challenge and allow the question to work its transformative effect.

My response to my question shifted as I approached my alcoholic Waterloo. When the friend of the previous paragraph suggested that I had a drinking problem, I exploded with anger. I knew he was more right than I was, but I refused to recognize his concern for me. As my drinking increased, the questions of others and my own questions began to work their transformative effect on me. These questions revealed the possibility of a different way to live.

These questions concern the meaning of one's life, one's identity. They are asked of us by others. We ask them of ourselves. However, we must answer them ourselves. As questions, they presuppose and reveal a limit. This limit is the imaginary line between what a person knows and what a person does not know. The knowledge to which I refer includes both the knowledge of fact, such as the circumference of a circle with x diameter, and the knowledge of value that underlies any given action. Questions presuppose a limit to one's knowledge. If this were not the case, one could answer the question promptly when it is asked. Besides a revelation of the limit to one's knowledge, a question is also an invitation. It is an invitation to go beyond one's previously achieved knowledge and acquire new knowledge in answer to the question. A question invites the answerer to move beyond the present known situation into the unknown.

As noted above, the question that eventually worked its transformative effect on me concerned alcohol. Did I have a problem with it? Most of the time the question came from someone else. It was not until the last year of my drinking that I began to incessantly ask myself that question. As long as my friends did not challenge my drinking, I had convinced myself that drinking was not my problem. I did not want to deal with my drinking because I enjoyed it. However, as the number of concerned people increased and as my own behavior became more and more erratic, I began to ask the question myself. As soon as I asked the question, it transformed my situation, however slight that transformation was at first. I moved from a situation in which I was drinking without an acknowledged concern to a situation in which my drinking was suddenly a major concern—not only for me, but for important people in my life. My life began to change because the question had become my question. As long as the question belonged to someone else, regardless of how important that person was to me, I could deny the relevance of the question. Having asked the question myself, I could never again lead the life I enjoyed at that time without the knowledge that a question had been raised about it.

This particular question demanded a yes or no answer. The yes or no that might have been given as an answer to the question rested on a judgment about the facts of the situation. The appropriate answer was yes if and only if the situation was such as to merit that answer. Was there sufficient evidence for making such a judgment? In my particular case there was sufficient evidence, and it was totally appropriate for me to say, "Yes, I have a problem with alcohol." In fact, as the last year of my drinking progressed, I knew that I was an alcoholic. The facts were clear to me; they had been clear to others for quite some time.

Notice, though, how the question can transform a situation. As far as I was concerned, my life was normal. It was true that I was having some interpersonal difficulties, but I thought that was a normal human situation. However, when the question concerning a possible alcoholic problem was raised, my perspective on my life began to change. Even though I continued to fight the implications of the question, and even deny the question, I experienced the results of looking at my life from this new perspective, that of an alcohol problem. I began to notice that many of my interpersonal problems were connected to my drinking alcohol. I began to notice my moods before, during, and after my drinking sessions. I had been convinced that my problems were either caused by the people with whom I was having a problem or they were caused by my own character flaws. I was either a victim of others' abuse or I was the great abuser of others because of my twisted character. The possibility that I had a drinking problem opened up new ways to understand the source of my interpersonal problems.

Questions introduce the possibility of new perspectives. They challenge us to look at a situation from a new point of view. Wonderful questions are those that suggest a novel way of judging or evaluating a situation. Such questions have tremendous power to transform a given situation for the better. Their transformative power rests in their ability to throw new light on one's life.

There are questions that ask about the facts: Am I an alcoholic? But there are also questions that ask about the values by which one lives one's life. After I made the judgment that I was an alcoholic, I was confronted by a new question: Is being an active alcoholic good? This question concerned the value of the factual situation that I had come to know in answering the question about my alcohol problem. I judged that I was an active alcoholic. Then I asked myself: Is that good? How I answered this question had ramifications for how I answered a further question: What am I going to do about my alcohol problem? The first question concerned the value of a given known situation: my active alcohol problem. The second question concerned the value of a possible course of action.

Take note of how transformative each of these questions can be. The first question suggests that I am able to make a judgment about the value, or lack thereof, of a given situation. I can judge whether or not being an active alcoholic is good. How I answer this question is a function of my affective, intellectual, and moral development, a subject which lies outside the scope of this essay. However, that I can answer this question is apparent. The question of value reveals my ability to make value judgments about my world.

The second question, "What am I going to do?" suggests that it is within my power to either maintain the status quo or to act in such a way that the status quo changes. Once again, this question reveals the possibilities of human responsibility. That I can assume, and have assumed, responsibility for my life is evident in the fact that my life has changed as the result of my decision to change the status quo.

Questions invite the questioner or the questioned beyond themselves in knowledge of fact, knowledge of value or ethical behavior. Questions indicate the limits of present knowledge and performance; they also indicate the possibility of transcending those limits. In my own struggle to come to terms with the life that was falling apart around me, despite my unwillingness to emerge from the darkness of my self-imposed ignorance, the questions with which my friends and family challenged me began the transformative process that brought me to that Sunday afternoon so many years ago.

MULTILEVELED COMMUNITY

Questions are asked by concrete persons. Concrete persons exist in concrete communities. Unless we are hermits, we are never so isolated that we have no contact with a community of persons whose lives impinge on ours and on whose lives we impinge by our words and deeds. The process of self-appropriation occurs in a community of people who are, more or less, also walking through this process. What kind of community exists around me and what kinds of ties I have with it are important factors in the journey toward authentic existence.

A community is always multileveled in this complex world of ours. Not all human relationships are equally valuable nor are they equally constitutive of the individuality and authenticity of the person. Communities are made up of families, circles of friends, circles of employment relationships, circles of voluntary associations, circles of local, state, and national political relationships. Today there is a growing awareness of the world community and the links that bind us together across oceans. These overlapping circles of relationship, which constitute human community at the end of this century, impact the development of the individual person.

The impact of these various circles within a community varies with the intensity of the particular relationship that the individual has within a particular circle. For example, my friend who challenged me about my drinking remained a good friend despite my consistent rebuffs of his expressions of concern. It was his consistency and commitment to our friendship that served as a key ingredient in my eventual adoption of his question as mine. His committed friendship was the catalyst for my own transformation. However, there were people with whom I worked who also expressed concern about my drinking. I did not like them or value my relationship with them. Consequently, their expressions of concern went unheeded for many years. We are embedded in multileveled communal relationships. Some are important enough for us to be a catalyst for personal growth, while others have little, if any, influence at all. It is important, though, to recognize that each person is a product of these many and overlapping relationships. One can never escape the influence of community.

Aristotle seems to understand the importance of community. He wonders how one can live life without friends. *Friends* for Aristotle is a term that covers all the relationships that I have claimed are constitutive of community. A friendship is constituted by a common bond. Friends are those with whom I practice the various virtues that constitute a happy life. In this Aristotelian tradition, I would claim that self-appropriation is not possible without a community of like-minded people. People who are also struggling to be true to themselves, struggling to anchor themselves in the truth of their heart, are people who can encourage others and model for others the path to authenticity.

The people who asked the questions that began my transformation and invited me into the process of self-appropriation were very important people in my life. The first person who challenged my drinking was my best friend. He asked me, "Mark, do you think you might have a problem with alcohol?" He took a huge risk. His understanding of, and commitment to, our friendship prompted him to take a very challenging stance toward my drinking. He later shared his struggle with me. He was not sure that he should say something, but he had been watching me slowly destroy my life. He loved me too much to remain silent. The people in my life who expressed concern about my drinking were people who understood that sometimes friendship and love call for taking positions with one's friends and loved ones that might be unpleasant. True to their own sense of self and the movement of their hearts, people in my life challenged me.

I was also being confronted by a variety of other sources in my community. In a graduate course I was taking at the time I was learning about the disease of alcoholism. By what seemed to be coincidence, I began to run into people who were admitted alcoholics and sober for multiple years. I had a spiritual advisor in my life who was also a recovering alcoholic. Through the prayer and meditation practices of my faith I began to be more honest about my life situation. All of these challenges and coincidences emphasize the role that a community, although multileveled, must have in the initial stages of self-appropriation.

The community is important in the ongoing process as well. My personal recovery from the disease of alcoholism would not have occurred if I had not been surrounded by people who were also recovering from alcoholism. The encouragement and support of my family and friends were a very important element in my recovery. My faith community also gave me a safe place to explore a new relationship with the divine that began to develop in the process of recovery. Both for the initial stages and for the ongoing process, the community serves a vital function for the individual person. Such a multileveled community will yield a range of relationships whose value to the individual will vary from almost nil to profoundly important. However, that range does not belie the necessity for a communal environment in which the individual can discover herself or himself.

THE ROLE OF THE HEART

The challenging questions and the supportive community moved me to begin thinking about myself in a different way. I could no longer pretend that nothing was wrong in my life because the question had been asked by significant people. However, I did not want to change. I did not want to make the decision that would lead to a revolution in my own way of life. As my understanding of the situation increased, it seemed that I was at a precipice. I either had to jump off into the unknown of a different life or turn back from the growing understanding that I was an alcoholic. But understanding alone was not sufficient to push me over the edge of that precipice. Authenticity is not merely the fruit of self-knowledge. The process of self-appropriation goes beyond self-knowledge as an intellectual endeavor and includes an affective dimension.

In his *Confessions,* Augustine, the fifth century philosopher and theologian, offers a telling description of the gulf that exists between knowing what one must do and having the willingness to do it. In Book VII of this work, Augustine recounts the moment when he understood clearly who and what he was as a human being in search of God. He understood the mistakes in judgment he had made along the path of his life. He understood what he must do to secure the peace of heart and mind that he sought for so long. He had to choose to live for God alone, searching for and fulfilling God's will for him. However, he could not make the choice for this new way of life. ". . . I was held back not by fetters put on me by someone else, but by the iron bondage of my own will."2 Augustine demonstrates the pull that one experiences in the pivotal moments of life when one must move into a new way of being. The head understands what must be done, but the heart does not want to move. The reasons for this may be many, but the fact remains that often the heart is not able to move in the direction the head indicates is best for the person.

What is this heart? By heart I mean the seat of the emotions or feelings of the person. I do not mean feelings like hunger, thirst, tiredness, or the like. I mean feelings that are intentional, that is, directed toward some person, thing, or idea. Anger, sadness, joy, gratitude, jealousy, fear, confidence, trust, and compassion are such feelings. Feelings are the link between self-knowledge and action consistent with this knowledge.

The feelings that constitute the heart are always oriented. They always tend in some direction. Their orientation can be discerned by the person struggling to achieve authenticity. Feelings may be directed to the maintenance of the status quo. That is, they may be self-regarding in that they are invested in the protection of the self that is, rather than exploring the self that can be. Feelings like fear, jealousy, sadness, and anger can function in this way. Feelings can also be self-transcending in that they are drawing the person toward the self who he or she can become. This is not an outright rejection of the self that is, but a recognition and openness to further development and the realization of untapped potential. These self-transcending feelings facilitate a movement into more authentic human performance.[3]

As I stood on the precipice and debated my next move, I found myself caught in a battle between my fear of losing what I had and a growing hope for what could be. This latter feeling is self-transcending. It does not regard what is; it regards what could be. This is the significant difference between the two kinds of feelings. For a long time I could not have imagined or have hoped for what could be. I did not trust the goodness of a future without drinking alcohol. By the time I began to come to terms with my alcoholism, alcohol was my crutch. It enabled me to feel good about myself. It enabled me to talk to people, to go to parties, to dance, and to be human. I could not imagine my life without drinking alcohol! What could there possibly be in a life without alcohol that I might want to move in that direction or even hope that it might be better than what I have with alcohol? However, as more and more people impacted my self-understanding through their questions and/or experience, I began to trust their encouragement and to hope for something better. Within me began to grow a sapling upon which I eventually was able to hang my future and leap over the precipice.

Herein lies a significant overlapping of the elements which I have discussed thus far. The community is a nurturing element in the process of self-appropriation if and only if it enables two feelings to grow. First, a community must be able to nurture a person's trust in those who are farther along on the journey of self-appropriation. Second, a community must be able to nurture a person's hope that the fruits of self-appropriation are a real possibility for her or him. A person who is caught in the feelings of fear, distrust, and despair cannot envision a future that is different from the present. However, a person who is surrounded by a loving and nurturing community can, and will, develop the feelings that will condition her or his ability to live a different future. That has been my experience. The knowledge of my alcoholism, on its own, would have never brought me to that Sunday afternoon so many years ago. However, that knowledge, combined with a loving community, nurtured within me a heart that could make a leap into the unknown. The community of friends, family, academic colleagues, and companions in faith loved me until I could trust them enough to leap into an unknown future without alcohol. This same community nurtured in me, through their example, a hope that this unknown future could be for me a happy and fulfilling destiny.

Without the requisite feelings a good idea remains just a good idea. In Augustine's language, without a will that is strong enough to break the chain of the old will, change is not possible. This new will is what I call the heart. Our heart must have an orientation that facilitates action consistent with what one knows to be the good for one's life.

THE CONSTITUTION OF THE WORLD

Questions suggest new ways of looking at one's life. A community nurtures the emergence of a self-transcending heart. A self-transcending heart enables the person to act in accord with her or his correct self-knowledge. Endemic to this process is the honesty that enables a discerning look at the reflection in the mirror. That honesty makes possible the final result of this process. A new world comes into existence, one of the elements of which is the new self that results from the process of self-appropriation.

The last element in the process of self-appropriation is the insight that what the world is today is, in some part, my responsibility. What the world can be tomorrow is, in some part, more or less, also my responsibility. Until that Sunday afternoon I was under the illusion that my world was not my responsibility. I wanted to live as if what I did and what I said were irrelevant to the rest of the people around me. The truth is that my words and deeds have a profound affect on the world in which I live. This claim is not egotistical; it is a sobering truth. The attitude that I bring to my life, the words that I use in my daily living, the actions that I take to procure that which I judge to be good for me are all ways I create the world as it is and as it will be.

The world to which I am referring is the human world of family, work, recreation, politics, economics, and religion. I am talking about the natural world to the extent that human action impinges on that world. I am talking about the world that is the result of responsible and irresponsible human action. It is this world to which I am responsible as a human person. How I raise my children will affect my children and their children. How I conduct myself as a supervisor on the job will affect the people in the workplace. How I decide to invest my money will have impact on a variety of people. The drifter is oblivious to this fact of human existence. Once I become aware that I am responsible not only for the ongoing creation of my own subjectivity but also am co-responsible for the ongoing creation of the human and non-human world, I can no longer claim to be a responsible subject if I ignore the ramifications of my actions.

For most of my life I did not understand how much my words and actions impacted on the people in my life. Even when I began to understand that truth, I did not appreciate it enough to begin to think more responsibly about my actions. It was not until I began to confront the truth about myself that I began to understand and appreciate my responsibility for myself and the world around me. In and through my actions a world is constituted. My actions can be blind, as are those of the drifter, or my actions can be open-eyed as a result of the process of self-appropriation. It is true that the drifter can at times stumble upon a very responsible approach to life. But it is also true that she or he can just as easily be irresponsible. A woman or man who has walked the journey of self-discovery that is self-appropriation will regularly understand the world-constitutive character of her or his actions. Couple this understanding with a heart whose intention is self-transcending and one has an individual for whom authentic action is a regular achievement.

CONCLUSION

The admission of my alcoholism was a turning point in my life. I have not been the same person since; my world has not remained the same. Questions continue to open up new possibilities to me, a community still surrounds me with its loving and nurturing presence, my heart has deepened in its self-transcending orientation, and self-knowledge has broadened. I struggle to live an authentic life. I would not want anyone to think that from that first admission of my alcoholism the struggles of my life ceased. The struggles have continued and are continuing. Authenticity is a precarious achievement. Since life continues to unfold, the challenge of authenticity is ever fresh. However, the grace of my life is that I have the tools with which to live the struggle. I am no longer a drifter; I am a self-possessed individual who recognizes and embraces his responsibility for himself and for the world in which he lives.

When I began my study of philosophy, some twenty years ago, my mentor taught me that the most important lesson that one learns from philosophy is the art of living life with open eyes. My eyes were blinded by the disease of alcoholism and the accompanying fear, rage, sadness, and isolation. Since I admitted my alcoholism and have been in the process of recovering from it, I have been able to respond to my mentor's suggestion. A life lived with open eyes is a life full of great joys and great pains. It is a life in which very wrenching questions must be faced. It is a life in which the rewards are posted in terms of dignity and integrity, rather than in terms of dollars and cents. The road is sometimes very hard to see when life becomes turbulent, but with the help of good friends, as Aristotle suggested so long ago, and a heart open to the Other, one can stay on the road. In the end, one understands that the road itself, and the struggle to walk it, are the goals of a life well lived.

NOTES

1. I am indebted to the work of the late Canadian philosopher and theologian Bernard J.F. Lonergan, SJ for the notion of self-appropriation and for the inspiration from which the reflections in this chapter flow.
2. Augustine, *The Confessions of St. Augustine*, trans. Rex Warner (New York: Mentor Books, 1963), 168.
3. An excellent analysis of the difference between self-regarding and self-transcending feelings is given in Erik Erikson's theory of human development.

STUDY QUESTIONS
1. How did Doorley move from drifting to self-appropriation?
2. In what ways can community with others help us in—or block us from—becoming ourselves?
3. What are the connections between a person's ethics and a person's identity?

The Birth of Personhood

Tabor Fisher

Tabor Fisher lives and philosophizes in Binghamton, New York. As a philosopher, she considers the political and ethical implications of seemingly abstract concepts like "person," "space" and "freedom." In the essay below, she thinks through the concept of "person" concretely, in the midst of the complex relationships out of which it is birthed.

"THE WOMAN'S BOND to her child is special," he assured me. "Men, after all, are alienated from their children from the beginning, while women are not." What followed was a discussion of the possibility of the maternal–fetal relationship providing a natural model for moral human relationships. I'm afraid I cannot provide a detailed analysis of that part of the conversation because I was too busy choking back my anger and disbelief to listen properly. A part of me listened and nodded at appropriate moments, but another part of me swirled in a medley of memories from my earliest relationships with Alec . . .

> *Hail Mary, full of grace, blessed are you among all women and blessed is the fruit of your womb, Jesus. Hail Mary, mother of God, pray for us now and at the hour of our death. Amen.*

I am lying on the couch in my living room. I am utterly alone. Blood is pouring out from between my legs. I am clutching the telephone, waiting for a ring. David has taken our first—perhaps our only?—child to his playgroup. I am waiting and praying. The telephone rings and I am instructed by the OB's nurse to come to the office immediately. But I have to wait for David to return. I repeat, over and over, "pray for us now and at the hour. . . ."

A month later I am standing at a photocopier making copies of a syllabus to hand out in the summer course I am teaching. My feet hurt and I am tired. I don't want to be teaching this summer because of the baby and its fragile grip on my uterus; but I have to work to pay the medical bills caused by the baby and its fragile grip on my uterus. I am thinking of the irony of this situation. I am also angry—angry at God for not either giving us this child or taking it, angry at the medical bills and insurance headaches. The anger, however, doesn't seem to touch me. I move efficiently, placing the pages on the glass, gently lowering the cover, lightly touching the button. I look out at the shimmering heat of a Tulsa summer afternoon, cool and comfortable in the air-conditioned building. I feel cut off from the world out the window and cut off from the lump that sticks out in front of my belly. I don't want to believe it is a baby.

Are mothers really less alienated from their fetuses than fathers or other people? I see Hugh Grant, in the movie *Nine Months*, sitting slack-jawed watching the sonogram of his son and suddenly becoming attached to him. Finally he is willing to sell the Porsche and buy a family car, to reconfigure his life so that there is room for the baby in it. I, however, at the same point in the pregnancy and after having seen two sonograms of my fetus, am standing at the photocopier trying to insulate myself from the belief that I am going to have a baby.

I suffered placental abruptions twice during my pregnancy with Alec. After the first, my doctor assured me that although we do not know why these things happen, he was sure that it would not happen again. After the second abruption, I was lying on the cold table in the hospital ultrasound room looking up at the screen and watching an active little fetus swim about. I held my breath and my husband's hand. The technician looked at me and said, "You should be relieved now. He's okay."

She didn't know that I couldn't believe anyone's assurances this time. She left the room to take the tape to the radiologist. I turned to David and made him promise that we would name this fetus and have a funeral if necessary. The image of a happy little creature on the screen seemed unconnected to the pain in my abdomen or the blood between my legs.

I was sent home to bed rest and a deep, quiet depression. I wasn't eating right and didn't care. The iron supplements I was supposed to take for my anemia hurt my stomach so I stopped taking them. During my first pregnancy I was the model mother-to-be. I didn't drink a drop, suffered through colds without any medication, hesitated before taking an aspirin. As I lay on the couch during my bed rest it simply didn't occur to me to worry about how I was eating. I couldn't believe that I was pregnant, so those careful mother-to-be behaviors didn't make sense.

Throughout both of my pregnancies I kept journals written to my fetuses.

After this second abruption I didn't write to the fetus for over two months. When I did I was as upbeat as possible, although I did express my concerns about how the pregnancy was going and how our relationship was being formed by the traumatic events we had suffered through together. I confided in the fetus:

> *So why has it taken me so long to write? Well, I got quite behind at work while I was out and it's taken me awhile to get caught up, but more importantly it's taken me longer to bounce back psychologically this time. I feel more tender to you than ever, but it's like there's a part of me that won't let myself believe you're there. I'm afraid of being too hopeful.*

It was another three months before I would write again, this time to tell the fetus that we had been scheduled for a cesarean section to guarantee that another abruption would not occur when I went into labor.

Writing to my fetuses was a strange experience. Time fell in on itself as I wrote to yet-unborn fetuses, imagining them as babies and yet expecting them to read the journals as thirteen-year-olds. My style shifts from baby-talk simplicity to complex philosophical discourse, often on the same page. I try to locate who it is I am talking to, and despite the time-shifting nature of my "audience," I direct my words to some imagined point. As I do so, do I "fix" the fetus in that point? Do I write it into being?[1]

The content of my writing was also transformed by my hypothesized relationships with these hypothetical people. I would imagine how a thirteen-year-old would feel to discover that I had such ambivalent feelings during my pregnancy. (I worry about it now as I write this article. How will Alec feel if he reads this years from now?) Unlike journals I write for myself only, I attempt to project a particular image in these writings. I write to explain, to soften the blow, to protect. I become maternal. I write myself into being as well.

I must reject the idea that the maternal–fetal relationships I have participated in were unalienated or natural. I worked at these relationships, struggling to forge them over barriers of distance and time. I worked relationships into the future and then cast them back into the present. I struggled to connect across three feet of empty air to a sonogram monitor and weave that back into my tormented womb. My relationships with my children, both before and after birth, were shaped by me and by the situations I found myself in. I struggled to create good relationships with my children. The morality of our relationships was not already given; it had to be achieved. Thus, my maternal–fetal relationships could not serve as a paradigm of natural and unalienated moral relationships.

Although I had been infuriated by my friend's suggestion that maternal–fetal bonds be used as models of moral relationships, our conversation prompted me to think about how women relate to their fetuses. And as I read about these relationships and discussed with other mothers what their pregnancy experiences had been like, I found myself thinking more and more about abortion. First, since the maternal–fetal relationship is at the center of one of the most per-plexing moral issues of our time, it seems unlikely that it could be *innately* moral. Second, thinking about maternal–fetal relationships in the context of the abortion debate turned my attention to the question of when a fetus becomes a person. In my relationships with my fetuses, was I relating to a part of myself, was I relating to autonomous individuals, or is the fetus neither of these—and if so, what?

The other day my two children, Adrian (7) and Alec (4), and I sat down and watched the video of Adrian's sonogram. The sonogram had been taken at thirty-five weeks, so the fetus was fully developed. Yet, my children could not find anything recognizably human in the video. They searched the gray blurs and static for discernible forms, calling out: "That looks like an alligator!" "There's a sunset and that's the ocean!" They saw doors, walls, stairways, and wa-ter. Finally, I told them what they were looking at and pointed out the beating heart, the rib cage, the shape of the skull. They still could not "see" it. And I found myself also frustrated, seven years later, trying to see what had struck me as so miraculous about the video when I first saw it.

Sitting next to me on the couch was a seven-year-old child who was defi-nitely a person. Before me on the screen was a shifting mass of gray static that I had thought of as a person in July of 1989. Now I wasn't sure. When had Adrian become a person?

David and I had wanted a child and set out to get pregnant. After three months the test paper in the cup of urine turned blue. I was so excited that I rushed to the mall, bought a small journal, and then went to the local library. I pulled a book on fetal development down from the shelf and read hungrily about what was happening inside my body. Then I sat down to write:

> *Dear Little One,*
>
> *I can't believe I'm writing this! I meant to begin by welcoming you to the world, but to be honest it's hard to believe you exist. Your father and I have been waiting and hoping for you—but now it is so unreal and I am a little bit afraid. All you are to me right now is a blue spot on a pregnancy test. I looked you up in a book on fetal development, so that maybe I could get a clearer picture of who I'm writing to. It seems you are a small, macaroni-shaped thingee—that didn't help much.*
>
> *You are about 16 days old . . .*

I must admit that I find myself naive and amusing when I reread this. The words flowed from me without difficulty that day, but I look back at them now and see numerous conflicts in them. The very fact that I was sitting there, directing my words to someone, implies the existence of a person. But I do not have a name for this someone; it is just "little one," and I cannot seem to locate this mysterious person. It vanishes in its medical existence as a blue spot and a "macaroni shaped thingee." Yet, it is "dear" and anticipated. I seem to want desperately to find and address a person who I am not sure exists.

I wrote this in 1988. Ronald Reagan was president and abortion politics were center stage. The public debate over abortion has been a driving force in the historical emergence of the fetus as an autonomous person in the public imagination.[2] Antiabortion movies like *The Silent Scream* used fetal imagery to attempt to prove "that the fetus is 'alive,' is 'human like you or me,' and 'senses pain.' "[3] In other words, the fetus is a person.

Presentations of fetal personhood were not restricted to the realm of abortion controversy, however. Routine sonograms were becoming a part of prenatal care, at least for those who could afford it, and the fetus was becoming a popular icon. After the "shy and secretive fetus" made "his" debut in ultrasound images,[4] it went on to virtual superstardom. It first caught media attention in *Look* magazine in 1962, then a cover story in *Life* in 1965 captured by Lennart Nilsson's "unprecedented photographic feat." Soon the fetus was landing choice movie roles, beginning with *2001: A Space Odyssey* (1968). A number of documentaries followed, like the previously mentioned *The Silent Scream* (1984) and Nilsson's "The Miracle of Life" produced for PBS's science show *Nova* in 1983. The fetus's most important role to date, however, may be its starring role in *Look Who's Talking* (1990), although it could have received a Best Supporting Actor Oscar for the dramatic cameo in *Nine Months* (1995) described above. As all true superstars do, the fetus has even lent its image for commercial purposes, starring in a Volvo ad in 1991 ("Is something inside telling you to buy a Volvo?").

All of this media attention did not pass by me unnoticed. Its effects on how I viewed myself and the fetus within me were not apparent to me at the time. But some women were beginning to note how the fetus was being thrust into the media spotlight and personhood. Rosalind Petchesky argued in 1987 that the fetal images presented both in abortion debates and in routine prenatal ultrasounds had an effect "not only on the larger cultural climate of reproductive politics but also on the experience and consciousness of pregnant women."[5]

When I wrote that first journal entry to what would be Adrian, I was a middle-class, Christian, white woman, secure in my marriage and prepared to stay home to raise my child. My social location embodied all the family values that would be extolled in later presidential campaigns: heterosexuality, marriage, patriarchy, security, responsibility.

I was the woman who could be the proper mother for the babies that antiabortion activists want to save. Susan Bordo has described how pregnant women are viewed as "environments" or "fetal containers" when the personhood of the fetus is stressed.[6] Sometimes women are forced to alter their behaviors drastically in order to provide the "proper" environment for the fetus. Bordo describes a number of cases of women forced to undergo major surgery against their will, sent to jail to prevent them from using drugs, or convicted of child abuse for drinking during their pregnancy or failing to follow their doctor's advice.[7] Because of my class position and the support I received through my marriage, I would be able to provide food, vitamins, rest, and security for the fetus with little difficulty. As a woman who was already positioned as a proper environment for a fetus, I did not have to restructure my sense of self in order to accept the fetus as a person. So, I can find myself sitting in the public library writing to a person inside myself only sixteen days after conception.

From that social position, viewing the ultrasound as an expectant mother rather than as a critical theorist, I was able to "see" a baby in the gray static. I wrote to the fetus:

> *Watching the sonogram was exciting. We saw your heart beating—it was awe inspiring. The last thing they showed us was your face and that was—I can't think of a word—wondrous, I guess, is closest.*
>
> *You had your fist up by your face as if you were leaning your head on your arm. You sighed and opened and closed your mouth a few times. It was magnificent. I think you have Daddy's nose. There you were, looking like one of us, moving, living—it really hits you at a time like that what a miracle life is.*

I read myself in this journal entry as the double of Hugh Grant's character in *Nine Months*. As he watches his son's ultrasound video his eyes fill with tears, then he smiles as he says, "His little heart's beating." I hear an echo of the antiabortion slogan, "Abortion stops a beating heart." I watch my understanding of my pregnancy get shaped by antiabortion rhetoric, even though I was not considering an abortion and even though I am pro-choice.

Petchesky differentiates between the public fetus, as presented on antiabortion bumper stickers and billboards, and the private fetus, as recorded in ultrasound photos tucked away in family albums. But she understands that these different kinds of images are interrelated. She points out that when women look at their private ultrasounds they "may see in fetal images what they are told they ought to see."[8] I believe this is what I saw when I viewed Adrian's ultrasound in 1989. Petchesky insists, however, that women are not passive victims of antiabortion rhetoric, nor are they a homogenous group. Depending on a woman's personal life history as well as her class, race, and sexual preference, she may view images of her fetus quite differently than she "ought" to.[9]

In 1992, as I viewed my second sonogram of Alec, I was in a different social location than I had been during my first pregnancy. I was now the sole financial support of my family. When Adrian was one year old, I began to teach full time at the local community college. David had left a paid position in the workforce to take on the job of caring for our home and child. My salary was less than a third of David's previous income. Our health insurance did not cover as much. As a working mother and with less money it was difficult to respond to the stresses my high-risk pregnancy presented to me and to my fetus. I was to stay off my feet, but I had to teach. I was no longer the ideal fetal environment. And since I could not find my place in the fetus-as-person/woman as environment model, I could not position Alec in that model, either.

As I think through my relationships with these two fetuses, I realize that it is not the two "people" involved who, by bringing their distinctive *person*alities together, define the relationship; but it is the relationship that defines the people. In both pregnancies, the evidence I was provided with did not clearly establish who or what the fetus was. I have described already how in my first pregnancy I was able and willing to ascribe personhood to the fetus—despite the countervailing evidence of a scientific photo of a "macaroni-shaped thingee." I must also note that by the time of my second pregnancy, the fetus had once more been splashed across the cover of *Life* (August 1990) and had starred in a major motion picture. This time both popular culture and the medical evidence weighed in on the side of personhood. I was affected by all of this; I would not insist on a name or a funeral for an amputated part of myself. But I was not able to respond to my fetus as if it were a person.

Some feminist theorists have argued that only one person can emerge out of the maternal–fetal relationship. Mary Anne Warren has defended birth as the proper moment to ascribe personhood to the child because up until that time the fetus shares a body with another person whose rights cannot be protected if the fetus is considered a person as well.

> [Pregnancy] is not just one of innumerable situations in which the rights of one individual may come into conflict with those of another; it is probably the only case in which the legal personhood of one human being is necessarily incompatible with that of another.[10]

She concludes, emphatically, "*There is room for only one person with full and equal rights inside a single human skin*"[11] [italics in original]. Discussing how women become fetal containers to accommodate the fetus's personhood, Bordo writes, "It is as though the subjectivity of the pregnant body were siphoned from it and emptied into fetal life."[12]

During my first pregnancy I considered my fetus a person; during my second I did not. Bordo's image of siphoning subjectivity from the mother to the fetus suggests that I should have felt like less of a person in my first pregnancy than I did in my second. However, my experience was the opposite. During my first pregnancy I felt like a queen. I reveled in the social approval I received and did not feel that I was paying a huge price for it. During my second pregnancy I felt I was being drained: emotionally, physically, and financially. If ever in my life I have felt that my subjectivity was being siphoned away, it was during that second pregnancy. As a middle-class housewife I seemed to have personhood to spare for the fetus; as a working mother, struggling with a high-risk pregnancy, I was drained.

In order to understand why my experience of being a proper fetal environment did not erase my personhood, it is necessary to look at larger relationships than the maternal–fetal dyad. Just as my body and my careful maintenance of it created an environment within which the fetus could enjoy personhood status, my middle-class home and neighborhood, well-appointed and carefully policed, provided the environment in which I could enjoy my subjectivity. I do not mean to present my position as a middle-class housewife as an ideal location; I am quite aware that the environment I was protected by could have been snatched away from me in a minute if my husband had divorced me or died or if he had lost his job. My security was precarious and not within my control. But during this period of time, my environment was maintained and I enjoyed the privileges it gave me.

The personhood which was siphoned off of me and provided to my fetus was replaced for me because of my social status. I did not feel the loss of money or energy, because I was provided with adequate health insurance and my husband was paid enough to allow me to take time off to have a baby. Just as I shared my subjectivity with the fetus, other people shared their subjectivity with me. People who paid insurance premiums, but did not have an insurance claim that year, paid my medical bills. Workers unknown to me made strollers and baby clothes in factories overseas in conditions I was unaware of. I benefited from their labor, grafting their substance onto myself.[13] Complete strangers who walked up to me in a store or a restaurant and congratulated me on my pregnancy, people who offered me a seat in a waiting room, or allowed me to go ahead of them in the line for the rest room, supported me and my fetus. All of these people, and many more, made it easier for me to give the fetus the environment that its public image as person demanded.

I know what extra hardships would fall on me as a pregnant woman if I did not enjoy middle-class status. During my second pregnancy, without adequate health insurance and with less money to pay the co-payment on my medical bills, I absorbed some of the cost of pregnancy that was paid for me by others the first time. There were many similarities between my pregnancies: I lived in the same place, used the same doctor, gave birth at the same hospital. But, I experienced my relationship with my fetus and my own personhood differently in part because of a change in my class position. Because of my (relatively small) change in social position and the emotional stress of a high-risk pregnancy, I had less personhood to share with my fetus. I can only imagine how I would be impacted if I were not white, or were single, or a lesbian, or on welfare. Would the grocery store clerk congratulate me on my pregnancy if I were paying with food stamps?

It is important to note here that in both pregnancies I was depending on the same social system for support, but that I was positioned differently within that system. A complete change in social systems, for example, if I lived in a rural setting with extended family accessible to me, would alter the personhood status of both myself and the fetus. Within the white, urban setting I lived in at the time, a loss of financial status diminished the support available for myself and the fetus. This would not and need not always be the case. Without social support it is more difficult to establish a person-to-person bond between mother and fetus, but how that social support is provided is not limited to the systems I related to during both my pregnancies (for example, individual nuclear family, employer-provided health insurance, and private doctors).

The relationship I enjoyed with my fetus in this first pregnancy is the kind of relationship that my friend had in mind when he suggested the maternal–fetal relationship as a moral model. I believe that what he had in mind was a natural and unalienated relationship. It seemed that he focused on the biological fact that the fetus and the mother are physically connected and assumed that the emotional and social relationships between the two would be as firmly and effortlessly connected as the umbilical cord, placenta, and uterus.

The energy required to construct myself and the fetus as full persons in an unalienated relationship during my first pregnancy was made available by other relationships forged in a particular configuration of social relationships. And those other relationships were not all, themselves, unalienated or models of moral connection. I had extra personhood, personhood to spare, in the first pregnancy, because it was provided to me through the work of others and my social privilege as a heterosexual, white woman. The model relationship I had with my fetus was only possible because of immoral relationships I had with others in our society.

It is ironic that in the case of my second pregnancy it was the uncertain connection between the uterus and the placenta that disrupted the relationship I had with the fetus. I want to affirm the physical nature of connections and disconnections, but, at the same time, I want to move away from an easy analogy or causal relation between physical connection and social/emotional bond. In an earlier version of this essay I discussed the experiences of a number of women, myself included, who shared their pregnancy experiences with one another and discussed their relationships with their fetuses. Feelings of separation or alienation were evident not only when the maternal–fetal connection was physically challenged but also when social pressures intervened. The greatest sense of alienation was expressed by a woman describing a teenage pregnancy. The child was conceived out of wedlock, and the parents were an interracial couple. The mother's schooling and future were thrown into chaos; her relationships with family, partner, and friends were strained; she ended up living in public housing. Her relationship with her now twenty-three-year-old child remains difficult.

My relationships with others are woven through, across, and around the multiple worlds we inhabit and the multiple axes of power that intersect those worlds. I think of how I am attempting to connect with you, the reader of this essay, knowing very little about you. Do we connect as women but disconnect due to class, education, race, sexuality, or a hundred other constructing influences? Do you exist in an academic world and feel at home with the apparatus of endnotes? My writing and your reading are not easy, instantaneous, or guaranteed modes of connection between us. As a writer I do not want to assume that I can write directly from my mind to yours. I write, dissect, edit, struggle. I have other people read and then—sometimes surprised at how they have understood me—I revise again. The communication I/you/we hope to have or end up having as a result of the writing and reading and struggling with this piece must be worked at in order to be achieved.

In the same way, my connections with my fetuses had to be worked at. I didn't automatically have an untroubled connection with them. Even in my first pregnancy, which appears to be the model of natural and unalienated connection between fetus and mother, I struggled with a relationship mediated by medical images and pro-life expectations as I wrote lovingly to a "macaroni-shaped thingee." The struggle in that pregnancy was easier than in the second. Part of the reason it was easier has to do with how I was positioned in a particular configuration of worlds.

In "Playfulness, 'World'-Traveling and Loving Perception," María Lugones discusses how people often exist in multiple contemporaneous "worlds," a concept she prefers not to define but to leave "suggestive."[14] In other writings she refers to "worlds of sense," with the feeling that these are networks both of people and of shared meanings.[15] Each world constructs the people in those worlds in different ways, and since people exist in multiple worlds, they also inhabit multiple and, at times, contradictory constructions. In Lugones's case she was constructed as both playful and not playful at the same time. In a similar way, a pregnant woman, or a fetus, could be both a person and not a person at the same time.

During my first pregnancy, the various constructions I experienced were not painfully different, and I was able to resist the very few depersonalizing constructions. In my second pregnancy I was trapped between contradictory constructions. In many worlds the fetus was constructed as a person and I was not. The fetus was constructed as a person in the abortion debate rhetoric, in social relations at the church I attended, within my extended family, and even in my relations with strangers who walked up to me in the grocery store and asked to feel my stomach! But my personhood was constructed away by this pro-life movement, which figured the mother as a fetal container. The repeated experience of people asking to feel my stomach reinforced that sense of being a fetal container. Would a stranger violate Bill Clinton's personal space by asking to touch his abdomen? Each time that question was asked, I felt erased.

As in the first pregnancy, I moved in other worlds that constructed me as a person; I was nourished by my relationships with my partner and Adrian, and I was a competent professional in a job I enjoyed. However, the high-risk pregnancy and the struggles I had because of financial difficulties mitigated my ability to be nourished by these worlds. My familial relationships were drained by our fear of losing Alec. My work was colored by the pressure to work more to pay for the extra medical bills, and my competence was strained by my physical condition.

I now see my failure to acknowledge Alec's personhood as a resistance to depersonalization. If I could see this pregnancy as a struggle that I, a person, was working through, I could feel some wholeness. But if I accepted my construction as a fetal container during this pregnancy my personhood would be erased, and since Alec's birth was uncertain, I might also fail at what should be a simple, mechanical task of being an incubator. Thus I held my self away from the fetus, walking around feeling detached from this little "person" who was continually being hailed and admired.

I do not often feel detached from Alec now. I enjoy a loving relationship with a delightful, energetic *person*. But the struggle to connect in ways that affirm both of us as persons continues. For example, when he gets demanding, ordering me to "Get me some juice, now!" we have to negotiate multiple constructions of what a mother is, what a woman is, and how children should behave. If I give in to the demand, will my personhood be erased? If I yell at him, overruling his will with my own, will his personhood be erased? The negotiations we perform in these situations are intersected by larger social networks, many of them sexist, some of them constructing children as property, and so on. Sitting in a church pew, I feel enormous pressure to keep my children under control. If I fail to do so, I will be judged a "bad" person. So I am tempted to minimize their personhood in order to protect my own. There are worlds in which it is easy to relate to one another in a way that affirms both Alec's and my personhood; there are other worlds where it is difficult for either of us to be recognized as persons.

I have argued that persons do not come together to form relationships; instead, persons emerge out of relationships. But those relationships are complex, involving many more people than the mother and the fetus. Some of the people involved may be imaginary (like the public fetus) and some may be removed by distance and time, like workers overseas. Personhood is distributed unequally among the participants in those relationships depending on how those relationships are structured. Any attempt to discover a paradigm for moral relationships must be made on a larger scale than the maternal–fetal dyad. Looking for a paradigmatic moral relationship cannot be a search for two people who are unalienated from each other. The social network that makes their unalienated relationship possible must also be examined. If the focus remains on the dyad, the immoral relationships that make the dyad possible will not only be ignored but will be unconsciously validated and reinforced. Therefore, the question must be how people in unalienated relationships came to be persons, how their personhood was birthed from a larger social framework.

NOTES

Muchas gracias a Neda Hadjikani for her encouragement to revise this piece and to Laura Duhan Kaplan and Dave Fisher for insights. I am deeply indebted to Jeffner Allen for conversation and her kindly critical comments on an earlier draft.

1. The idea that the fetus can be called into a particular kind of being is based on the Althusserian concept of interpellation or hailing. For more information about this idea in general, see Louis Althusser, *Lenin and Philosophy, and Other Essays* (New York: Monthly Review Press, 1972), 127–86. For an application of the concept of interpellation to the fetus in particular see Ann E. Kaplan, "Look Who's Talking, Indeed: Fetal Images in Recent North American Visual Culture," in *Mothering: Ideology, Experience, and Agency*, ed. Evelyn Nakano Glenn, Grace Chang, and Linda Rennie Forcey (New York: Routledge, 1994), 121–36.
2. A number of theorists have discussed the historical emergence of the personhood of the fetus. See Rosalind Pollack Petchesky, "Fetal Images: The Power of Visual Culture in the Politics of Reproduction," *Feminist Studies* 13:2 (summer 1987): 263–92; Carol A. Stabile, "Shooting the Mother: Fetal Photography and the Politics of Disappearance," *Camera Obscura*, 29 (January 1992): 179–205; Susan Bordo, *UnBearable Weight: Feminism, Western Culture, and the Body* (Berkeley: University of California Press, 1993), 71–97; and Kaplan, "Look Who's Talking."
3. Petchesky, "Fetal Images," 267.
4. Dr. Michael Harrison's description of the fetus in the *Journal of the American Medical Association* in 1981, quoted in Petchesky, "Fetal Images," 276.
5. Ibid., 265.
6. Bordo, 80–82.
7. Ibid.
8. Petchesky, "Fetal Images," 280.
9. Ibid., 278, 280.
10. Mary Anne Warren, "The Moral Significance of Birth," *Hypatia* 4:3 (fall 1989): 61.
11. Ibid., 63.
12. Bordo, 88.
13. Marilyn Frye develops this concept of grafting another person's substance on to oneself in *The Politics of Reality: Essays in Feminist Theory* (Freedom, CA: Crossing, 1983).
14. María Lugones, "Playfulness, 'World'-Traveling, and Loving Perception," in *Women, Knowledge and Reality: Explorations in Feminist Philosophy*, ed. Ann Garry and Marilyn Pearsall (New York: Routledge, 1992), 281.
15. María Lugones, "Strategies of the Streetwalker/*estrategias de la callejera*" (unpublished manuscript), 6–7.

STUDY QUESTIONS

1. What made Fisher's relationship with the fetus during her second pregnancy a difficult one?
2. Do you think that "a mother's love" toward her children offers a good model for behaving ethically in all kinds of situations?
3. What does it mean to say a person inhabits different "worlds"? How might a person's social status in these different "worlds" affect her or his sense of self?

Discipline or Domination: An Ethical Dilemma in Childrearing

Charles Kaplan

Charles Kaplan is a professor of psychology at the University of North Carolina at Charlotte, and a psychologist in private practice. As a clinician and researcher, Kaplan focuses on the intellectual development of children. As a father, however, he faces the unique challenge of putting his abstract theories into practice.

I HAVE ALWAYS thought of myself as a nonviolent person who abhors domination and the assertion of power in interpersonal relations. Even as a child, I didn't like it when my friends were "bossy," nor was I comfortable asserting my will over my playmates. This, of course, made me rather an easy mark for those in the neighborhood who didn't share my perspective. Other children found that they could take advantage of, or even bully, me. Years later my parents would tell the story about the time when I was four that I came running home in tears from Joey Moskowitz's house because he made up all the rules for our games. "Why don't you tell him you won't play with him anymore if you don't get a turn at being the leader," they suggested. "But he's my friend," they claim I said. "I can't be mean to him."

What I wanted was for Joey to share power with me because it was fair and reasonable. Fourteen years later, when I was an eighteen-year-old college freshman, chafing under my parents' domination over my autonomy, I again appealed to reason and fairness when they told me not to bother coming home for Thanksgiving without first getting a haircut. They didn't listen to reason and I didn't go home. That's when it finally began to dawn on me that people are often unfair and unreasonable in their dealings with one another. Much to my dismay, I saw that instead of routinely looking for ways to share power, the human impulse seems to be to gain and maintain control, using coercion and domination if necessary.

I went on to become a child psychologist, and perhaps not surprisingly, one of my interests has been discipline and parent–child relationships. For years I have counseled parents about gaining their children's cooperation by keeping lines of communication open, reasoning with them about appropriate behavior, and using logical consequences to discipline. I have taught that harsh discipline is unnecessarily punitive and that spanking is abusive and teaches children to be aggressive if they can't get what they want through other means.

But, that was B.C. (Before Children)! Life has its own way of intervening and wreaking havoc with theory, and my two precious children have made me confront a painful reality. For example, when I communicate clearly and patiently to Hillary (age 2 1/2) for several days running that she mustn't dump her cup of water on the dinner table because it is wasteful, messy, and bad manners, and if she does it again she'll have to leave the table, and she gets a gleam in her eye and very deliberately does it anyway (and then refuses to leave the table), I am left with no choice but to dominate. Sometimes physically, by picking her up and carrying her bodily to her room while she shouts "Put me down! Put me down!"

The situation I describe here is not an isolated one—Eli, in his own way, is equally a challenge. Nor are our children monstrous discipline problems, a case of "the children of therapists and ministers are the worst behaved" syndrome. On the contrary, they are slowly learning manners, reciprocity, and respect for others. Hillary and Eli are simply exercising their human impulse to control, to be in charge, and to do so coercively if necessary. Clearly, children need to be socialized—to enter into a consensus with the larger community about acceptable and unacceptable behavior—and it is my job as a parent to accomplish this. But must I dominate and coerce in order to socialize? If only they would be fair and reasonable!

Given my background, this is very complex for me. The practical utilitarian parent side of me simply does what needs to be done without thinking too much about it. The clinical psychologist side of me rationalizes that children need and want limits. But the philosopher/theorist side of me is troubled. How can someone who abhors violence and domination be so quick and so cavalier about using it to socialize his own child? Yes, I consider the disciplinary act I described as an act of violence. Throwing an adult female over my shoulder and carrying her off kicking and screaming would certainly be an act of violence. How does such an unacceptable act become acceptable when the recipient is a small child? If there is a difference between an adult and a child (and surely there is), then how is that difference to be characterized? And, in that characterization, where is the line on one side of which sits a person who may be ethically forced into submission and on the other side of which is a person who may not? What criteria are used to judge which side of the line a person is on?

My field of psychology is surprisingly silent on these philosophical questions. In our literature, discipline is typically addressed empirically by describing statistical relationships between various disciplinary styles of parenting and outcomes such as social or intellectual competence. For example, the best known work of this type is that of Diana Baumrind who compares the competence of children raised by authoritarian, authoritative, and permissive parents. She notes that permissive parents have few expectations for their young children in terms of maturity and self-reliance. Not surprisingly, Baumrind finds that these children often develop behavior problems and are low achievers. However, both authoritative and authoritarian parents set high standards for their children and exert considerable control over them. The difference between these two parenting styles is in how control is exercised. The authoritarian parent dominates the child completely, does not permit disagreement with their authority, and favors forceful, punitive methods of control which do not diminish as their children become more mature and competent. The authoritative parent also exercises control, but consciously attempts to permit enough autonomy and self-will to allow the child to develop a sense of personal agency and self-reliance. The authoritative exercise of control diminishes over time as children demonstrate greater competence and greater social maturity. Baumrind finds that children of authoritative parents are typically socially skilled, responsible, independent, and achievement oriented, whereas the children of authoritarian parents are often more uncomfortable socially, rely on external guidance and structure, and are neither internally motivated nor achievement oriented.[1]

Baumrind's illuminating empirical work is somewhat comforting as, of course, I see myself exerting authoritative control rather than authoritarian control over my children. I look forward with smug self-assuredness to knowing my competent, self-reliant, achievement oriented teenagers! However, although I understand the "how-to's" of authoritative parenting, I am still left with many of the same unanswered philosophical questions about it. Why are domination and coercion acceptable over some individuals but not over others? Under what circumstances are domination and control appropriate? desirable? even necessary? When, from an ethical perspective, must they stop? In sum, what are the philosophical foundations of authoritative parenting?

The theoretical literature in psychology is, unfortunately, no more helpful than the empirical literature in addressing these questions. This literature addresses the issue of discipline only indirectly, if at all, through theories of personality and personality development such as those developed by Sigmund Freud, Carl Rogers, and Erik Erikson. These theories focus on the nature of the adult personality and how it is shaped through childhood experiences, including childrearing practices.[2] Coercion and the assertion of power over children are rarely discussed specifically, and, in fact, recommendations for disciplinary practices are rarely explicit. Rather, methods and techniques of childrearing are generally *inferred* from the theories by practitioners and authors of books for parents, sometimes with surprising inconsistencies. For example, Freud's psychoanalytic theory has as its basis the notion that human beings at birth are a mass of instinctual impulses that require taming over the course of development in order for the child to develop into a civilized adult. One might easily infer from this notion that heavy-handed, perhaps even coercive, discipline is necessary to accomplish this socializing goal. Instead, methods of childrearing based on psychoanalytic theory tend to emphasize the need to avoid emotional damage to children as they work through the very difficult psychological conflicts of childhood. The result is the very same permissive parenting style that Baumrind roundly dismisses as ineffective!

When developmental psychologists look to philosophers to guide their thinking about the nature of childhood and the developmental needs of children, they most often cite (and oversimplify) the ideas of Jean Jacques Rousseau, Thomas Hobbes, and John Locke. In his book *Emile or On Education*, Rousseau described children as actively involved in their own development, questioning and exploring the physical and social world.[3] He is often interpreted by psychologists as suggesting that children have an intuitive sense of right and wrong that is simply misdirected by society. Childrearing, then, would require carefully structured experiences intended to elicit and facilitate children's inherently good traits. Coercion and domination should not be necessary to bring these about, as long as the right experiences are provided. Well, either Emile was nothing at all like Hillary and Eli, or my wife and I are failing miserably to provide the "right" experiences! Would it be irreverent to point out that Rousseau is reputed to have put his own babies up for adoption? It is certainly tempting to imagine Rousseau discovering the hard way that coercion was the only way to ensure that his children had only the "right" experiences, at all times played only the "right" games, in the "right" way, and with the "right" people!

In his book, *Leviathan*, Hobbes describes a state of nature in which uncivilized human beings compete violently for scarce resources. Civilized behavior comes about when an absolute sovereign sets up a totalitarian regime.[4] Psychologists interpret Hobbes as taking a perspective opposite to Rousseau, that children are inherently selfish egoists who need authority figures to restrain and control them for their own good. Hobbes's notion makes intuitive sense from the perspective of parents of young children. Unfortunately, he seems to hold out no hope for developmental growth, as adults are viewed by Hobbes as equally self-interested and in need of strong authority. Thus, a Hobbesian perspective on childrearing would suggest that domination and coercion are and must always be necessary, *throughout the lifespan*. It is interesting to juxtapose

Hobbes's view of human nature with Baumrind's description of authoritarian parenting. The authoritarian parent might be described as a leviathan, maintaining tight reins of control throughout development, leaving the adolescent (and presumably, the young adult) just as dependent on authority figures for direction and guidance as the child was. Here, obviously, is where my own thoughts and practice differ from both Hobbes and authoritarian parenting. The goal of socialization must surely be to *free* individuals from authority figures, replacing external control with what psychologists call self-control—personal beliefs, convictions, and values that transcend the need for a controlling authority figure.

Locke falls between these two philosophical extremes, describing children as possessing neither an inherent sense of right and wrong nor a selfish egoism. Rather, in *An Essay Concerning Human Understanding*, Locke describes the child as a *tabula rasa*, a "blank slate," which is written upon by experience.[5] Locke does not discuss childrearing in this strictly epistemological work. But in the context of our discussion, it seems clear that parents and other agents of socialization are the providers of children's formative experiences. Thus, children will simply develop the beliefs, convictions, ethical standards, and values (or the lack thereof) that experience teaches them. Now, I can't speak for others' children, but mine appear to have some text written on their slates in their own handwriting! Undeniably, Hillary and Eli are learning from the socialization experiences we provide. But watching them vigorously and determinedly pursuing their individualistic agendas, sometimes literally in spite of our best intentions to teach them something else, makes me wonder just how blank that slate really is.

In his *Second Treatise on Civil Government*, Locke speaks more explicitly about the process of childhood socialization, even hinting that children are not the passive recipients of experience suggested by the *tabula rasa* metaphor. The purpose of this *Treatise* is to argue for a democratic republic in which mature individual citizens safeguard their freedoms when they demonstrate informed civic responsibility by making wise choices of elected officials. Locke argues that children must develop a capacity for responsibility before they are able to become members of the republic. He describes a transition in the child's political equality and frames this issue as a developmental need for external control.

> Children, I confess, are not born in this full state of equality, though they
> are born to it. Their parents have a sort of rule and jurisdiction over
> them when they come into the world and for some time after, but it is
> but a temporary one. The bonds of this subjection are like the swaddling
> clothes they are wrapt up in and supported by in the weakness of their
> infancy. Age and reason as they grow up loosen them, till at length they
> drop quite off, and leave a man at his own free disposal.[6]

Locke is describing a socialization process in which children are subjected to a degree of control that is not required—or desirable—once they become responsible adults. By framing this developmental process in terms of inequality transformed into equality, he suggests a rationale for the *temporary* domination and coercion of children as a means to an end: liberty. Locke seems to be describing the task of Baumrind's authoritative parents who assert parental control as a means of nurturing their children's social and personal development, loosening the "bonds of subjection" as their children grow.

In her (not so new) book, *Towards a New Psychology of Women,* Jean Baker Miller echoes Locke's ideas about "temporary inequality," illuminating this issue further by specifying what it might look like. According to Miller, the goal of a relationship of temporary inequality is to end this unequal relationship. The "superior party" in the relationship is described as having "more of some ability or valuable quality which she/he is supposed to impart to the lesser person."[7] Thus, from this perspective, children are temporarily unequal because they lack some qualities that their parents possess. The goal of socialization, then, is to teach them what (presumably) their parents already know. But what are these valuable qualities that children must learn before they can be considered equals? If I take Locke's thoughts seriously, these must be the qualities that enable adults to be competent citizens who exercise their liberties, participate as equals, and contribute positively to their communities. It seems these qualities would include the character traits of self-control, personal responsibility, trustworthiness, fairness, and respect for and caring about others. Engendering these qualities is such an important socialization goal that authoritative parents will use coercive methods if persuasion and reasoning are not successful. The message to the child is, "I feel so strongly about the importance of this issue that I will 'pull rank' in order to make it happen."

So, judicious use of coercion may sometimes be a necessary socialization strategy, but it is not sufficient by itself. The authoritative parenting model goes beyond any of the philosophies discussed here in suggesting that, even in the coercive act itself, I need to model in myself the qualities that I wish to see in Eli and Hillary. If I am to teach a lesson beyond "I am more powerful than you and can work my will on you if I so choose," I need to exercise my own self-control, trustworthiness, and respect for and caring about them. Thus, when I am at my authoritative best, I articulate my expectations clearly in order to demonstrate that there is a lesson plan and that discipline is not capricious. In order to demonstrate that "using our words" is the preferred approach to conflict resolution, I reserve coercion for those situations in which persuasion and reason have already been tried. And I avoid coercion in the heat of an angry moment in order not to model that power assertion is a way of dealing with people when you are angry at them.

So, Hillary is now a precocious four-year-old possessed of a creative and energetic agenda all her own. She is very clear in all matters about what she wants to do, as well as when, where, how, and with whom. Let's listen in on the following interchange to see how Socialization 101 is going. The scene takes place in the family library where Hillary is eagerly engaged with "Hidpix," the computerized version of the much beloved hidden pictures feature from *Highlights for Children*. She has already been on the computer for an hour, more than long enough in our estimation, and it is now time for dinner.

> *Dad*: OK Sweetheart, dinner's ready. Time to shut down and come eat.
> *Hil*: NO WAY! I want to play Hidpix some more.
> *Dad*: Sorry, Hillary. Dinner is on the table, and besides, after half an hour on the computer you start getting frustrated.
> *Hil*: (folding her arms in defiance and shouting) I DO NOT!!! I'M NOT COMING! I DON'T LIKE EATING AND I'M STAYING RIGHT HERE.
> *Dad*: (with a quiet edge in his voice) We can't stay healthy if we don't eat, so this isn't your choice. And if you want to play Hidpix tomorrow, you need to get up and come now.
> *Hil*: (grabbing the chair and howling) NO O O O O!!
> *Dad*: (reaches over and turns off the computer, still quiet, but clearly annoyed) OK Hillary. The computer is now off for the night and I'm carrying you to the kitchen table. What will happen if you fight me?
> *Hil*: (with resignation in her voice) I'll spend the rest of the evening in my room. Humph!! Daddy, can I have some pasta?

What do you know. Perhaps I'm growing into this business of domination for the purpose of socialization! But one last thing seems clear to me as I contemplate the depictions of children suggested by the philosophies of Rousseau, Hobbes, and Locke: Children cannot be adequately characterized as "noble savages," "selfish egoists," or "blank slates." Such monolithic characterizations overlook the fact that children's individualistic temperaments will make each one different from the next in their intuitive understanding of right and wrong, their tendency toward unrestrained egoism, and the ease with which socialization experiences can be imprinted upon them. So I need to add flexibility to my list of important qualities to model in myself and insist on in Hillary and Eli. Can we ever hope to live up to these Herculean standards of parenting? Not a chance, as long as we also possess the qualities of fatigue, frustration, anger, inconsistency, and other human frailties. We can keep our philosophies in front of us, but only as guideposts and goals to keep us on track when we react rather than think, yell rather than talk.

1

NOTES

1. Diana Baumrind, "Current Patterns of Parental Authority," *Developmental Psychology Monograph*, 4 (1, Pt. 2, 1971).
2. Richard M. Ryckman, *Theories of Personality* (Belmont, CA: Wadsworth, 2000).
3. Jean-Jacques Rousseau, *Emile: or, On Education*, trans. Allan David Bloom (Harmondsworth, England: Penguin, 1991).
4. Thomas Hobbes, *Leviathan*, ed. J.C.A. Gaskin (New York: Oxford University Press, 1998).
5. John Locke, *An Essay Concerning Human Understanding*, ed. Alexander Campbell Fraser (New York: Dover, 1959).
6. John Locke, *The Second Treatise of Civil Government*, ed. J.W. Gough (Oxford: Blackwell, 1948), chapter 6, section 55.
7. Jean Baker Miller, *Toward a New Psychology of Women* (Boston: Beacon Press, 1976), 4.

STUDY QUESTIONS

1. What specific conflicts between ideals and realities did Kaplan face when he became a parent?
2. Should parents try to match their styles of discipline with the expectations of society? What if the social expectations are unclear or if they vary according to race, class, geographic region, or gender?
3. Under what circumstances are domination and coercion ethically acceptable?

What's Wrong with Bribery?

James B. Sauer

Jim Sauer is associate professor of philosophy at St. Mary's University, San Antonio, Texas where he specializes in social philosophy and ethics. He has published in both philosophy and economics journals. His interest in bribery started when he was in Africa and was often expected to pay bribes (he didn't!). It was renewed by his students, many of whom report that bribery is a way of life in their native country of Mexico.

DINNER WAS OVER and an animated conversation had started around Margaret Ross' recent personal problems.[1] Margaret was a successful businesswoman who ran her own financial consulting firm. Some months earlier she had been sued by a client for "bad advice." It was a nuisance suit, but her lawyers had recommended that she settle because it would be less expensive than going to trial. "Besides, we never know what a jury might decide," her lawyers told her. Margaret had heard from a "friend of a friend" that money passed to the court bailiff in sufficient quantity for everyone would get her case dismissed on first hearing. "Your case will never go to trial," she was told. The bailiff was one part of an elaborate bribery scheme to get cases like Margaret's dismissed. Margaret felt that settling the suit out of court would be an admission of wrongdoing. But, as her lawyers advised, she could not be sure what would happen in court. So, while paying the bribe was more expensive than settling, she decided to pay the bribe. Because the scheme was under investigation by state police, she had been caught. Promised immunity from prosecution, she had been a witness in the trial of the judge who was the key figure in the scheme. He had been accused of taking money for favorable decisions from the bench.

"I don't know how I got involved at all," said Margaret. "It just seemed the easiest way out to me at the time. It was stupid, I know. But I knew the suit had no merit. I hadn't done anything wrong. But the legal system has gotten so screwed up this just seemed like another loose screw to me. So I paid the bribe and got the case dismissed on first hearing."

Bill Meyers, a lawyer, said, "But you ought to have known the bribe was wrong—not just legally wrong but morally wrong."

"Sure I did. But that's easy to say now, but things weren't so clear then. It was just the easiest way out when I had a business to run and no time to spend on the lawyers' games."

"But that's how these things go, don't they? Bribes always look like the easy way out. But the easy way is not the right way. Besides, your lawyers would have taken care of the legal details. That's what they are there for."

"But they were part of the problem," said Margaret. "They were advising me to take the easy way out and settle out of court although I wasn't liable for anything. So don't talk to me about the easy way out being the problem with what I did. I was just making the system work the way it had worked for other people. I just got caught."

Bill added testily, "But that's the point Margaret. You tried the easy way out-side the system. You just wanted to make things work for you. But suppose you had done something wrong, paid the bribe, and gotten the same dismissal. I am sure you'd agree that would be unjust and wrong. That's the point here. Bribery is always wrong because it puts our personal interest over the interest of the com- *social contract* munity or what is true or fair."

Bill had scored his point. But he was being just a little bit too "open and shut" about the problem of bribery. Willa, our hostess, jumped in, "Bill, I think you're rushing to judgment here. Margaret's situation was not exactly like the four representatives at the state house who each took ten thousand dollars for their vote on the new telecommunications bill. Their votes were openly 'for sale.' Lobbyists not only wined and dined them, but offered them money for their votes on the bill. They took it, and if we believe the evidence, they had done so before. Given they were the swing votes, the bill was bought and paid for. They were willing to sell their influence. What is wrong here is clear cut. They sold their votes and influence. Isn't this what is wrong with bribery?"

"Sure," said Bill. "But think about it, Willa. It takes two to make a bribe—a giver and a taker. In Margaret's case, the judge sold his office by taking the bribe. His decision was influenced by the money he took. It was dereliction of duty. One wrong. But two wrongs don't make a right. People who offer bribes are not only legally guilty, but morally responsible too. They know bribery is wrong and offering the bribe is wrong. Bribery isn't exactly like going out and buying a computer! Public officials have a duty to act fairly and impartially. That's a public trust. To sell that is to sell something that doesn't belong to them to sell. Offering a bribe is encouraging the wrong. So in a way giving and receiving bribes is a kind of stealing and lying. You'd agree that stealing and lying are morally wrong."

Willa responded, "Bill, you're being too cut and dried here. Margaret didn't go looking for the judge. The judge was corrupt, willing to take the bribe, before Margaret came on the scene. She was just using what was openly available because the judge was corrupt."

"That's true. But Margaret asked the judge to ignore his public duty in favor of her interests. That's morally wrong. We recognize that in the laws against bribery that cover both taking and offering bribes."

It seemed to me that Bill had missed Willa's essential point. I tried again. "Bill, I think you have a point. It is certainly what most people would think. Bribery is wrong because it buys favoritism. So the wrong of bribery is that it is unfair and unjust because it seeks a private benefit from a public trust. But I am not so sure we can be so open and shut about it. Let me tell you my story. I had my first introduction to bribery twenty years ago. I have had many experiences with bribery since then, but the first time is the one that I will always remember. I was on a jitney bus between Kananga and Mbuji-Mayi, two large provincial capitals in Zaire. I was traveling alone to get home. No one knew I was in transit. I had been working in Kananga temporarily and decided on the spur of the moment to return to Mbuji-Mayi. It was a beautiful day and I was enjoying the trip. About five miles outside Mbuji-Mayi, the police stopped our bus at a roadblock. Roadblocks are common in Zaire. The police and military use them to control population movement and to supplement their meager salaries by demanding a payment to pass from bus and lorry drivers. I didn't think anything about it. This did not concern an expatriate like me. It was a local affair. I didn't think anything about it until a policeman in fatigues and carrying an automatic rifle pulled me from the cab of the bus and told me I was under arrest. He shuffled me to a small group of people from the bus sitting under a tree waiting to be taken to jail.

"I was in a panic. No one knew where I was. Police don't give prisoners a phone call even when the phones worked. There is no bail. Trials are nonexistent. Jails are dirty, dangerous, and unsafe. Without family to feed me I would go hungry. I was in trouble and didn't know what I would do.

"Gradually from my companions under the tree, I learned that I had been arrested because I had paid my bus fare with a bill withdrawn from circulation that morning. The driver had used it to pay his bribe to the police. So as not to be arrested himself, the driver told the police I had given him the bill for my fare. So my crime was currency violation. But this didn't make any sense. I had gotten the bill from the bank that morning! One of my more knowledgeable companions laughed and said mysteriously, 'That doesn't matter. You're in Zaire. You just have to understand how things are here and don't worry about it.'

"After about an hour, our group started to dwindle. Someone would get up, walk over to the police, squat down to talk, spend a few minutes in animated conversation, get up and then start on to Mbuji-Mayi leaving the rest of us behind. This continued for several hours. As the day was drawing to an end, the policemen started laughing and pointing at me. This was uncomfortable. Maybe their unusual catch amused them or maybe they were deciding who would walk me the five miles or so to jail. One policeman got up and came over to me. For the first time he took my identity card, told me that I had used illegal currency, and walked away. My identity card became an occasion for heated discussion among the policemen. But still, even with the sun starting to set and their normal tour of duty at the barricade over, the policemen waited. Another policeman walked over: 'Mutoka (white guy) are you stupid? You are arrested for using illegal currency.' Back in the group more animated conversation among my guards. They called a child from a hut over to them. The child listened intently and then walked slowly and shyly over to me. 'Tatu (sir),' the little boy began. 'Who are you?' 'Jim Sauer,' I replied. 'No, Tatu, are you a minister—a priest?' 'Yes.' Silence. 'Muambi (preacher), there is a problem here because you don't understand why you have been arrested.' 'I used illegal currency.' 'No, Muambi, you don't understand. You have to pay.' He walked away back to the police. As he did, it finally dawned on me. What the policemen expected me to do was pay a bribe for my release. This was what those who had disappeared had done. They had understood. I had not. So I had sat under a tree waiting to go to jail for six hours. Finally a sergeant shuffled over. 'Muambi, go on. You will never understand.' Believe me, I went. But the police never understood either. They thought I had sat under that tree for six hours unwilling to pay the bribe when I just hadn't understood what they meant by arresting me!

"Now years later, I wonder if I would have paid the bribe if I had understood the meaning of my arrest. Would I have sat under the tree on the road to Mbuji Mayi so long? It would have been easy to pay the bribe. It would have amounted to little more than my dinner in the local hotel where I had planned to eat that night, but it was food for a week for one of the policemen's families. I could have easily argued, as many do, that bribery is part of the culture.[2] It enters into the predictable habits of their social routines. What would be wrong with paying the bribe? Others had and left. Certainly few things are as so every day and casual in many parts of the world as offering and receiving bribes.[3] And yet something felt right about not paying, even if that was because I didn't understand that was what was expected. I think there is something wrong with bribes but it is not exactly Bill's clean-cut argument about public duty."

Jim Edwards, a successful local contractor, looked surprised at my story. "I don't understand the problem here. There wasn't much you could do but pay— if you'd understood that's what you were supposed to do. Sometimes," he said, "there's not much you can do. It is the system. It why I have been so angry at what happened to Margaret. It's just the system and I have a good example. I have to give city safety inspectors a little something to sign off my sites. In my business, coordinating various parts of a big project depends on having building inspectors sign off on each stage of the work. If I waited until they got around to my site, then I could have things hung up for days losing money the whole time. I can't stay in business if I lose money. But a few dollars gets them to the site when I need 'em. I get the sign-off. The work continues. No one's hurt. Everyone's a little better off. What's the problem? For me, it's just part of the cost of doing business."[4]

His wife, Willa, chimed in, "Yeah, it's a little like a tip in a restaurant.[5] Waiters don't do so well. We know that and we tip. Well, city building inspectors aren't paid much either. If the city paid 'em a decent wage then maybe we wouldn't have to work this way. But this is the way the system is. It is just expected—just like a tip. You wouldn't say a tip was wrong would you?"

"Willa," I said, "I grant that you seem to have a point when you say that tips seem morally neutral. There may not be anything morally wrong with tipping. We tip all the time. Waiters, bellhops, hairstylists—even contractors, I bet, get gratuities and gifts sometimes from satisfied customers. But is what you're paying the building inspectors really a tip? Isn't it more like a fee for a service? I pay you X dollars for inspecting my building site when I need it."

Willa answered, "Yes, but that doesn't change my point. Tip, fees, or whatever. There's no harm done. Everyone benefits."

"I am not so sure that is true, Willa. It is true that city building inspectors are paid low salaries compared to other engineers and technologists. That might be part of the problem. But let's take a closer look at your argument about tips. Suppose I show you that tips aren't necessarily morally neutral, would you then grant that the money you pay the inspectors might be morally wrong?"

"Yes."

"Well let's look at tips. To it keep it simple we'll just use the example of tipping in America. The purpose of tips in American restaurants is to supplement low wages. It is a system that has grown up that allows restaurant owners and others to justify paying low wages. Owners argue that the posted restaurant prices are for prepared food not service, and since service people receive tips they should not bear the full cost of wages. However, in France, the menu prices are for food, but the bill contains a *prix complet* or the fee for the service. The French model seems a bit more honest and predictable than the American system. First, you know up front that food service is a separate charge. The charge is clearly stated in the menu. Second, service wages are such in France that restaurant and bar service is a respectable career for many people. This is different from the U.S. where the food service industry is notorious for being a short-term, high turnover occupation that contributes little to a local economy. So maybe tipping itself is not morally neutral because it perpetuates an unjust, unfair wage, and it means that certain jobs really don't enable people who perform them to participate completely in the economy. We can argue that they can support themselves, at least for a time, but doesn't work contribute more to our lives and society than just self-support?"

"What do you mean?" asked Jim.

"Well, it contributes dignity and cultivates the skills of public living. I know that sounds abstract, but it is not as abstract as it sounds. Pride in our work, pride in accomplishment, being paid a just wage for fair labor, and respect for our work are important public, and not just personal, values."

"Ok," said Jim, "maybe tips aren't morally neutral. But you've still not dealt with my objection. There are still some systems that work better because of bribes, the construction industry is one."

"Jim, I know there are a lot of people who would agree with you. But there still may be a problem. Let's get back to the inspectors. The purpose of the inspectors is to assure an independent judgment of safety and code compliance for public use facilities. Users, like me, depend on the independent judgment of the inspectors. That is why they are paid by government and not contractors. Isn't one condition of the bribe not only a timely inspection, but a quick sign off on safety documents? The independence of the inspectors is not assured, if a significant part of their income comes from the contractor. Wouldn't you say that if I bribed an inspector to pass faulty work that I had done something morally wrong?"

"Sure. It's the inspector's job to assure the safety of the work for the public. It's a safety issue. It's hard to spot good construction from bad when the walls are up to hide mistakes or substandard construction. Most people don't have the technical knowledge to know good construction from bad. So, I guess it is a confidence thing, too, even when we don't think about it. Having the inspections creates a habit of public trust. It's just not something we think about much."

"Exactly. I think you have hit on a key insight, Jim. The inspector's job, her role, is to inspect and certify the work of other people for being up to code and safety standards. Bribing the inspector to pass bad work is to break a kind of taken-for-granted trust. So we can agree that bribing the inspector to pass bad work is wrong."

"But wait a minute," said Jim, "I am not bribing the inspectors to pass bad work. I am just making sure they come to my building site when I need them to be there. If they find bad work I expect them to say it is bad work."

"Sure that is what you expect. But what does the inspector expect, or better, understand as the meaning of the transaction?"

"Well that's never said. You just don't handle things like this like that. You just know how it's done."

"Exactly. That's part of the problem. Doesn't that 'you just know' of the bribe set up the possibility of misunderstanding, like I misunderstood the road police in Zaire? What's expected in the bribery transaction, because it is hidden and under the table, is not open. That's how it differs from buying a camera or hiring an accountant. In those transactions expectations are clear because of the role of a sales clerk or accountant. But when you give money to an inspector— even if it is just to get to your site when you need her—there is much less clarity, more ambiguity, because the inspector's role is to inspect the building. That is what she is paid to do and clearly her salary is paid not by you but by the city to assure an independent judgment. Right?"

"Yeah."

"But when you pay the inspector outside the rules so to speak, don't you cloud the issue? I mean what rules govern what an inspector ought or ought not to do when you have paid the inspector something extra? It clouds the issue. What have you purchased?"

"That's easy. I have paid for a timely inspection. I still expect the inspector to make an independent judgment. You're making this whole situation harder than it has to be."

"Maybe I am. But how do you know that the inspector shares your expectation and just does not assume you have bought her signature on any kind of work?"

"Well you just have to trust the inspector. It is just the way things are."

"But we know something about the trustworthiness of the inspector who accepts your 'little extra' don't we? Having taken your bribe, we know she cannot be trusted to do her work in a timely manner. Doesn't this count against fully trusting that she will report defects in a building site?"

"I think you are exaggerating."

"Not really. Just being accurate. If someone tells a lie doesn't this make them a liar?"

"Of course. But that doesn't mean that they lie all the time."

"No, but it means they will lie. Knowing that they lie, are you inclined to trust them as much as you did before you discovered that they were liars?"

"No. That happens all the time. I trust my employees' word until I find out otherwise. When I find out I can't trust their word, then I am more careful to check out what they tell me before I depend on it."

"How is the example of the inspector taking a bribe any different? One of their duties is timely inspection of building sites. But you get a timely inspection only when they get a little something extra. No harm you say. Well, by your own admission there is a harm. They are less trustworthy. There is some doubt, no matter how little, that their judgment is open to being influenced by valuable considerations. This is exactly what a bribe is, isn't it?"

"Yes, I suppose you have a point. But what you don't see is that this is the way the system is. No grease, no progress. You have to realize that these guys are as busy as a one armed paper hanger in a fan factory. There are always too few inspectors and too much work. A little guy like me can't afford to wait on the inspectors."

"I understand that. Time is money. But you have hit on two more problems. First, this is the way the system is. But isn't it also true that the 'system,' as you call it, has been built up over time—bribe by bribe—to the point that inspectors expect to supplement their salary with your gratuity making it necessary for you to pay the bribe to get the work done that they should do by virtue of their job? Wouldn't it be better—that is more desirable—to work on city hall to hire more inspectors and enforce timely inspections or whatever?"

"Sure but that's not my job. I can't spend the time working on that and build buildings, too."

"That's true. But what you spend on bribes could be spent hiring others whose job it would be to lobby city hall or join a group trying to reform salaries, procedures, or whatever. Wouldn't this improve the life of everyone in the community as well?"

"I suppose so. I hadn't looked at it that way before. What you're saying is that by bribing inspectors I help continue the system that requires the bribe."

"Yes."

"And that there might be a better way to solve the problem of timely inspections by using what is spent on bribes to fix the system and that would increase rather decrease habits of public trust."

"Yes."

Willa, who had been silent, spoke up. "That might work in Jim's case because he has a stake in the outcome and influence on the system. But what about a different kind of situation? For two years Steve and I lived in Nuevo Laredo. We'd go over to Laredo to shop for what we could get on the Mexican side. We did it all the time. Most of the time it was just easier to give money to a customs official to get through the lines without a hassle. This situation is different from Jim's example in two ways. First, no one's life is at risk. Second, bribery is a way of life. As a foreigner I don't have any influence on Mexican life. When in Rome do like the Romans, I say."

"Willa, you're right. It does seem harmless and only money might be involved. But are you sure you didn't have any influence on the Mexican way of life? Let's suppose the value of what you were bringing back into Mexico had a duty of $25.00. I suppose you might have offered five or ten dollars to the inspector to let you through the line. So in essence the Mexican treasury comes up short $15.00. This doesn't seem like much. But multiply it by all the possible customs transactions in a year and the amount becomes enormous.[6] This money is money that the government has lost to its revenue base. It might have been used to pay salaries, support health care or economic development projects. In any case, fifteen dollars never enters the Mexican economy. This is another problem with bribery. It diverts resources from public to private use. Data is

sparse because bribery by its nature is a hidden, unrecorded transaction, but the best estimates are that a bribe diverts 15 times the cost of the bribe from public to private use. It would be a little like you deciding at tax time to pay one fifteenth of your taxes to Uncle Sam and spend the rest on what you decided was best. We might want to be able to do this, but could we conduct any kind of public life if everyone did it?"

"No. Sometimes I don't like how my tax money is spent. But taxes, even if I don't like 'em, are meant for a public good. If I find a reason they're not, then I have to try and change that, not just quit paying taxes or insist that they only support what I want them to support."

"Exactly. But many bribes are transactions that effectively bypass the public good for a private one. This is not just true of things like customs duties. For example, bribery is often used by businesspeople to reduce competition. Not long ago several Honda officials were indicted and convicted because they accepted money from dealers to give the 'dealer paying grease' preferential treatment in getting cars to sell. This violated their contract with dealerships to provide stock for sale on a fair and equal basis."

Robert, a regional sales manager for a large regional manufacturing company, spoke up. "That's not a good example. That was just illegal—a breach of contract. The contract could have been written differently to permit premium payments for high demand models. But I have an example. How about the practice of giving gifts to purchasing agents to favor certain companies or product lines over others? I lost a big contract this week because my competitor had locked in his bid by paying off the purchase agent of another company. When I confronted the guy on it, he just said it made good business sense to lock in contracts. He didn't see anything wrong with what he did. But it doesn't do much good to bid on contracts when you know that is happening."

"That's a good example of another problem with bribery. It reduces competition. Competition lowers prices. Lower prices benefit everyone. Bribery raises prices. So bribery also converts public goods like lower prices to a private benefit. In effect everyone pays the cost of a bribe. This is not fair or just. Maybe more important though, is the attitude of 'What's the use?' Bribery lowers our willingness to engage in public processes like competitive bidding. It raises mistrust in public life."

"Wait a minute," said Willa. "You're making it sound like any time we offer money or privileges to someone to do something that they ought to do because it's their job or role or whatever is wrong. But we use gifts and rewards all the time to motivate people. In the company we use incentives to reward motivated people. We also show our gratitude to suppliers and subcontractors with gifts at Christmas and birthdays. And when Steve and I first had children, we started using treats to get them to sit still, clean their rooms, and things like that.

Now that they are older, we use the car and the curfew hour when they get good grades and stuff. It teaches them responsibility."

"Does it really? Or does it teach them that they can use their position to benefit themselves rather than acting responsibly? It seems to me to be setting up a relation between a desired performance and a reward, such that the reward is the motivation rather than the willing performance. The reward is an inducement to act in ways you want them to act. Your expectation is that without the reward they will not act in that way. This seems harmless, but I am not sure this is the habit you want to encourage either for your business or your home."

"Now wait. You're going too far there. These are rewards not bribes. Besides what we are teaching is not what you say, but habits of responsibility." Willa was obviously angry.

"I know what you intend to teach, Willa. But what is the response that is really responsible? Is it to do what they have promised to do or ought to do by virtue of their position in the job or place in the family? Or is it the response to the link between reward and position? I think it is the latter, and—in no matter how small a way—you are setting up the conditions of bribery as a recurrent scheme."

Cooling the moment, Anibal, who had been silent all night spoke up. "Willa, I am not so sure that Sauer has gone too far. I think I am starting to catch on to what Sauer means. The order of social routines is made up of thousands of little transactions. These transactions are largely a matter of habits. For example, buying and selling is a set of habits and shared expectations reinforced by a lot of small transactions everyday. Every time we buy and sell we reinforce the habits of the scheme. If the scheme is good, then the habits to maintain it are good, too. But you can flip that over; some habits condition bad schemes. So even what we might call harmless bribes are teaching people, especially children, habits of using their social position to benefit themselves. That does undermine trust, because we can't depend on people to do what they are responsible for doing, or say they will do, without a personal inducement or reward and that's what a bribe is."

Steve jumped in again. "I think I am starting to see what is going on here, too. You're saying that interactions among people, what you call transactions, have a predictable structure to them and the structure, not the intention, either contributes to the overall of good of the scheme in social relations, or in fact, contributes to a kind of decline by reducing the good yielded by the scheme."

"Not exactly, but close. I am not saying intentions are not important. But I am saying that the operative routines of society are a form of order that increases or reduces a human good by the way they enable or frustrate our efforts to meet the needs and desires of many people over long spans of time. Bribery and many other kinds of transactions like extortion, robbery, theft, and the like convert the public good of order to a personal or private good. It collapses all goods into private ones."

Margaret finally jumped back in, "I think I have an example. In a company I worked for there was an unstated rule to win at any price. Some of the younger guys took this to mean that anything was fair game if the company benefited. A couple of the guys started spending small amounts of money on suppliers—a dinner here, golf there. But the little things got bigger and bigger. Finally it was taking several hundred dollars to get each contract. Worse, those of us who disagreed with what was happening saw our production stats go down. Management got on our backs, asking why we couldn't produce like the 'golf game mafia.' Eventually it got so bad I left. That's why I opened my consulting business. I wanted to operate in an open, clean-handed way. I guess I lost sight of that by bribing the judge. It really did seem like it was just the system, but it was the system that was unjust. I contributed to that no matter how unintentionally."

"Let me see if I've got the idea," said Anibal. "We have hundreds of little choices to make everyday. Those choices bring a future into being. If I lie regularly then I become a liar. On the other hand, if I am honest, then I become an honest person. It's like our actions create a world. I can create a world of hospitality and trust, or I can create a world of enmity and mistrust. How I choose to act in my environment has varying degrees of impact on the environment. One choice leads to continuing to spew pollutants into the air and that has an impact on the world I live in. Choosing to obey the traffic laws has an impact on the world of other drivers. So, by choosing to engage in bribery or not has an impact on the world of public life. What you're saying is that it comes down to choices."

"Yes, but notice that each choice sets up a framework for the next choice. Each time I pollute the environment it becomes harder or more costly, or takes more effort to choose a clean environment. Each time I pay a bribe—not matter how small—it becomes harder to reverse the payment of bribes."

"Or we all know that one little lie often get us started on ever more lies to cover the first lie."

"Yes, something like that."

"Hey, this circle starts to explain how bribery moves from merely offering a bribe to the expectation of bribes. When people start expecting to be paid something extra for what they do, we move from a bribery world to an extortion world. We all agree that extortion is morally wrong. To demand something from someone to do what you ought to do anyway is like stealing or robbery."

"I hadn't though of it that way. So choosing to pay bribes to get construction inspectors to get to my sites on time actually contributes to the world that makes paying these bribes necessary in the first place. What works to my benefit in the short term actually undermines a larger good, not just for me, but for everyone from other contractors to clients."

"Yes, it undermines habits of public trust and confidence in the reliability of public schemes to deliver their goods."

"It also starts to explain the situation you were in Zaire. The police arrested you to get the bribe. Arresting you was unfair and unjust, but understandable given the habits in place. But to pay the bribe only reinforced the conditions that extorted the bribe in the first place. When you think about it, I start to understand why there was a problem. Still, I think I would have just paid the bribe."

"I suspect if I had understood what was expected of me, I would have paid it, too. But I didn't understand and so didn't pay the bribe the policemen expected. What was interesting though was what my Zairois colleagues said when I told them the story. They said it was a good thing that I didn't pay the bribe—even if only accidentally—because 'missionaries don't pay bribes.' This was a reminder that a world without bribery was possible. 'Besides when the police realized that you were a preacher, they knew you would not pay. So they let you go.' What my friends were saying is that there were different sets of routines and habits in place for people like me. Those who had gone before me had created a different world for the missionary. I could have changed that—no matter how little—if I had paid the bribe that was expected. What was unfair, I think, is that there were two worlds. A world of bribery for the African and a world without bribery for the missionary. I guess this is the real reason I keep coming back to the problem of bribery. Justice and fairness—what we might call human progress—depend on the kinds of worlds we bring into being through our choices. We might disagree about what we ought to do, but I think we agree that what we do aims to bring a better situation or a better world into being."

"And by undermining trust, converting public goods into private benefits, and sacrificing the long term for the short, we do create a less desirable world. This is what you mean, isn't it?"

"Yes."

Jude, a probation officer, added, "That starts to explain something that I see everyday in the gangs. Many of them are willing to try new ways of solving problems and creating community. Most of them don't like the life offered by gangs. They see it as the only option they have. But when we offer them a chance to engage in dialogue with the police, for example, they turn us down flat. They tell me that 'the fix is in.' What they mean is habits of public trust have been eroded too far. They have little confidence in the system, but the system is not so much a system as a set of transactions that build up confidence over time or fail to build up confidence. So 'the fix,' what they see as bribery and corruption in public life, is answered with the only alternative they think they have. So what you've got is a loss of public confidence and trust. That goes on long enough and the breakdown makes 'gangsterism' completely rational. Gangs are, in their own perverse way, a kind of order—a predictable set of transactions—in what gang members see as a very disordered world."

Steve took up the conversation. "That's not a bad example, even if it is hard to relate it to any single act of bribery. But here is a another story that is similar. Last year a friend of mine was covering a news story in Mexico.[7] People in small villages had started taking the law into their own hands. What put my friend on the story was an incident where people burned a man alive who had molested and murdered a village girl. There was no trial or anything. Just outrage. The guy was dragged into the village square, covered with old tires, doused with kerosene, and set on fire. Officials in Mexico City told my friend this was an isolated event and those guilty of the murder would be tried and punished. Nosing around, my friend found that people reacted the way they did because the accused man had not been arrested or even questioned by police. Lack of police action just seemed to be expected. As one man put it, 'Justice is for sale here. If you have some coins, you can buy some. If not, they just listen to your story and nothing happens.' Continuing to investigate, my friend discovered that this sentiment was not isolated but widespread. To get the police to do anything requires payment—not just to the local policeman but to the district and regional police commissioners.[8] Moreover, there is a pattern of vigilante justice throughout the state in response. People are taking justice into their own hands. As a prominent merchant in Santiago Tolman told him, 'We are tired of waiting for justice.' A parish priest told him, 'There is anger and a feeling of necessity that people comply with what they promise.' A sociologist in Mexico City told him, 'People no longer expect that social institutions will respond when and as they should to perceived incidents of injustice.' What my friend concluded was, in spite of government reports that this isolated, in Mexico 'the evidence of lost faith in the government's ability—or desire—to protect and to serve is everywhere.' "

"What a story," said Jude. "Maybe that really gets at what is morally wrong with bribery better than anything we've said tonight. There is a problem with merchandising order and predictable social routines. But is still easy to pay to get what one wants. I think this was Margaret's point from the beginning."

"Sure it is," said Steve, "but the fact that it is easy does not mean that it is morally right and that has been topic of the conversation. I have been convinced that bribery is not just legally wrong. It is morally wrong because it systematically distorts the social relations that are condition of the possibility of our meeting whole ranges of goods for many different people over relatively long periods of time. Choosing to pay bribes has consequences that are not as obvious as getting what one wants like construction inspectors to my sites. Sure, it is easy to pay the bribe and get the inspection. But I also have to ask myself is it right. I don't think it is because of the distortions it creates."

Margaret, somewhat angrily, retorted, "That's easy to say from the comfort of your dining room, Steve. You did not have the decision to make that I did. I only did what I had to do."

"Exactly, Margaret," answered Steve. "You felt you had to because bribery had become a normal routine at the courthouse."

"What a horrible vision you make such a little act out to be," Margaret argued. "Can it really so bad that a bribe to the judge becomes a bribe to the police and so on like your Mexican story?"

"That's what the evidence suggests can happen," said Steve. "That does not mean it has to happen that way. But more harm than good seems to come from offering and taking bribes."

Margaret, miffed, ended, "I still say I made a decision that you really have not had to make."

Anibal, ever the peacekeeper, said, "Yes, that is true. None of us faces the exactly same decisions as anyone else. We make our decisions and accept the consequences which raises another interesting question: Are the consequences we suffer for our actions always just?"

NOTES

1. This essay uses the old philosophical device of the dialogue to try and answer the questions posed in the title, "What is Wrong with Bribery?" The dialogue is imaginative, based on a cluster of conversations I have had over the years in a variety of contexts. While the framework is imaginative, the content is not. Every story in the story is true.

2. There are five arguments offered to justify the moral neutrality of bribery: (1) everybody does it; (2) bribery is necessary in order to do business in some cultures; (3) reciprocities (gifts, gratuities, tips and bribes, etc.) are formally indistinguishable; (4) prohibitions of bribery are unenforceable; and (5) the social effects of bribery are trivial or nondemonstrable. Arguments 1–4 are, on close analysis, circular and fallacious. Argument 5 is based on a mistake of fact. As will become clear later, these arguments, or better, moral rationalizations, are based on a form of common sense that actually promotes social decline rather than fosters social progress. I concede that bribery is a widespread practice that enters into the production of a standard of living in many societies, but this is not the question being addressed in this essay. The question is: "Is bribery moral, immoral, or morally neutral?"

3. John T. Noonan Jr., *Bribes: The Intellectual History of a Moral Idea* (Berkeley: University of California Press, 1984) offers a detailed history of bribery in human culture both historical and contemporary. He concludes that (1) bribery is universal in human cultures but it is also (2) universally regarded as "shameful." Herb Brooks, "The Cost of Bribery," *Human Systems Management* 12:3 (1993): 205 estimates that bribes equal 1% of the U.S. gross national product (an estimate of the value of goods and services produced in a given year). However, as Brooks accurately says, bribery is a hidden transaction and so difficult to measure. Bribery has become so common in developed countries that the codes of ethics of almost all professional associations contains a prohibition of offering or taking bribes. All states and the federal government have laws against bribery. My point is bribery is an everyday experience even in the United States and Europe. Bribery is not just a phenomenon of underdeveloped countries.

4. Steve's position is not an uncommon one in many businesses. However, the practice is illegal in the United States. But many countries consider bribes legitimate business expenses and are deductible for tax purposes. This is the case in Austria, Australia,

Belgium, Canada, Denmark, France, Germany, Greece, Ireland, Luxembourg, the Netherlands, New Zealand, Norway, Spain, and Switzerland.

5. Everyone is familiar with the practice of tipping. A tip is a small gift or gratuity for services rendered. For example, the money left at the table in a restaurant, given to a bellboy in a hotel, or to a hairstylist etc. are tips. Its moral connotation is "very good." A fee for service (discussed below) is a publicly known payment for services rendered. For example, payments made to a doctor, lawyer, or accountant are fees for service. Its moral connotation is that such payments are appropriate.

6. I do not have figures for Mexico, but a recent World Bank study showed that in 1976 Nigeria lost 480 million dollars from goods smuggled into neighboring countries. In developing countries like Mexico this loss of revenue is not negligible—especially given that this is revenue lost to public goods such as economic development, health care, and public administration.

7. Reported in *The San Antonio Express News*, September 15, 1996, 1A. Bribery has become a focus of interest and concern in relation to community, economic, and political development. See, for example, the address by Dr. Frene Ginwala, Speaker of the National Assembly in Parliament of the Republic of South Africa, "The Role of Government in International Corruption," delivered to the European Business Ethics Network Conference, September 19, 1996. She cites the following statistics. In 1995 there were 100 cases in which foreign bribes undercut the ability of U.S. firms to win contracts valued at 45 billion dollars. A recent UN study estimates that between 1988 and 1992 the top ten arms exporters sold 20 billion dollars of arms to developing countries. At least 15% of this was paid to politicians and military chiefs as bribes. She argues that international corruption is in many instances tacitly supported and actively encouraged by many Western countries.

8. The *mordita* (the little bite) is common in Mexico. Police often stop cars, hold out their hands, and demand *por la coca* (for a soft drink).

STUDY QUESTIONS

1. According to Sauer, what is wrong with bribery?

2. Should an individual be held responsible for immoral behavior if a social system encourages it?

3. Can you think of other conflicts between the needs of the individual and the needs of a society? What ethical solutions to the conflicts might you propose?

PART II

Social and Political Philosophy: Social Locations and Political Commitments

Introduction

PERSONAL EXPERIENCES SPARK particular challenges that generate philosophical questions. People living in different social contexts will raise different kinds of philosophical questions. Contemporary philosophers often follow sociologists in defining social context in terms of an individual's race or ethnicity, national origin, economic class, gender, and sexual orientation. A person's treatment at the hands of others is often affected by these variables. One radical branch of social and political philosophy examines the effects of these variables on human experience.

More traditionally, social and political philosophy studies the nature of human communities. What frictions arise when diverse individuals and groups try to live together? What kinds of social structures ease those frictions and make collective activity possible? What kinds of collective activities lead to justice in societies? And, finally, what kind of treatment of people should be considered just? Economic freedom? Flexible work schedules? Gender equality? Ethnic stratification?

The essays in this section lie at an intersection between traditional and contemporary radical social/political philosophy. Each essay deals with its author's growing understanding of justice. Each author, regardless of her or his social location, wants to live in a society that helps as many people as possible flourish. Depending on the particular abundance or deprivation they have seen, however, each author defines justice and injustice slightly differently. Each author identifies a different arena in which social change will bring about greater justice.

In his essay, "Conversations with Russian Philosophers: The Importance of Dialogue in Political Philosophy," American philosopher William C. Gay emphasizes the importance of understanding the everyday context in which political philosophies arise. He describes his initial impressions of his Russian professional counterparts. He found them naive in their political understandings, overly ritualistic in their professional behavior, and cynical about the wrong things. However, when Gay learned more about their day to day lives, he realized that he was the one making the mistakes by interpreting their behavior as if they lived in a U.S. context. To do political philosophy effectively, Gay concludes, philosophers from different countries need to experience daily life under each other's systems and not merely trade the philosophies generated by those systems.

In her essay, "Memoirs of an Unconventional Mother," Martha Satz directly addresses the ways in which her experiences as a mother shaped her views on justice and equity. As an older, single, adoptive mother of biracial children, she did not have the same opportunities for support of her parenting as more conventional mothers. She realizes how helpful it would have been if her employers and colleagues had made allowances for her: allowing more time to complete assignments, paying childcare fees during attendance at professional conferences, giving more family leave time. All parents should receive these benefits, she argues, even if people who are not parents do not receive a parallel benefit. Justice does not require treating everyone equally, that is, exactly the same way, but equitably, in accordance with individual needs and the contributions he or she is making to society.

Robert Jensen, in "Hearing Voices and Telling Stories: Resisting Domination in Everyday Life," describes the gradual changes in his lifestyle that led to a commitment to resist unjust domination. As his situations and practices changed, so did his thoughts; as his thoughts changed, so did his practices. Changes in his family, new understandings about his sexuality, conversations with friends, and books by remarkable philosophers all affected him. Gradually he became aware that the everyday practices of watching television, eating meat, driving automobiles, and consuming pornography contribute to unjust domination—of people's minds, of animals, of the environment, of women, of children, and of some men. He shows that we can change our everyday practices in order to take a political stand.

In "Being and Playing: Sport and the Valorization of Gender," Leslie A. Howe speaks of her experiences as an avid player of the male-dominated team sport of hockey. Playing hockey raised her consciousness of sexism and motivated her to speak out against sexist practices in team sports. In Canada, hockey is often experienced as the ultimate site for learning and enacting masculinity. As such, women are often not welcome as teammates—even on explicitly co-ed teams. This leads to an erosion of team values of respect and cooperation and to a lack of self-respect even among accomplished women athletes. Team sports has the potential to develop some of the best human qualities, but gendering a sport blocks both male and female players from achieving moral and athletic excellence.

In "Engendering Ethnicity: The Economy of Female Virginity and Guatemalan Nationalism," Luna Nàjera tries to understand why her parents reacted to her rape by directing their anger at her. According to Nàjera's analysis, Guatemalan Latinos take pride in their ethnic superiority. It is considered a Latina woman's job to preserve the integrity of ethnic and class divisions by having sexual relations only within a socially approved marriage. She proves her social worth by remaining a virgin until marriage; if she fails to remain a virgin, her family may consider her to be socially worthless. Nàjera finds the system of social stratification unjust, for divisions are often justified by discriminatory stereotypes. Further, the system has disastrous consequences for women who are raped or otherwise sexually active, for they are sacrificed by the community in order to maintain it.

In "Looking Backward, Moving Forward: Phenomenologies of Time and the Apology for Slavery," Laura Duhan Kaplan comes to a new understanding of racial injustice when she, a white American, helps an African-American family whose car has broken down. A blatant display of racism against the family by a white neighbor shatters some of Kaplan's illusions about the progress the United States has made toward racial equality. She realizes that time seems to have moved in a spiral, rather than in a straight line. Old unresolved issues reappear in new forms. Therefore, any apology or restitution for slavery by the U.S. government must address contemporary forms of racial injustice.

QUESTIONS TO GET YOU STARTED

1. What services do you expect government, family, and religious institutions to provide? Why?
2. How do acceptance and rejection by these institutions affect a person's sense of self?
3. What are some everyday practices that establish divisions—or connections—between social groups?
4. How might a person's experiences affect his or her idea of what justice is?

SUGGESTED READINGS

Dewey, John. *Democracy and Education.* New York: Simon and Schuster, 1997. Dewey (1859–1952) describes an ideal democracy in which groups learn to evolve in response to one another's needs.

Freire, Paulo. *Pedagogy of the Oppressed.* Trans. Myra Bergman Ramos. New York: Continuum Press, 2000. Freire (1921–1997) explains that education for political change begins with careful listening to students.

Hobbes, Thomas. *Leviathan.* New York: Cambridge University Press, 1996. Hobbes (1588–1679) argues that a totalitarian state is necessary to control the disorganized impulses of human nature.

King, Martin Luther Jr. *Loving Your Enemies, With Letter from a Birmingham Jail and Declaration of Independence From the War in Viet Nam.* New York: AJ Muste Memorial Institute, 1981. King (1929–1968) explains why nonviolent direct action is the best way to fight oppression and solve political conflicts.

Montesquieu, C. de. *Spirit of the Laws.* Montesquieu (1689–1755) argues that different political systems are appropriate for different cultures.

Plato. *Republic.* Trans. Allan Bloom. New York: Basic Books, 1991. Plato (c. 427–347 B.C.E.) describes a utopian society in which each person is educated for the good of the state and the soul.

Williams, Patricia J. *The Alchemy of Race and Rights.* Cambridge, MA: Harvard University Press, 1991. Williams (1951–present), a law professor and a descendent of slaves, tries to make sense of the concept of property.

Wollstonecraft, Mary. *A Vindication of the Rights of Woman.* New York: Dover, 1996. Wollstonecraft (1759–1797) argues that gender inequality makes any kind of political equality impossible.

Conversations with Russian Philosophers: The Importance of Dialogue in Political Philosophy

William C. Gay

William Gay teaches philosophy at the University of North Carolina at Charlotte. His teaching, publications, and community service are oriented toward exposing and reducing violence in everyday life—from offensive language to international war. He also works closely with Russian philosophers and published, with Tatiana Alekseeva, *Capitalism with a Human Face: The Quest for a Middle Road in Russian Politics* (1996).

FORTUITOUS CIRCUMSTANCES AND dogged determination secured for me an unusual portal onto the dramatic changes associated with the dissolution of the Soviet Union. My vantage point is both academic and personal, both theoretical and practical. From the time of Gorbachev's *glasnost* until the present day, I have worked with philosophers at Moscow's Institute of Philosophy.

My experiences have led me to re-examine my understanding of political philosophy, a field in which I have worked for two decades. What does it mean to "do political philosophy"? Within political philosophy, this question has traditionally been focused on the relation between theory and practice. Philosophically, positions have been staked out that give a priority to one over the other or which posit a dialectical relation between the two.[1] In this essay, I wish to address in a nontraditional manner what it means to do political philosophy and how this approach leads to a re-evaluation of the relation between theory and practice. To do so, I will employ a narrative method in which I reflect on my experiences with Russian philosophers. While I have learned much from my experiences in Moscow, I have found especially fascinating my observations of and conversations with some very colorful characters. Two of these characters are Oleg Bezrouchkin and V.S. Stiopin, and I will focus on them.

From a vast cast of characters with whom I have become acquainted in Moscow, I have chosen to focus on Oleg Bezrouchkin and V.S. Stiopin because of their starkly contrasting positions and because, while I initially regarded each as naive in different ways, I eventually learned that it was I who was equally naive. Oleg Bezrouchkin is a young man at the beginning of his professional life, and V.S. Stiopin is an elderly man nearing the end of his career. Both are members of Moscow's Institute of Philosophy, Oleg an aspiring graduate student and Stiopin the established Director of the Institute.

Interestingly, I refer to one of these characters by his first name and the other by his last name. I do not recall having heard Oleg referred to by his last name, and I have not heard anyone call Stiopin by his first name—Viacheslav. The issue is not one of the difference in the difficulty of pronunciation but of difference in authority. Still, while my position in the profession is clearly above Oleg and below Stiopin, I have learned from each, but not as much in the numerous professional meetings I have had with them as during informal conversations with them.

Oleg the Myopic Communist

Oleg Bezrouchkin has ruddy cheeks and a constant smile. He is slender, wears wire-rimmed glasses, and smokes whenever he can. Oleg is a graduate student at the Institute of Philosophy, and he is in Tatiana Alekseeva's section on political philosophy. While he regards himself as fairly sophisticated, Alekseeva frequently characterizes him as having "Paleolithic thinking" because of his myopic devotion to the Communist Party, and commands him, if he wants to remain in her section, to master English. All things considered, he holds up fairly well under such criticisms and demands.

I first met Oleg in 1991, shortly before the dissolution of the Soviet Union. He was proud of his membership in the Communist Party yet also had many questions about the American political system. As part of his research into political philosophy, he interviewed me several times. On one sunny, crisp May afternoon, we strolled around Red Square and discussed American politics. I quickly realized that he had a very idealistic view concerning U.S. political campaigns. He believed that they focused on candidates presenting coherent and comprehensive policies to an electorate that would make its selections based on a judgment about which policy positions were closer to their own political philosophies.

Of course, other members of the Institute of Philosophy were Party members; it was virtually unavoidable for those seeking professional success throughout the Soviet era. However, during the Gorbachev era, younger intellectuals were generally critical of the Party, as Alekseeva obviously wanted Oleg to be. They tended to be anti-Soviet and pro-United States. Still, Oleg was one of the top graduate students at the Institute. He was in the Department of Political Philosophy, and he clearly had social skills, as well as language skills, that were superior to many of the other graduate students. For example, he could discuss Hobbes's political philosophy in a competent, sophisticated manner and he had some familiarity with contemporary U.S. political philosophers, such as John Rawls.

So, why would a bright young man like Oleg have such naive views about the Communist Party and American politics?

Maybe he was not so naive. Surely, just as I regarded him as naive, he saw me as equally naive. Maybe he simply did not know enough about how U.S. political campaigns are actually conducted, while I equally failed to know enough about what functions the Party served for young people in the Soviet Union who wanted a moral system for a guide in their lives.

Through conversation, I corrected his idealism about how U.S. politics functions and he corrected my cynicism about the moral status of Soviet communism. Marxism began as a critique of capitalism, especially of its exploitation of workers. Marxism also placed the interest of the species over that of the individual. For this reason, Marxism provided values that should guide the organization of societies and the conduct of individuals. From my studies of orthodox (Soviet) Marxism and Western (non-Soviet) Marxism, I knew that the CPSU (Communist Party of the Soviet Union) regarded Marxism as a scientific system, not as a moral vision. But when I visited in Oleg's home, I learned things that are not found in official Party propaganda or in critical Western analyses. I got to know a young man who, though not raised to be religious, still found himself looking for meaning and value in his life. For him, the summer Pioneer camps gave him the sense of community and moral vision that he needed. He displayed with pride memorabilia from these days—photographs, badges, ribbons, and certificates of membership and achievement.

At that time and for years after, Soviet Communism represented to many an ideal of equality and justice; it provided a model that enabled Oleg and countless others to make reasoned moral judgments. Of course, he knew that the practice of Soviet politics often fell far short of the ideal. But he knew that, whatever the Party might say about scientific Marxism, for many young people like himself it evoked an emotional response that led to a moral passion: He had faith that the ideal of Soviet communism served to advance peace and justice on a global scale—even if it had not done much at all in the past or even though it was not doing that much in the present, at least possibly, and he believed probably, it would or could do so in the future.

Oleg, like most of us, had no basis for assuming that other people, even

Americans, might think in ways that were significantly different from his way of thinking. So, he interpreted political campaigns in the United States according to his ideal of how he imagined they would occur in Russia if free, multiparty elections were to be held. If uninformed interpretation is naive, then I must have struck him as naive as well. In fact one of the lessons to be learned from exchanges such as the one in which I have participated is that when successful people from different cultures find one another's behaviors and views to be naive, it may well be an indication that each is simply operating out of the structural roles and with the cultural assumptions into which they were socialized. Since members of these groups are intelligent, knowledgeable, and professional, we need to move beyond initial recognition of our respective naivetes. To do so requires dialogue like the one Oleg and I had.

Once I found out in some detail where he was coming from in asking his questions about U.S. political campaigns, I realized that our conversation was a breakthrough for me as well. I could now better understand other Russian academics. Likewise, having through Oleg corrected some of my own naivete about attitudes among some toward the Party, I could now better interpret what I heard Russian colleagues saying about the benefits of the former Soviet system and about their frustrations with Russia's recent turn toward democratic politics and a market economy. I now saw that while some were indeed Party hacks and opportunists, others were more like Oleg, finding in the Party a sense of idealized values amid a sea of cultural nihilism.

I regret to say, Oleg has for now at least left the Institute. He may even abandon his dream of becoming a professional philosopher. Instead, he has turned to woodworking. In his small shop and with the help of several employees, he makes cabinets and other household furnishings. I have not yet had a chance to talk to Oleg about why he left the Institute. When we talked about political campaigns, I registered the cynicism of someone who has grown up with political campaigning with its attendant opportunism, scandals, and corruption. Oleg, having not witnessed any genuine elections until the post-Soviet period, had been able to maintain a loftier view. Then came the national campaigns for the Russian Parliament in 1993 and for the Russian presidency in 1995. These elections were hardly devoid of opportunism, and reports of scandal and charges of corruption were rampant. Perhaps, it was all too much for Oleg. Learning the truth about U.S. political campaigns had been hard enough for him. Now he perhaps has come to regard Russian politics in the same cynical manner as I regard U.S. politics. I do not know, but I suspect I will find out this is his view if I can find another afternoon to stroll around Red Square with him and discuss recent political campaigns in Russia. I hope Oleg has not permanently turned his back on philosophy. But regardless, I know I can still learn much more about Russian political philosophy by talking with him than I can from turning to articles in the press or even academic works on Russian politics.

And I hope he can say the same about what he learns about U.S. politics from talking with me.

STIOPIN THE BUREAUCRATIC "CHIEF"

V.S. Stiopin is a survivor. He is a tall, thin man with white hair and thick black-frame glasses. I first met Stiopin in Moscow in May 1991, shortly before the attempted coup in August. He visited my campus for the first time in November and December of 1991, shortly before the dissolution of the Soviet Union. Needless to say, the tensions of these times added to the intensity of our interchanges. I saw him again in Moscow in 1995 and again in Charlotte in 1996.

Because of his opposition to the Soviet Union's invasion of Czechoslovakia, Stiopin's career was sidelined for many years. Eventually, he had entered into his record that he was guilty of only a minor infraction, and he was able to return to positions of prominence, eventually, under Gorbachev's *glasnost*, becoming the Director of Moscow's Institute of Philosophy. He obtained this position during the last years of the Soviet Union and now, several years after the transition to post-Soviet Russia, he still retains this position.

Actually, post-Soviet Russia has largely retained the institutes run by the former Academy of Sciences of the U.S.S.R. (The Russian government now calls them institutes of the Academy of Sciences of Russia.) The Russian government has not even reshuffled personnel very much. However, it has eliminated the institutes that were run by the CPSU. The scholars from these institutes have had difficult times finding new jobs.

So, Stiopin was lucky given his personal past and recent political transformations. Still, when you see Stiopin, you see someone who acts like a "chief." He is clearly the one in command at the Institute, behaving in much the same way as other typical bureaucratic chiefs during the Soviet era and now in the initial post-Soviet period. Some habits die hard; maybe, some never die. At least in the case of hierarchicalism, Russian society seems fairly constant. There may be a rhetorical shift to talk about democracy, but Russia's millennium of authoritarian rule seems to be alive and well in many spheres of supposedly democratic Russia. All of us, Russian and American alike, refer to this chief as "Professor Stiopin," even "Academician Stiopin," or, at times, simply as "Stiopin," but never less formally. No one interrupts him.

Despite his behavior as a bureaucratic chief, Stiopin has other sides to his personality. One of the more surprising for me was his keen interest in professional basketball in the United States. When I asked more, I learned that as a young man he had been a member of the Beloruss (White Russia) national basketball team. He told me that he dreamed of someday attending a professional basketball game in the U.S. Well, I was able to help make his dream come true. During one of his visits to Charlotte, I called the Mayor's office and explained I had a group of Russian scholars participating in a program on democracy at my university. I asked whether the mayor might help us secure some complimentary tickets to a Charlotte Hornets basketball game. I was able to obtain some tickets for a Friday night game at the end of the Russians' visit. Usually, when I would go to the hotel to pick up Stiopin, I had to wait several minutes before he would come down from his room. Not this night. He was standing in front of the hotel waiting for me. He even insisted on eating hot dogs and drinking beer at the game instead of going out to a restaurant for our dinner that evening. He wanted the full, typical, American experience while attending a professional basketball game. Throughout the game, he would stand and cheer when Charlotte took the lead. At one point, and in one of his few spontaneous remarks in English, he said, "I love this game! I love this game!" He might be a "chief," but he also knew how to be a regular fan at a U.S. basketball game.

Stiopin is also an extremely gregarious person. Initially, I thought he did not understand how professional conferences were to be conducted. My presumption turned out to be another case of my naivete. Later, as I observed more, I realized Stiopin was paying attention, even day after day at a conference at which almost all papers were delivered in English (which meant, since he has very little understanding of English, he had to listen to simultaneous translations that were whispered into his ear). Frequently, he would jump into the discussion and talk very passionately and at great length.

What I have come to realize is that Stiopin is a real intellectual but not of the sort with which Americans are familiar. At our conferences, professors generally read technical papers focused on a narrow topic and argue in a tight manner. Members of the audience do not speak until after a presentation has been completed and then only when called on, and usually members of the audience do not speak very long or very passionately but rather coolly and logically. Stiopin, like other Russian intellectuals, shows his brilliance by doing precisely the opposite. He speaks extemporaneously and throws his net wide, drawing from recollections of the vast Russian literary tradition and Russia's millennium-long history of authoritarianism in politics. Within this intellectual framework and also making connection with 19th- and 20th-century Russian philosophy, he articulates his philosophical points.

At the organized Roundtable discussions on democratization in Moscow and Charlotte, the Americans, at both locations, prepared and read papers. The Russians, who never read papers in Moscow, did prepare them for meetings in the United States. They actually knew us better than we knew them. On a couple of occasions, I have had the opportunity in Moscow to speak to faculty groups in one of the departments at the Institute of Philosophy. I found that what worked best was for me to make a few provocative remarks and ask for questions and then pursue a genuine dialogue, rather than stage a "performance" in which I read a lengthy paper. In other words, through observation of Russians like Stiopin and by conscious self-remodeling of my behavior, I was becoming more like Stiopin.

One final lesson that I learned was from the occasions when Alekseeva and other Russian colleagues would coach me before my meetings with Stiopin about the Scholar Exchange Agreement between the Institute of Philosophy and my university. On the first such occasion, back in 1991, I thought they were coaching me so that I could suggest to Stiopin some of the things that my younger and closer Russian colleagues wanted out of the exchange. How naive I was. Only in 1995 did I come to see that they recognized that I and other Americans are naive about the politics of such meetings. The expectation is that a participant in an exchange at such a prestigious institute needed to make a case for its benefits. I needed to show the advances that would come to the institute (and, of course, its director) of continuing and expanding the exchange.

I tended to regard these visits to Stiopin's office as "breaks" in which the leaders on each side sipped tea, munched on sweets, and exchanged pleasantries. No, these were the real work sessions. This was the time when deals were to be proposed and agreements struck. These were the crucial sessions, despite the appearance to a Westerner that they were informal and insignificant opportunities to chat over refreshments during breaks between formal sessions of the Roundtable discussions. Next time, I will be better prepared and act more appropriately without coaching or as the result of coaching that I will now better understand. In other words, I will become even more like Stiopin.

CONCLUSION

Even when I do more traditional political philosophy in Moscow, such as delivering a lecture, I am also always involved in activities that take me a step further away from this more traditional role. This step away from traditional philosophizing occurs when I participate in the numerous informal dialogues that take place at these conferences. It also occurs when I observe and reflect comparatively on what I see and then ask myself how their style, when it strikes me as naive, might make perfect sense in their context. What I have come to see is that political philosophy can be done in a very practical and successful way through personal interaction.

On reflection, I realize that through such observations and conversations I do more to advance political philosophizing than I do in my formal papers delivered at the Institute and elsewhere. What Oleg and I had read and theorized about one another's political systems were very idealized and frequently misrepresentative accounts. Our conversations, though dealing with only a few details, brought us to levels of insight and understanding that our professional papers flew over without so much as a bump of concrete comprehension in their unfolding of pre-packaged distinctions. Our conversing let us know that in our conferencing we were more like ships passing in the night than political philosophers engaged in a project of mutually shared theory construction.

Similarly, while I might regard Stiopin as a bureaucratic chief and he might see in me an American unprepared to wheel and deal, we are both naive in these perceptions. Stiopin knows how to get things done in his system, and I have learned to accommodate their style and to conduct myself accordingly in meetings in his office. Likewise, he and the other members of the Russian delegation have learned to conduct themselves in public forums in the United States in a manner that lets them appear to Americans as rigorous professionals. Of course, they are quite professional in their own way, but it would not be easily recognized if they behaved here as they do in their institute in Moscow.

As a result of these experiences, I cannot accept a definition of "doing political philosophy" that is restricted to delivering and publishing professional papers. When political philosophy is separated from practical politics, the exigencies of the real world are glossed over. Ironically, such political philosophy has lost sight of its *raison d'être*. Granted, Plato argued for the primacy of theory over practice in *The Republic*. However, the driving force behind his argument arose from his own practical involvements in and frustrations with concrete, real-world political life. My own experiences with Russian philosophers, while hardly as extensive or significant as Plato's involvement in politics in Athens and Syracuse, underscore that when political philosophy loses sight of the concrete, real-world political life that spawned it, its theories remain not only abstract but also truncated—if not outright distorted.

The positions on theory and practice in political philosophy do not provide useful models for dealing with the inadequate pursuit of peace or democracy by Russia, the United States, or the rest of the global community. If I want to advance peace and democracy, I would be ill-advised to do so exclusively by means of pursuing traditional political philosophy. Laura Duhan Kaplan, in writing about how abstract philosophy does not advance justice, states "it serves the world quite poorly for a great intellect to waste its time spinning elegant abstractions which do not make the world, nor the lives of anyone within it, better."[2] At the least, abstract theories need to be put into words and projects that connect with everyday life. Plato himself, after spinning out his ideals and theories in *The Republic*, calls for practical action, for the least change that would advance society toward the actualization of his conception of justice.[3]

I do not know what the "least change" is that would advance Russia, the United States, and the global community closer to peace and justice. However, I do know that during the period of my involvement with Russian philosophers, the global community has faced some serious military and humanitarian crises which have received little attention within political philosophy.[4] At the end of the Soviet period, two significant U.S. military interventions occurred. In December 1989, Operation Just Cause occurred with the invasion of Panama. In

January 1991, Operation Desert Storm occurred with the Persian Gulf War. Then, in the immediate post-Soviet period, humanitarian intervention was made into Somalia while the slaughter in Bosnia initially went largely unchecked—as it later did in Rwanda.

How much political philosophy do we need in order to be able to analyze these events? And despite its theoretical sophistication, why does political philosophy so seldom address such pressing problems of actual everyday life? Do our political theories really help us in dealing with such all-too-frequent everyday manifestations of injustice and cruelty? They may give us the conceptual tools, but by themselves they do not engage us practically.

Marx said philosophers have only understood the world and the point is to change it.[5] I make a similar point when I say that political philosophy needs to turn to the practical and concrete concerns of everyday life.[6] This move can occur in conversations with friends and colleagues. I have learned this lesson from shifting from conferencing to conversing with colleagues in Moscow.

I cannot accept that we are doing political philosophy only when or even especially when we are conferencing. I affirm that we are also and especially doing political philosophy when we are conversing outside formal meetings. In a stroll along the Arbot with a Russian colleague or during a dinner party in a Russian home, I have done relevant and serious political philosophizing with more impact on my understanding and that of my Russian counterparts than has occurred in the discussions at Russian-American philosophy conferences. A truly robust political philosophy, capable of engaging the problems of everyday life, may well have as its springboard genuinely open dialogue instead of the typically disengaged monologue of abstract theory construction. So, to do political philosophy, we need to begin by talking with one another; we need to converse about the political realities of everyday life and how we can ameliorate them.

NOTES

1. For the priority of theory, cf. Plato, *The Republic of Plato*, trans. and ed. Francis MacDonald Cornford (Oxford: Oxford University Press, 1945), 177–78; for the stress on practice or observation, cf. Alfred Jules Ayer, *Language, Truth and Logic* (New York: Dover Publications, Inc., 1952), 31–32; for the dialectical relation, cf. Georg Lukács, *History and Class Consciousness: Studies in Marxist Dialectics*, trans. Rodney Livingstone (Cambridge, MA.: The MIT Press, 1971), 3.
2. Laura Duhan Kaplan, "My Father the Philosopher: Body and Mind, Hopefully Intertwined," in *Family Pictures: A Philosopher Explores the Familiar* (Chicago: Open Court Press, 1997), 60–70.
3. Plato, *Republic*, 178.
4. One exception occurs in the work done by members of Concerned Philosophers for Peace. Special issues of *Concerned Philosophers for Peace Newsletter* have been devoted to The War Against Iraq (11, no. 1; spring 1991), Bosnia and Somalia (13, no. 1; spring 1993), and Haiti (14, no. 2; fall 1994).
5. Karl Marx, "Theses on Feuerbach," in *The Marx-Engels Reader*, 2nd ed., ed. Robert C. Tucker (New York: W.W. Norton, 1978), 145.
6. Cf. my essay, "From Wittgenstein to Applied Philosophy," *The International Journal of Applied Philosophy* 9, no. 1 (summer/fall 1994): 15-20.

STUDY QUESTIONS

1. Gay offers several examples of situations in which he felt he genuinely gained political insights. What are some of the situations and the insights?
2. How is it possible to gain philosophical insights merely by getting to know people?
3. How is political philosophy connected with the quest for peace and justice?

Memoirs of an Unconventional Mother

Martha Satz

Martha Satz, an assistant professor of English at Southern Methodist University, has published many essays drawing on her dual academic background in philosophy and literature. She is currently at work on a book on adoption, race, and literature. This book integrates her experience as a single person who adopted two biracial children with a study of cross-cultural adoption in literature, law, and popular culture.

AT THE END of last semester, a student in my interdisciplinary women's studies class presented me with a necklace, a string of African beads from her collection. Although thrilled by her offering, I did not register the surprise I first experienced on receiving such a token, for I have grown accustomed to the ceremonial way some students choose to mark their taking leave from my class. I accepted the gift in the spirit in which I thought it intended, an external symbol of a life-altering experience. Last semester one young woman wrote that at the beginning of the semester she had been contemplating plastic surgery to fulfill her boyfriend's ideal of beauty, but by the end, she had decided against the operation—and him. A young man reported that he brought the subject matter of the class home to his fiancee each week and as time went on they reconceived the plan for their lives—factoring in her career plans as well as his. A woman reconsidered her relationship to what she had regarded as her difficult mother-in-law and saw her anew as heroic. These transformations occur, I have come to believe, because students bring with them a simmering brew of personal issues, often unacknowledged and unexamined. When the class furnishes them a theoretical framework and an occasion to consider these concerns in an intellectual, experiential, and emotional way, the ferment produces radical alterations.

For these reasons, I always include the topic of motherhood in the curriculum, in particular the reconciliation of mothering and career. Such an inclusion, I believe, extends the student an anticipatory favor, for the topic consumes almost every woman I know. And no mother of my acquaintance has resolved the issue to her satisfaction. A close friend of mine with a prestigious career wistfully confided to me that when her sons were young, she had resigned herself to being third in importance to them—after their primary caretaker and their father. An acquaintance, a newly appointed administrator, was intent on attending an intensive twelve-hour a day, three-week institute with an infant in tow and was aghast that the conference made no provisions for nursing mothers. But she was more shocked by a feminist friend who did not share her outrage. "You can't climb Mt. Everest with a baby strapped to your back," her friend had remarked. But primarily, I consider this topic because of my own obsessive interests. For the last twenty-seven years, motherhood and its relation to career has occupied a central place in my consciousness.

In my classroom, students discuss issues of equity and parenthood; these questions, it seems, cut to the marrow of all our beings. Never are arguments more passionate or personal. All of us have something vital invested in examining and evaluating our own upbringing and our stance toward perpetuating such a model. Young students imagine their future lives—with or without children. And all of us live and work alongside parents and feel strongly, it would seem, in that regard. Of course, I bring my own life experiences to these conversations, but only very gradually do I share my perspective with my students. I do not want to skew the direction of discussion or unknowingly silence certain viewpoints.

In the class, we consider Felice Schwartz's proposal to create an alternative career path for women, a recommendation nicknamed the "Mommy Track" from her article's initial publication in the *Harvard Business Review*.[1] Schwartz assumes that women are more costly to employ because of the facts of maternity and suggests that working mothers would happily sacrifice pay and promotion for a more flexible schedule. We read as well Barbara Ehrenreich and Deirdre English's scathing response exposing and questioning Schwartz's assumptions and suggesting another viewpoint entirely.[2] Although Ehrenreich and English expose Schwartz's dubious premises, that working mothers do in fact have the freedom to decrease their incomes and that mothers rather than fathers should shoulder the responsibility for child care, the authors reserve the brunt of their attack for Schwartz's underlying assumption that individual parents must resolve child care issues—not business or society at large. In contradistinction to Schwartz, Ehrenreich and English suggest that if business and society are not conducive to family life then it is the work environment and society at large which must change.

Almost all the students balk at Ehrenreich and English's challenge to their customary ways of thinking. At the core of their beliefs lies the view that having children is an individual decision for which parents must take responsibility. This response is almost universal—nineteen- and twenty-year-olds in agreement with older students who are themselves mothers. If anything, the mothers hold the belief more adamantly, painfully aware of the challenges faced and the sacrifices made to be in the class. With some pride, they cling to the belief that society should not have to make any accommodations for them at all.

In class discussion, I gently push at the students' assumptions drawing from my own recent experiences. Doing so feels restorative to me because in past years, at a momentous time in my life, I shared the students' assumptions and suffered greatly from so doing. I have recovered from my own situation, and in the intervening time my views have undergone revolutionary change.

As a result of my altered perspective, I propose that in the business world the chief caregiver of young children should be accorded more latitude, the option of having more personal or sick days, a work schedule that will accommodate the needs of small children, flextime. "It's not fair!" most of the younger students angrily protest. They talk of having to work weekends on jobs because coworkers with families can't. One young woman speaks resentfully of another woman in her office "getting off" all the time to take her child to the doctor. For the first time a visible rift does arise in the class. I see the faces of the mothers in the class tighten in anger. One finally erupts, "When I take my child to the doctor, I'm not 'getting off.' I'd much rather be at work." Another student, the most scrupulous and intelligent in the class, quietly recounts an incident. "Last semester, the only time I ever mentioned my children to an instructor, I called the day before the final to explain that I might not be there because my daughter was having a severe asthmatic crisis. He replied that there were lots of other students who didn't want to be at the final either." She pauses, shaking in outrage. Students talk passionately trying to make others understand. The younger students almost unanimously pleading fairness, which they translate as equality—everybody must be treated the same.

We read a brief *New York Times* article that supports the view that all workers be treated the same.[3] The article recounts the grievances of single people in the workplace who feel indignant about personal leave time for parents that they as single people are not accorded. The article cites with approval a company that accords as much status to the employee who wishes time off to practice the bongos or to pursue mountain climbing as the one who wishes to take off to care for a sick parent or child.

I argue against this perspective, declaring that some reasons are just more important than others, and society should recognize that hierarchy. Taking care of a child is more important than playing the bongos. Society has a vested interest in the next generation. There exist all kinds of societal precedents to indicate that equitable treatment is not always identical treatment. We make special provisions for the handicapped, for those with learning differences. In a moral sense, we should be able to take into account the personal situation of someone in the workplace. Indeed, granting a person who is involved in caretaking more latitude may be treating that person equitably, enabling that person to be as productive as other workers. Students counter with the objection that the handicapped and the learning disabled have no choice in the matter, but parents do elect to have children. I appreciate the massive psychological weight of their objection.

With a great deal of trepidation, I cite inconsequential examples from the margins of my experience. I am the only person in my department with a child under the age of eighteen. Moreover, I am a single parent. Some things that are trivial inconveniences for others constitute a hardship for me. Shouldn't I be excused, for example, from advising students in the late afternoon? Students inquire whether I have always felt this way or only since I have had a child, covertly implying that my intellectual position is simply a disguised form of self-interest. I am tempted to answer their question in full.

Some years ago, when I made a series of unconventional choices, I also had certain assumptions about how those decisions would be regarded by my colleagues and by my institution. I took a preemptive stance to the attitudes I assumed they would adopt, acting in accordance with my presuppositions.

As a single person, I adopted two biracial (Black and White) children—with a sixteen-year gap between the two adoptions. Ten years ago, when my son was a freshman in college and I was in my early forties and just after having received tenure, I adopted my daughter. I was at a moment in my career when I was intensively involved in scholarship and at the brink of what I and my department believed would be a somewhat delayed scholarly flourishing.

When I adopted my daughter, I believed that many in the department would take it as a betrayal, reneging on an implicit promise. And, as reported to me, many did. Responding to the anticipated voices, I did not request a maternity leave or a reduction in course load. Although I received the call about my newborn daughter the first week of the semester when changes could have been made, I continued to teach the three different courses that constituted my schedule and administer the course of which I was coordinator. Further, I simply assumed that I would honor the commitment of revising a conference paper requested for an upcoming anthology and write the conference paper that had been accepted on the basis of an abstract. By an unhappy coincidence, my father was taken to the intensive care unit the day I received my infant daughter, and he subsequently died that semester.

Because I had adopted my son at the age of two and a half, I did not appreciate the stress of one person's taking full-time care of a newborn. I had child care only for the times when I was in class. My mental state quickly began to degenerate simply from sleep deprivation. All the courses I taught were writing intensive, and papers went unreturned for longer and longer periods. Occasionally, I couldn't stay awake long enough to read the assignment, so I didn't show up to class, or if I did I was incoherent. I felt unremittingly guilty—guilty toward my students for unreturned papers and shoddy classes, guilty toward my colleagues for lapsing in my collegial duties, guilty toward my father for not being involved sufficiently in his care, guilty toward my daughter for taking my attention away from her to do work. I was a bad person, a failure. I had told everyone that I could do everything, that my work would be unaffected. But I had lied. Some female colleagues bragged about me. I was doing everything. I had missed only one class. I was amazing. Only I knew the horrible truth—everything was falling apart, especially me.

In March, when my daughter was ten weeks old, I sensed that my father's death was imminent. I journeyed East to say goodbye to him and give him a glimpse of his new granddaughter. After returning, I decided that although surely I could write the conference paper, probably this was one commitment that I didn't need to honor, meaning as it would traveling East the following week. The chair of the session was very understanding in contrast to the woman editing the anthology. I called the latter to say that I just wouldn't be able to make the deadline. "I have an infant and a dying father," I started to explain. "And an obligation," she rejoined firmly. Ah, yes, an obligation. I would meet it. My father died the following week. I wrote the paper in a sleepy haze, stringing words together not knowing if they were meaningful or not.

At the end of the semester, the chair of my department called to tell me in a tragic voice that there was very bad news, a student was protesting a grade. "She's citing missed classes and papers returned late?" I asked. He responded sadly and affirmatively, as we both remained silent for a minute contemplating my negligence.

Time has passed and other attitudes have joined with my colleagues' views that I have willfully and perhaps self-destructively thwarted and retarded my scholarly career. Because I am heavily involved in women's studies and minority literature, my personal situation has furnished me with experiential credentials. I am the only one in my department who can speak personally about balancing maternal and professional concerns. I am not Black, but I have two minority children, and this fact means that I have a demonstrably greater vested interest in minority studies. I am introduced with pride when we are recruiting minority candidates. As an outgrowth of my activities as mother, I have developed a children's literature course which emphasizes the problematics of race and gender. I think that my department respects me, what I have achieved personally and how I have integrated the personal with my professional life. But now that my daughter is ten, I have had the leisure to re-evaluate my experience of her infancy, seeing much of it as a product of self-victimization, much of it the product of fallacious institutional and societal thinking, and much of it open to difficult far-reaching questions.

The unorthodox nature of my motherhood magnified the issues of individual responsibility in my particular situation. I was single, I already had a child, I was in my forties, and I elected the adoptive route to motherhood. Consequently, in a number of ways, I was defying conventions and expectations in becoming a mother of an infant. Had I been in a similar career situation, but a thirty-something married woman who became pregnant, I do not think that issues of professional betrayal would have arisen for my senior colleagues or for me—at least not with such vigor. Had the circumstances of my maternity been more conventional, I believe my motherhood would have been accepted more readily, and I would have been routinely accorded a maternity leave and arrangements to accommodate my situation. Perhaps more importantly, I would have asked for these things and taken them as my due. Certainly, it may be argued that becoming a parent is always the result of a choice or series of choices. However, clearly, my motherhood was the product of more self-conscious choices than most situations of parenthood. I had to decide that contrary to popular wisdom, a single White woman in her forties would make a good mother for a biracial infant daughter, and that I wished at my age to take on this additional life-long commitment. Secondly, I had to find an adoption agency willing to make such a placement and then persuade the agency of the wisdom of so doing. I had to furnish evidence of my financial and emotional capacities for taking on this responsibility. I had to pay the agency a considerable sum. All of these things I did because I was convinced that adopting my daughter was a good idea. Without going into great detail, I will enumerate some of the reasons. I had a good track record. My biracial son was emotionally grounded, academically successful, and comfortable with his complex identities. Biracial children were still difficult to place so that the adoption would be of societal benefit. Also, although my life had been difficult, I had flourished as a scholar/mother.

Yet, in spite of all these good reasons for my becoming a mother again, my actions indicated that I believed my motherhood needed further justification, that I believed I was not as entitled as others to societal support. But if I presumed, as I do now, that all parenthood is entitled to societal support, and if I further assumed, as I do now, that all parenthood is a result of choice, then, in all consistency, I should have believed that my motherhood, although the result of unconventional, self-conscious decisions, was also entitled to such support.

Evidently, I did not. I believed that because I was breaking with convention I needed to take complete responsibility for my decision. I have since concluded that although I had argued against those I imagined believed that my motherhood was inappropriate, I believed them on some level and therefore accepted the view that I would have to take on more of the responsibilities of motherhood than others. But now that my second adventure in motherhood is no longer a bold experiment but a mundane fact of my existence, now that the once theoretical reasons for my second motherhood undergird my life, now that younger women look to me as a positive role model, I realize the deficiencies of my former thinking. I realize I am more similar to other mothers than different from them.

I also recall with horror some of my colleagues' views and wonder at their power to infiltrate my thought. Some of my colleagues believed that I had adopted a child to thwart my scholarly career, that I unconsciously feared success and chose to adopt a child as a way of holding myself back. When I first heard the view, I feared the hypothesis might be true. But almost immediately I realized what a warped position such an idea represented. If one evaluated success only in terms of a scholarly career, then indeed one could pass this judgment. But this view assumes an exceedingly narrow view of success. Seeing a child as an unconscious instrument in the thwarting of one's career is to see life as if it were measured only in the dimension of career advancement, a view I fear some of my colleagues hold.

I am also ashamed to admit that I caught myself subscribing, contrary to all my other views, to the idea of natural motherhood. I viewed my motherhood, in contrast to the thirty-year-old married woman of my imagination, as an artifice and thereby less deserving. In my more clear-thinking moments, I do not believe that there is any such thing as natural or unnatural motherhood nor could I conceive of any way of distinguishing the two.

But now having discussed the oddity of my particular situation, let us talk of the general question of whether motherhood or primary caregivers should be given institutional support to accommodate their particular situation and whether such treatment constitutes unfair treatment. Take for example the issue of travel funds. I resumed conference-going when my daughter was thirteen months old. That first conference was a ghastly experience. My little girl destroyed the motel room, smeared cream cheese on my manuscript, cried heartwrenchingly when I left to deliver my paper, constantly struggled to escape from her stroller, but broke into a headlong run whenever she was put down. Only on the shuttle from the hotel to the airport did she give me a moment's peace, falling asleep on my lap as I clutched my briefcase. A young woman attending the conference regarded us and whispered, "This is my dream." I saw in her mind's eye the rosy vision of herself with briefcase in one hand, baby in the other, career and motherhood in perfect balance. I didn't want to disillusion her by recounting all my difficulties. However, I venture to say that attending that conference had been a good deal harder for me than for most participants. And more expensive. While some conferences have free or low-cost child care, this one did not. Would it have been absurd to ask my department to subsidize my child care, surely a professional cost of attending the conference?

But when I have ventured such ideas, I have heard troubled responses from others. Let me note two of them. One woman of my acquaintance says that she has personal costs arising from conference attendance as well. She owns two cats and when she goes to a conference, she must board her cats and if, as frequently happens, one of her cats should acquire a urinary tract infection at the vet, then the bills really mount up. Should her department be responsible for such personal expenses arising from her conference attendance? I think I understand the spirit of her objection; it is what logicians term a *reductio ad absurdum* refutation. Surely no department should pay vet bills. Logically, if one considers the conclusion absurd, then one must say that a premise is absurd, in this case, that a department should pay personal expenses. However, I do feel comfortable with the principle that one can make a moral distinction between children and cats and reasonably assert that child care is more than a personal expense.

Another concerned response comes from an administrator: "How am I going to make judgments about everyone's individual needs? One colleague needs to secure care for his elderly father, another a babysitter, another a housesitter. Once we open the door to everyone's particular situation, it makes my job as administrator untenable." I feel sympathetic toward this administrator's increased difficulties, but, in fact, administrators make complex judgments all the time, balancing the performance of one faculty member who has an outstanding teaching record with one whose teaching is perhaps less strong but who does more research. Perhaps, though, this administrator feels discomfort because such a policy would require her to make judgments in a nontraditional area—need.

But there is a yet more deeply rooted objection against the idea that primary caretakers be given additional levels of support, in my experience arising most often from female colleagues. The perspective surprised me initially because it expressed anguish in an area where I had not dreamt or perhaps remembered it lay. "You mothers have so much already," a friend tearfully confessed to me when I shared an early version of this paper with her late one night, "love, warmth, family. When you grow older, there will be someone around to take care of you. I will have no one. Things do have a way of evening themselves out. Now you want more benefits too. It's not fair. I have chosen to be alone, and I deserve to be rewarded for the things I've sacrificed."

On a human level, I find this argument affecting. And I think my response reminded me of how morally invigorating it can be to be to see something from another, opposite perspective. In my musings, I tend to concentrate on the things I lack, particularly time and money, and I often succumb to jealousy when I perceive the great expanses of time, as it seems to me, that my colleagues possess. But on listening to someone who was envious of me, who focused on what I had that she did not, I shifted my perspective, treasuring what I did have.

And it is not that I suddenly realized my children's material or strategic value, for who knows who will care for me when and if I am old? However, once again I appreciated their contribution to the quality of my present life. I must confess, though I have not publicly uttered the words before, to my own belief that those with children have a richer, more profound life that those who do not. And this insight did make me temporarily ashamed of thinking of my children in terms of increased need. But in a practical sense, they do represent such need, and it is on the practical dimension my university deals with me. And reciprocally, if in years to come, my children can provide for me materially or practically, and my colleague is alone, then I believe society should provide for her, but of course that consideration takes us far afield from this paper.

Quoting my female colleagues and disagreeing with them saddens me and painfully reminds me of that semester when my daughter was an infant. Sadly and ironically, those I most wanted to keep faith with were my feminist friends on campus. For me that meant I wanted to prove for them that women could be mothers, even single mothers, and be every bit as productive as scholars and teachers. Some of them bought into my self-delusion. They cheered me as I stumbled on. But as they proclaimed me "super woman," their perceptions became another set of expectations to which I felt I had to rise. In contrast, I remember with gratitude the sentiment of a perceptive woman colleague when I returned from my father's funeral and confessed that I couldn't go on. She said, "Thank God. I wondered when you were going to acknowledge that."

I think women, in particular, while encouraging themselves and other women to destroy gender stereotypes, to pursue careers of all kinds, should also acknowledge the strains and limitations childrearing creates for anyone who does it. Simplistic as it sounds, they must acknowledge the finitude of individual human beings. The only thing that finally alleviated my guilt that fateful semester was the insight, obvious though it should have been, that I was failing because I was human. I simply physically could not do more. I was in an impossible situation. I had too many obligations.

In this essay, I have offered my view of institutional policy toward those with particular needs in caring for children. But I could not offer my position without relating the story from which my revelation arose. My story and the insight it produced are the tangible means I wish to present in exchange for my students' offerings of gifts, stories, and insights. As we hear each others' stories, I believe we correct and expand our moral vision.

NOTES

1. Felice N. Schwartz, "Management Women and the New Facts of Life," *Harvard Business Review* 67, 1 (Jan–Feb 1989): 65–76.
2. Barbara Ehrenreich and Deirdre English, "Blowing the Whistle on the 'Mommy Track,'" *Ms. Magazine* 18 (July 1989): 56–58.
3. Lena Williams, "Childless Workers Demanding Equity in Corporate World," *New York Times*, May 29, 1994, 1.

STUDY QUESTIONS

1. What are some of the conflicts Satz has experienced as a working mother? How did her assumptions about motherhood contribute to the conflicts?
2. Should the resolution of the conflicts be the responsibility of society or of individuals?
3. Is treating people equally the best way to treat them fairly?

Hearing Voices and Telling Stories: Resisting Domination in Everyday Life

Robert Jensen

Robert Jensen is a professor of journalism who also teaches in the honors and freshman programs at the University of Texas at Austin. His research and scholarly writing have focused on freedom of speech and media, specifically issues around sexual violence and pornography. He also regularly commits acts of journalism in the mainstream and alternative presses, and is involved in a variety of progressive political groups and activities.

I HAVE A SECRET to share, one I have always been a bit nervous about saying out loud: I hear voices sometimes, and sometimes the voices tell me what's right and what's wrong. And sometimes I do what the voices tell me.

These voices come from different places, including from within me, and from different people, in different tones at different times. Some I feel more than I hear. Some I miss the first time around, or even the first few times around. These are mostly human voices, but I am coming to understand that the other animals and the plants and the rocks have been talking to me as well, though I haven't known how to listen.

This does not mean that moral theory and political principles have no place in my ethical decisions, or that I never rigorously reason my way through an ethical issue. It is simply to acknowledge that moral decision making is almost never solely about rules and reason, no matter how much we may want to believe that it can be. Like most people, when I tell stories about my moral decisions I often ignore the role of those many voices in my coming to moral judgments. When I spell out a rationale for my actions to others, I usually try to construct well-reasoned arguments that will persuade others, both of the right-ness of my moral decision and of just how clever I am. This can seem more com-forting than sorting out the sometimes complicated mixture of reason and emo-tion, intellectual insights and intuitions, empirical evidence and hunches, that may have led me to a certain moral decision. Making sense of that complex mix of factors can be difficult, but our lives and moral conversations would be en-riched if we told those stories more often.

   This essay is about those voices and how they have shaped my moral and political decisions about everyday-life choices concerning meat, pornography, television, and automobiles. I will start by describing the moral and political framework that I eventually developed to make sense of those choices. From there I will move backward to explain in more detail how those choices origi-nally appeared to me and which voices spoke to me as I muddled through the questions. I will end with a discussion of why any of this is worth discussing and how it guides my life.

RESISTING DOMINATION IN EVERYDAY LIFE

My choices not to eat meat, use pornography, own a television, or own a car are linked by ideas about justice and sustainability. The concept of justice has been the subject of much debate in philosophy, but here I will define it simply as "the human plea for decent lives."[1] The quest for justice, in my view, involves resis-tance to oppressive systems that maintain unequal distributions of power and resources that are unjustified and requires the search for ways to give voice to those who are silenced by such systems. My ideas about sustainability come pri-marily from the sustainable agriculture movement, which focuses on satisfying human needs in a way that takes nature as measure and is capable of maintain-ing an ecosystem's health, and hence its productivity and usefulness to humans, indefinitely.[2]

   The central assertion underlying my philosophy is that systems based on the dynamic of domination and subordination are not only unjust but unsustain-able. In contemporary America, we live with a number of unsustainable and un-just cultural, social, economic, and political systems (racism, ethnocentrism, sex-ism, heterosexism, state-corporate capitalism) that result in problems familiar to us all: disparities in access to resources; unjust distributions of power based on those disparities in wealth and/or identity markers; institutionalized discrimina-tion; horrific levels of physical and sexual abuse; the disintegration of human community; savage attacks on nonhuman life and the natural world; the degra-dation of work in industrial and postindustrial capitalism; and unchecked ag-gression against less powerful people and nations.

   These systems of oppression, and the inequalities they produce, are rou-tinely naturalized in our society, taken as "just the way things are." One of the reasons these systems are so entrenched is that the domination-subordination dynamic on which they are based is commonly rendered invisible by both ide-ological obfuscation and the exercise of raw power. The result is a system that is unsustainable and unjust. A fairly simple, but powerful, principle underlies my argument here: The imposition of power and authority by a person or group on another person or group can never be assumed to be obviously correct, but must always be justified. As Noam Chomsky argues, "[A]ny structure of hierarchy and authority carries a heavy burden of justification, whether it involves personal re-lations or a larger social order. If it cannot bear the burden . . . then it is ille-gitimate and should be dismantled. When honestly posed and squarely faced, that challenge can rarely be sustained."[3]

With this focus on domination and subordination, there are clear, and sometimes urgent, questions we face on a macro scale, such as the need to op-pose our government when it participates, directly and indirectly, in sanctioned massacres of people in less powerful nations. There also are issues that involve work at many different levels, such as the complicated questions of law, eco-nomics, and social relations involved in the struggle for racial justice. To under-stand certain everyday-life issues as moral and political questions does not mean that everyday-life questions are all there is to morality and politics, just that those questions are part of our moral and political lives. This framework has helped me focus on the moral and political aspects of everyday behaviors that are often seen as unproblematic in moral and political terms. By exploring each decision in more detail, I will elaborate on the different philosophies that have shaped my moral and political understanding of the world.

Again, it is important to emphasize that the choices I will describe fit within this framework but does not mean that my decisions were made simply by as-sessing the issues, applying a principle, and coming to a clear and clean resolu-tion. My views have evolved over time, and the choices were made partly by evaluating the questions within the evolving framework and partly by the messier process of listening to those many voices. That is, over time I have come to see how these choices I will describe are part of an overall project of resisting the dynamic of domination and subordination in all parts of my life, but at the time I first made the choices I did not necessarily understand them in that sense.

In short, I've been making it up as I go along.

In viewing these everyday-life issues as moral and political, I am not sug-gesting that anyone who chooses differently than I do is necessarily unethical. We live in a complex society in which the choices are not always clear and the consequences of choices cannot always be reliably predicted. People of good faith with common goals can disagree about the importance and efficacy of all these choices. Indeed, I have close friends and allies who choose differently than I, and I feel no need to renounce them or their choices. A kind of epistemolog-ical humility is necessary given that what we do not know always far outstrips what we do know. Those caveats, however, do not undermine the argument I make for why my moral and political choices in these areas are good moral and political choices, even though I cannot sensibly demand that others accept them as the only possible ethical choices.

From here, I will describe in some detail how these choices became clear to me.

MEAT

I believe that the choice not to eat meat is one way to resist the unjust and unsustainable domination of animals by humans in the contemporary economy. Here's how that all started for me.

In a writing class I was taking in 1985, then-*Washington Post* columnist Colman McCarthy gave a guest lecture about the craft of writing, and he also spoke of his Christian pacifist philosophy. One important aspect of that discussion was his opposition to violence, including war, abortion, and the slaughter of animals for food. I am not a Christian, nor have I ever been except in the most superficial cultural sense. I also have never been an absolute pacifist; I believe that in certain situations, violence to resist injustice can be justified. And I do not agree with opposition to abortion on pacifist grounds. But I was struck by McCarthy's conviction, honesty, and willingness to talk openly about his faith and philosophy. And his discussion of vegetarianism struck a chord with me. I didn't leave the room a vegetarian, but about six months later I ate my last meal that included a dead animal. While McCarthy's talk did not directly cause me to give up meat, it certainly influenced me.

By the time I heard McCarthy speak, I had read the traditional utilitarian argument for animal rights[4] and had found it sensible in certain ways but not compelling. And by that time I had developed a strong critique of the everyday violence—within the family, in sports, etc.—that pervades so much of life in contemporary America. While not a pacifist, I had come to the simple conclusion that less violence is better than more violence, and that I should act in ways to reduce the amount of violence in the world.

So, I do not offer an airtight argument against killing animals at all times and places based on their moral status but rather a critique of the way in which animals in this society are raised and killed for food in the commercial meat industry.[5] Because I live, and have always lived, in a city, any meat I eat is most likely to come from a supermarket, the product of a factory farming system that involves the use of large amounts of drugs and chemicals, inhumane containment methods, and the mass slaughter of animals. I believe that system is unjustifiably cruel and violent. Because humans can live healthy lives on a plant-based diet, it seems to me to be an easy choice: reduce the violence, cruelty, and inhumane treatment of other living things that share our capacity to feel pain. Do it for them, do it for ourselves, do it to make the planet a less cruel and violent place.

Why did McCarthy's short talk have such an effect on me, especially given that I did not share McCarthy's Christian faith nor accept his pacifist argument? I think his words touched me at least in part because he spoke honestly, without apology for the strength of his convictions but also without any hint of contempt toward those who might not share his position. His voice reflected the quiet but animated power of a person at peace with his own choices. That does not mean that McCarthy is not capable of righteous indignation at other times and places. But in that class, rather than telling me what I should do, he told his story, and that story resonated with me. His talk was less a lecture and more an invitation to reflect on the question. I did not have to agree with him completely to accept the invitation, and that invitation led me down a similar, though not identical, path. It was, in short, McCarthy's ability to live his philosophy honestly in front of others that touched me; it was the gentleness in his voice that spoke to me.

PORNOGRAPHY

I believe that the choice not to use pornography is one way to resist the unjust and unsustainable domination of women by men. Here's how that all started for me.

When I began my doctoral program in media law and ethics in 1988, I became interested in the legal questions surrounding pornography, which led me to the radical feminist critique of pornography and of the sexualization of male dominance. The central assertion of this view, which I will sketch only briefly here, is that sexuality and compulsory heterosexuality are a crucial site in the social subordination of women.[6] The sexual ideology of patriarchy eroticizes domination and submission, and pornography is one of the vehicles for that ideology in contemporary culture.[7] One result of the patriarchal sexual system is widespread violence, sexualized violence, and violence-by-sex against women, children, and in certain situations, vulnerable men. Pornography's role in this includes the harm to women, children, and some vulnerable men in (1) the production of pornography, (2) having pornography forced on them, (3) being sexually assaulted by men who use pornography, and (4) living in a culture in which pornography reinforces and sexualizes women's subordinate status.[8]

My interest in this subject was as much personal as intellectual. Like most American men of my generation, I grew up using pornography, and I had accepted the argument that pornography was about sexual liberation. But somewhere in my gut, I was never comfortable with the act of purchasing women's sexuality on paper and film.[9] My initial response to the feminist critiques was resistance, but I kept reading because, while I did not want to accept the conclusions, the writing of these women resonated with me. Even though I was skeptical, their work seemed to explain how the world worked and how I felt. At some level, I suspect I knew that I was starting on a path that would result in change, not only in my intellectual life but in my personal life as well. I was nervous. But I kept reading.

In particular, I kept reading the books of Andrea Dworkin, one of the strongest and clearest of the radical feminist critics of the gender and sexual politics of our culture. Her books are full of passion, anger, careful analysis, and compelling calls for justice. Like McCarthy, the power of her words is in their honesty, but her voice is different. Dworkin is, in some ways, not gentle, and she is not hesitant to hold men accountable for their actions. Dworkin does not turn away from the painful realities of sexual abuse and does not soften her critique to make it more palatable.

Because of this, Dworkin, and feminists like her, are often labeled man-haters. In a male-dominant world, it is perhaps inevitable that attempts to hold men accountable will be labeled "hatred." Still, I have always found that reaction odd. For two main reasons it never occurred to me while reading Dworkin that she hated men. One is that, even though her writing is blunt, there is a gentleness beneath it, a loving affection for people, women and men, just as there is underneath McCarthy's gentleness, a passionate intensity. I have always assumed that this affection fuels Dworkin's work. Second, I came to realize that the system that Dworkin describes not only harms women and children but also constrains the lives of men. There are material rewards for those who dominate, but they come with the heavy price of a emotional and spiritual impoverishment.[10] In that sense, it is in the self-interest of men as well as women to read Dworkin's work.

Once I understood some of these things, my personal life changed. I was married through the first years of this process, and as I write this I am divorced and have come out as a gay man. The story of those changes is complex and painful—in many ways still too painful to recount in public. But when we decide to open ourselves up to change, we can never know where change will lead us. Part of what opened me up to change was not simply the evidence and analysis presented by feminist critics, though that analysis is powerful and, for me, has yet to be refuted. Crucial to the process by which I came to know about gender, sex, and power was the distinctive voice of Andrea Dworkin. It is a voice that touched me and that stays with me.

TELEVISION

I believe that the choice not to own a television is one way to resist the unjust and unsustainable domination of cultural life by a handful of powerful corporations and the advertisers who keep them in business. Here's how that all started for me.

Like most Americans of my generation, I spent a good part of my childhood in front of a television set. I continued to watch throughout my teenage and college years, though the amount of time I devoted to television steadily decreased. For most of my 20s, I owned a television but watched infrequently as I began to understand that I was watching the few shows I still enjoyed more out of habit than conscious choice. And I began to realize that when I used the television as a tool to relax—as in, "I was too tired to do anything, so I watched TV"—I didn't feel very relaxed afterward. I was beginning to listen to an inner voice that was telling me that this activity, taken for granted by virtually everyone around me, did not seem to produce many tangible benefits in my life. TV was supposed to relax me, but I didn't feel very relaxed. TV was supposed to entertain me, but it didn't seem very entertaining. TV was supposed to inform me, but I couldn't pinpoint any particular useful information coming my way through the box.

So, I began to move from a focus on the question, "What's on TV?" to the question, "Why is the TV on?" I started paying attention to how I felt before, during, and after watching television. I started asking questions about how television changed my interaction with the people around me and with the nonhuman world. I read some of the critiques of television,[11] though it was more my own experience than anyone else's analysis that fueled my questioning. As this process went on over the course of several years, I became more convinced that television was, on balance, a destructive technology in my life. But by that time, I was married to someone who enjoyed television. So, I couldn't unilaterally decide to get rid of the television in our house.

That became possible when my wife and I split and I moved into an apartment. By that time, I had decided not only that I would live without a television but that I wanted my son to have the experience of living without one when he was with me. I was committed to giving my child something I had not had—a space, albeit limited, to live away from the television. Despite warnings from friends that my son, who was three years old at the time of the divorce, would whine constantly for the TV when he was at my house, I held firm. So far my son, who is five at the time I write this, has adapted just fine to life in a television-less home during his time with me. My ban is not absolute; I have watched television at the homes of friends on rare occasions, and I sometimes use videotapes in teaching. But I remain unconvinced by friends who tell me that I am missing wonderful things by tuning out, to the degree possible, of television culture.

As I have tried to make clear, my analysis of television as an agent of domination developed over time and strengthened my resolve not to watch. But the initial questioning was vague and grew not out of an intellectual exercise but out of the voice inside me that said, simply, "Something is not right here."

AUTOMOBILES

The choice to not own a car is one way to resist the unjust and unsustainable domination of the nonhuman world by humans. Here's how that all started for me.

The contemporary American economy is extractive, not sustainable, and is based on a viewpoint that sees the world not as a system to be maintained but as a resource to be exploited. To the degree possible, I believe there is a moral imperative to reduce our connection to, and complicity with, the extractive economy. This is not an easy task, in part because we live in a world in which systems and structures of power that have a major role in structuring the patterns of our lives care little, if anything, about these questions. The automobile is one of the best case studies of these problems.

On the criteria of sustainability, the widespread use of automobiles is a horrendous debacle. The cars on the road just in the United States require huge amounts of resources and energy to build and maintain, and dump vast amounts of pollutants and toxins into the world. The social patterns that develop to fit the car culture breed isolation and disconnection. Automobiles are smelly, loud, dangerous, and the source of one of the most incredible delusions of the modern era—that owning your own car brings freedom.[12] Certainly there are productive uses of automobiles, but the costs that come with widespread ownership of automobiles so outstrip their contribution to human flourishing that they easily can be branded a quintessential industrial evil.

Yet it can be very difficult to live in much of contemporary America without a car, and most people who can afford a car own one. My decision to finally give up my car came only a couple of years ago, again prompted in many ways by my divorce and the opportunity to rethink how I wanted to live. Going carless was relatively easy for me because I live in a warm-weather state that makes year-round biking possible, close enough to my job to bike to work; there are grocery and drug stores within walking distance of my home; I live in a city with a bus system; and I have a number of friends who own cars and graciously offer me rides to events that are difficult to get to by bus or bike. For people without some of these advantages, living without a car can be difficult, if not practically impossible.

It is ironic that the person who had the largest role in my decision not to own a car, my friend Jim Koplin, drives a car himself. This final example of moral and political decisions in everyday life is another reminder that our moral vision is best expanded through conversation with others, not commandments from another. I don't drive a car in large part because for the past nine years I have been conversing with Jim about the natural world, sustainability, technology, and our choices in an industrial world. It has been those conversations with Jim, and reading done with him or at his suggestion[13] that have shaped my view of the automobile. In those conversations and readings it became clear to me that compelling concerns about justice were linked to equally compelling concerns about sustainability. Until I met Jim and began thinking more seriously about questions of technology and the natural world, I on occasion had cursed cars (as we all do, especially when they break down or get stuck in traffic) but I had never seriously considered living without one.

Jim has made a choice to continue to drive based on his particular situation, which is quite different from mine. In fact, if I were in his situation, I also likely would own a car. Although Jim's view of these issues has influenced me considerably, his choices are not necessarily my choices. I respect Jim's moral and political commitments, I value his knowledge and wisdom, and I take seriously his decisions about how to live. Because of the length and depth of our friendship, Jim's voice—even when he is not present in the room with me—speaks to me and with me as I struggle my way through life. But I do not always do as he does, nor does he always do as I do. We both understand that the modern industrial world often offers us difficult choices, and that each person makes those choices under varying constraints and with different options.

MUDDLING THROUGH

As I have emphasized, to say that a question has moral and political implications is not to say that there is only one possible ethical course, or that the right thing to do is always obvious, especially in a complex society. Some moral/political questions are fairly clear, and we should not hesitate to make clear judgments. For example, if a man were to ask me whether I thought it morally acceptable to have sex with a woman who had not consented, I would tell him that it is wrong, and if he does it he is wrong, and that he should not do it. To suggest that any other answer is possible, I would argue, is to forfeit your humanity.

The choices I have discussed here vary in this respect. I think the case against pornography is so overwhelming that any man who uses mass-marketed heterosexual or child pornography cannot claim that he cares about women and children while he continues to support an industry that violates women and children so routinely.[14] Though the questions are not identical, I have reached a similar judgment about lesbian and gay pornography.[15] On the other end of the scale, I think the decision not to own a television is of a very different kind; the connection of television to domination is clear to me, but I cannot argue for a clear moral and political imperative that puts on us the same demand that pornography does. The case against automobiles is stronger than the case against television, yet the constraints on us are greater; so, I would argue that we all should strive to reduce our automobile use in whatever way feasible.

Perhaps the most difficult case for me in public discussion is vegetarianism. I am committed to a life without meat, and I believe the world would be a better place if we all made such a commitment. But I also realize that it is possible for people to kill animals in a manner that is respectful and sustainable. This has long been the case in many indigenous cultures, and it is the case in my own culture among respectful hunters. Still, I do not hesitate to say that I find eating industrially produced meat to be difficult to justify morally and politically.

At the very least, I want to suggest that we have a moral and political obligation to routinely examine the costs of our pleasures and conveniences. Pornography provides sexual excitement, but at what cost? Meat tastes good, but at what cost? Driving is sometimes more convenient than walking, but at what cost? Television can be amusing at times, but at what cost? Sometimes these costs are borne by others and sometimes by ourselves. Sometimes it is the entire planet, both its living and nonliving elements, that pays for our entertainment. In a culture consumed by consumption, we can start to be more morally and politically responsible to the planet and to each other by consuming less, buying fewer things, making better use of the things we already have. In short, we should ask ourselves every time we step up to a cash register to purchase something, "Do I really need this, and what is the real cost, beyond money, of buying it?"

This is not an argument against pleasure or for a rigid asceticism. I revel in the pleasure of good food that is well-prepared, the pleasure of conversation, the pleasure of imaginative literature, the pleasure of playing with my son, the pleasure of a lake's cool water on a hot day. There is no end to the pleasure that this world offers us at little or no cost. My argument is not against pleasure, but for justice and sustainability, for a sensible balance of pleasure to cost. Such a focus on costs is not easy. These four choices hardly exhaust the list of everyday-life questions relevant for someone trying to resist the dynamic of domination and subordination that structures so much of our lives. Many of the choices we have to make are more difficult than the ones I have discussed here, but one does not need answers to all the questions before acting on the answers that we can see clearly.

How should we sort out all these issues? There is no grand moral or political theory, with a corresponding rule book, that answers these questions. As humans always have done, we muddle through using a combination of myth, history, intuitions, empirical evidence, logic, conversation, and informed guesswork. Whether we acknowledge it or not, we listen to voices. If that is the case, then perhaps the most crucial moral and political tasks we face are struggling to hear as many voices as possible, learning to train our attention on voices that come from the powerless, voices that challenge our most deeply held notions, voices that are pushed to the margin by unearned privilege and power. It also is our job to tell our stories honestly, to search our own minds and bodies to understand how to frame the questions and how to piece together our answers.

PAIN, EMPATHY, AND MORAL VISION

As part of my struggle to tell an honest story, I will end with a partial account of my search to understand myself and my motivations in these areas. One of the things people sometimes ask me is, given that my culture gives me vast amounts of unearned privilege for being white, male, educated, and in the professional class, why would I advocate political positions that would seem to undermine all that privilege? It is easy to understand why people who are oppressed would critique systems of oppression, but why would someone so firmly rooted in various oppressor classes pursue such critique?

The answer is, of course, complex. One obvious point is that my privilege allows me to do it. Because my position in life gives me status and a stable income, it is in some ways easy for me to critique—I'm a professor who gets paid to think aloud in public. So far in my life, none of the things I have said or done in opposition to systems of domination has threatened me to any great degree. I realize there are potential punishments for resisting the dominance of certain systems and ideas, but to date I have escaped most of those punishments.

Also, the choice of whether or not to speak against and resist systems of oppression is, in the vernacular, a no-brainer. Once a person faces the choice, the alternatives of ignoring oppression and thereby unconsciously supporting it, or of consciously participating in oppressive actions, become increasingly ludicrous. How does one survive with any self-respect in a racist and sexist society, for example, without resisting racism and sexism? How does one maintain the belief in one's own dignity when denying the dignity of others? I believe that this accounts for much of the willed ignorance in the world: People understand that knowing too much about oppression can lead to difficult choices, so they sometimes choose not to know. At various times in our lives, I suspect we all have relied on such a tactic. I have no doubt that I still resort to it when I feel too overwhelmed to cope. But it is a tendency that needs to be resisted.

But there is another level to this question for me. Systems of domination and subordination produce deep and intense pain in the lives of real people. Different systems produce different kinds of pain; for example, the pain of poverty is not exactly like the pain of rape, which is different than the pain of being excluded because you are not white. But no matter how different our experiences, we can recognize each other's pain. It is called empathy, and I believe that it is, unless suppressed or distorted, a characteristic of being alive. And once we understand that the dynamic of domination and subordination underlies this pain, we can see more clearly that eliminating that dynamic is a central component of our work in this world.

So, while all pain is not equal, the distance between us can be bridged in part by understanding the pain of others and our own pain. There are two primary ways in which I experience this. First, I was raised in a world that forced me to deny, repress, and lie about the emotional and sexual desire for men that I felt throughout my life. Most of the people in that world gave me the choice of acting on that desire at great risk or burying that desire to avoid the risk. It has been only recently that I have realized that either choice stole from me a basic human right: to love without fear. There is a pain in that loss that I carry with me today and which is tapped whenever I hear the stories of people who are subordinated in other ways. Again, this doesn't mean all oppression is equivalent, only that understanding our own pain can help us understand not only the pain of others but the systems that produce this pain.

All of that is fairly easy for me to address. But it is only part of the story, only one of the sources of my own pain. Like all of us raised in the United States, I have been a child in a culture that claims to adore children but, in reality, too often ignores them. Most of us have memories of realizing that, as children, our opinions, needs, and dreams were irrelevant simply because we were children without power to demand attention from adults who often did not seem to care. The consistency and sheer number of stories of this—in such varied sites as families, churches, schools, sports teams—leads me to conclude that our society, as a whole, cares little for children. That does not mean that large numbers of us don't struggle to be good parents, teachers, and caretakers, but that the culture is structured so that the denigration of children is fairly routine. For some of us, that routine denigration was taken to more extreme levels through abusive intrusions into our psychological spaces and/or bodies. The pain attached to those experiences for me is intense, and I often can feel those emotions kick in when I hear the story of someone else who has been hurt through cruelty or domination.

The point of highlighting this pain is not to demand sympathy, but rather to focus on how many of us have lived on the subordinate side of the domination-subordination dynamic. As we get older most of us acquire some privilege, even if it is just the privilege of being adult and powerful over children and animals. Some of us choose to turn our backs on what we may have learned and seek to dominate. At various times in my life, I have given in to that; it is easy to exploit privilege, and the culture does little or nothing to foster more humane and just behavior. But we can choose a different path, away from domination, toward empathy, compassion, and equality. I believe that is the path of sustainability and justice. While the right answers are not always clear, the choices are ours to make, or to turn away from.

NOTES

1. Mari J. Matsuda, "Pragmatism Modified and the False Consciousness Problem," *Southern California Law Review* 63 (September 1990): 1768.
2. Wes Jackson, *Becoming Native to This Place* (Lexington: University Press of Kentucky, 1994).
3. Noam Chomsky, *Powers and Prospects* (Boston: South End Press, 1996), 73.
4. Peter Singer, *Animal Liberation*, 2nd ed. (New York: Random House, 1990).
5. Jeremy Rifkin, *Beyond Beef: The Rise and Fall of the Cattle Culture* (New York: Dutton, 1992).
6. Andrea Dworkin, *Letters from a War Zone* (London: Secker & Warburg, 1988) and *Intercourse* (New York: Free Press, 1987); Marilyn Frye, *Willful Virgin* (Freedom, CA:

Crossing Press, 1992); Sheila Jeffreys, *Anticlimax: A Feminist Perspective on the Sexual Revolution* (New York: New York University Press, 1990).

7. Andrea Dworkin, *Pornography: Men Possessing Women* (New York: Perigee, 1981); Catharine A. MacKinnon, *Feminism Unmodified: Discourses on Life and Law* (Cambridge, MA: Harvard University Press, 1987) and *Toward a Feminist Theory of the State* (Cambridge, MA: Harvard University Press, 1989).

8. Andrea Dworkin and Catharine A. MacKinnon, *Pornography and Civil Rights: A New Day for Women's Equality* (Minneapolis: Organizing Against Pornography, 1988), 41–52.

9. Robert Jensen, "Knowing Pornography," *Violence Against Women* 2 (March 1996): 82–102.

10. Robert Jensen, "Men's Lives and Feminist Theory," *Race, Gender & Class* 2 (winter 1995): 111–25.

11. Jerry Mander, *Four Arguments for the Elimination of Television* (New York: Quill, 1978).

12. James J. Flink, *The Automobile Age* (Cambridge, MA: MIT Press, 1990); Jane Holtz Kay, *Asphalt Nation* (New York: Crown, 1997).

13. Wendell Berry, *What Are People For?* (San Francisco: North Point Press, 1990) and *Sex, Economy, Freedom and Community* (New York: Pantheon, 1993); Jackson, *Becoming Native*; Kirkpatrick Sale, *Rebels Against the Future* (Reading, MA: Addison-Wesley, 1995).

14. Gail Dines, Robert Jensen, and Ann Russo, *Pornography: The Production and Consumption of Inequality* (New York: Routledge, 1998).

15. D.A. Clarke, "Consuming Passions: Some Thoughts on History, Sex, and Free Enterprise," in *Unleashing Feminism: Critiquing Lesbian Sadomasochism in the Gay Nineties*, ed. Irene Reti (Santa Cruz, CA: HerBooks, 1993), 106–53; Robert Jensen, "Getting It Up for Politics: Gay Male Identity and Radical Lesbian Feminism," in *Opposite Sex*, ed. Sara Miles and Eric Rofes (New York: New York University Press, 1998).

STUDY QUESTIONS

1. How are Jensen's choices about meat, pornography, automobiles, and television examples of resisting the dynamic of domination and subordination?

2. Can you think of additional examples of everyday practices that are, or ought to be, the result of ethical choices?

3. Is sustainability a good measure of justice? Why or why not?

Being and Playing:
Sport and the Valorization of Gender

Leslie A. Howe

Leslie Howe is a professor of philosophy at the University of Saskatchewan whose research and teaching interests are mostly about the constitution and understanding of the self. She is a competitive rower and hockey player, holds coaching certification in both sports, and also participates in a number of other athletic activities. An abiding concern for her both philosophically and practically is how to integrate reflective, athletic, and ethical existence. She is not related to Gordie Howe.

HOCKEY IS CANADA'S game. It may also be Canada's national theatre. On its frozen stage, each night the stuff of life is played out: ambition, hope, pride and fear, love and friendship, the fight for honour for city, team, each other, themselves. The puck flips one way, bounces another, and the players set out to control and direct it. It takes them where they never planned to go. It tests them. And in struggling to get it back, with the millions who watch in the arena or by television, the players find out who they really are. Like the bearpits in Shakespeare's time, we attend hockey games as our popular theatre. It is a place where the monumental themes of Canadian life are played out—English and French, East and West, Canada and the U.S., Canada and the world, the timeless tensions of commerce and culture, our struggle to survive and civilize winter. (Dryden and MacGregor, 101)

We tend to think of sports as mere trivial addenda to our lives, but as the above quotation suggests, sport reflects who we are at a particularly deep level and serves as a vitally important medium in shaping our personal and cultural identities. It so happens that for Canadians the sport that does this above all is hockey; in most of the world it is soccer. For Americans, matters are more complicated: baseball, football, and basketball carve up the collective psyche in variously complementary and perhaps contradictory ways. I will be talking about hockey because that is the sport I know and love, but most of what I say will, I think, be applicable in one way or another to other sports and other societies. No matter what sport we are talking about, however we participate in it, whether as spectators or players, its influence is at once subtle and profound. For women, the definitions of self that sport provides are frequently negative and even destructive (as indeed they are also for men, in some respects). But the direct involvement of women in sports, especially the traditional competitive ones, also presents an immensely valuable opportunity for the redefinition of the female self.

HOCKEY AND GENDER

Most of us can recognize quite readily the phenomenon to which Dryden refers: how sport fashions our national, civic, and economic identities. What we usually manage to avoid reflecting on, however, is the way sport shapes us as individuals, that is, as individuals of a particular gender. Sports, as we humans play them, are never simply a series of purely physical motions of the body. Rather, they are complex normative structures of social interaction that effectively define, embody, and enforce the socially appropriate limits of human being and behaviour. And the most notable way in which traditional sports, at least, do this is by telling us what it means to be male or female.

> "Only real men play hockey." These are the words from a popular song that appropriately became the anthem of ice arenas. (Tretiak, 28)

Hockey, as it is commonly conceived, as it is sold to the public, and as it is taught to young boys, is a hypermasculine game. Playing hockey, where it is a culturally significant sport, carries ultimate social validation for males. To play hockey is to be a man. In fact, the virtues extolled for hockey players are those most central to the traditional conception of masculinity ("manliness"): strength, courage, physical skill, solidarity, and, especially, aggression. These have become exaggerated, and heavily romanticized, to the point where "heart" (the most valued characteristic for North American players) is equated with a willingness to hit every opposing player in sight with as much punishing force as possible (preferably, to take him right out of the game), to play despite injury, and to fight whenever challenged, even when the game is well lost. It is a game where the smart player is one who knows how to do all these things "at the right time," that is, when it will most advantage his own team. Size and power are valued above all; skill, finesse, and careful playmaking are secondary and frequently suspect qualities. A player who is a superior skater and puckhandler, but hesitant to drop the gloves if pushed around, is assumed to be not tough enough (not man enough) to play the game and a target for the other team, as well as a liability to his own. "Character" in this context means a willingness to "mix it up," whether on one's own or one's teammates' behalf. One must not show any weakness, physical or otherwise, as this will be construed as a failure of masculinity, which failure demonstrates one to be unfit for the game. Hockey defines itself not only in terms of exaggerated masculine traits, but it interprets those traits as being in absolute opposition to any that might, in the remotest way, be thought of as being feminine or, more to the point, effeminate. Thus, at the most fundamental level, hockey excludes as antithetical to itself any trace of the feminine, and exalts itself as the pinnacle of purely masculine attainment.

Except . . . not all hockey players are men. Women have played hockey almost since the game was invented, though in considerably smaller numbers and without any significant encouragement. In fact, the gender disparities in funding, recognition, and opportunities continue to be grotesque even as women's involvement in the sport mushrooms at local, national, and international levels. The root cause of this continuing pattern of neglect is our socially constructed definitions of gender. These definitions of gender are maintained and deepened by the exclusionary self-definitions of our traditional sports. For example, women's hockey is not funded properly or supported because "obviously" hockey is a man's game. Such a circular definition works against women who seek to participate in the sport.

Every Tuesday and Thursday morning for two seasons I get up at 6:30, eat a bowl of cereal and a handful of aspirins, and head for a freezing arena in the west end of Montreal to play recreational "oldtimer's" hockey. It's supposed to be the faculty and staff of the university, but few of the players are. Some are students, some are just guys who know guys: overweight and middle-aged accountants, realtors, dog food salesmen. It's mostly men, but usually, one of the women from the varsity team plays with us. We play on opposite sides most of the time; she plays left; I take right wing or defense. I'm supposed to check her. Sometimes I manage it; most of the time I don't. She doesn't do anything really extraordinary; she just does everything really, really well. That's a very significant accomplishment in a game as complex as hockey. Most of the guys I've played with have only one, maybe two, good moves, usually flashy ones, and if you play with them enough, you can always see it coming. She's on the national team, and later this particular year she will win a gold medal at the world championships in Lake Placid. Now, she's here, pulling a deke on me that I will remember for the rest of my life, and I

*have to decide whether to be humiliated or inspired. Ultimately, I choose to
be inspired. But I suspect that she's really only playing at quarter speed—just
getting in a light workout before class. So, there's a women's tournament here,
and some of us go to watch her play for real. The teams are good ones, from
Canadian and American universities. The Americans have expensive
equipment and drill like the Red Army. But our team goes out and whips
them all. Our player double-shifts, plays the point, and looks at the end of
each game like she's ready to start another. We cheer excessively when she
scores—as if we somehow had something to do with it. At one point, one of
the guys turns to the rest of us and, his voice full of genuine admiration,
offers the highest praise he can think of for her: "You know, when she skates
you can't tell she's not a man."*

How do women deal with the problems associated with trying to participate in a sport that is not only masculine, but antifeminine?

My plan for a deck of hockey tarot cards failed for want of the truly
feminine. I could make some figure a woman in the game; Canada's
women's team is the best in the world, and maybe I could push the
notion until it does not matter, woman or man—just The Player. But I'd
be lying. This is not why I love the game, or why its symbols work like
runes in my language. This is a game the women watch, its gentler
moments taken in their image: The Trainer, running to the Fallen Man
Beside the Boards, cradling the face now loose and looking skyward in
his hands, smoothing his hair with a towel; the Equipment itself,
stockings, girdles, garters. At the time I did not understand what the
woman next to me at a hockey game was trying to teach when she
wondered aloud whether she would find a better lover in another woman
as the players below us skated the warm-up, around and around their
own side of Centre, lofting long, lazy Pucks at their Goalie. There is a
Mask on my face, the game divides us. Again I've come to a profession of
love in words I cannot use for you, with all the women left in the stands
where I demand that you sit and love it all. (Harrison, 19)

I first heard these words spoken by their author in a nationally broadcast
presentation of his poetic interpretation of the game and its embedded emotional culture. What came across most clearly to me, as a hockey player and a
woman, was at once the poetry's heightened sentimentality and its unquestion-
ing celebration of the masculine mythos of hockey. I noticed that women fea-
tured only as a superfluous and confusing complication of the rapturously male
experience. Indeed, even "The Feminine" in the above poem is represented pref-
erentially by a male. It seemed to me that I had just been told that I did not

exist, and that what I had thought I had loved all these years and worked so hard at was really something to which I could have no intuitive access. To add to the insult, not only had I been dismissed from something that is as central to my being as oxygen, but my own identity had been ludicrously misappropriated in order to valorize that from which I had been so summarily excluded. In short, I was infuriated.

When I was a little girl, the skating proprieties were communicated very clearly: boys got hockey skates and girls got figure skates. At the local park, there were two ice surfaces: one reserved for hockey and the other open to everyone—unless it was needed for hockey. I wasn't very interested in either figure-8's or frilly little dresses, so I hardly skated past the age of 9 or 10. It would never have occurred to me to be interested in hockey. That was for boys, much more obviously than the other "boy" things I was interested in: science, construction sets, and so on. It was almost 20 years later that I started to skate again, on hockey skates this time, playing shinny and, sometime later, hockey proper, at first recreationally and then competitively. Usually I would be the sole woman, or one of only a very small number of women, playing with men until I gradually shifted into women's hockey, joining a local women's league and eventually playing on a university women's team.

THE EPISTEMOLOGY OF RESPECT

What I found through all my various hockey experiences was that there was almost always a profound dissonance between male perceptions of the game (which are inevitably assumed to be normative) and those of women. We would look at the same action and offer radically different descriptions of what had happened; we would look at the same player and make quite incompatible assessments of his or her abilities. It seemed as though we were seeing different things.

When I later met other women hockey players, I found that they would tell similar stories. It seemed to be a recurrent experience for many women playing the game with men. What they would frequently find is that the men would not respect them—no matter what their relative skill level. It seems as though the male players come to the game with a pre-formed readiness to see the women as unqualified, compared to men, even when they do in fact play as well or better. What all this suggests is the influence of an epistemology underlying the attitude of respect.[1]

> *I'm sitting in the referees' room where I change after the game, listening to the guys in the next room yelling about the game, each other, about whether Patrick Roy can carry the Habs again this year, whatever. The walls don't go all the way to the ceiling, but they've never noticed and don't realize that I can hear everything they say. Their enthusiasm for their own athletic*

accomplishments leaves me more breathless than the game does. I resolve never to make assumptions about my own standard of play. They have decided that I'm useless because I can't pick up a pass (what pass?) and that the varsity player is so good she's almost as good as them. I cringe with embarrassment when I realize how pleased I am when they say I skate like her. At the end of the season they decide to go to a strip-joint on St. Jacques to celebrate.

Our respect for other persons is normally based on certain judgments we make about them, based on our experience of them. But those judgments about what we experience are themselves contingent on a network of presuppositions we carry with us about what it is that we are likely to experience. For the most part, we do not see what we do not expect to see. Very often, we anticipate what our senses actually present to us, leaping to conclusions about what we are seeing before we see it. Thus, if we expect a person to act in a certain way, or to do well at a specific activity, we are inclined to "see" them do so; that is, we interpret what we do see as satisfying that expectation. Our world works so much more smoothly if it follows regular and predictable patterns, and so we look for confirmation of pattern in our experience. What doesn't fit is discarded or discounted, usually without our being fully conscious of what we are doing. To a great extent this is unavoidable—if we didn't do this, we simply wouldn't be able to function: Information has to be ordered in some way or other to be information, that is, informative, and this means fitting what we get into some pattern that we can recognize and use without a great deal of epistemic fuss. Most of the patterns we use are underdetermined by experience. In other words, either they are preconceived or they elaborate on whatever it is that is really presented to us. We have to remind ourselves now and again that this is what we are doing and be ready to revise the patterns we use since there is no a priori reason to suppose the patterns we are presently using to be optimal. Where the accepted patterns have not been consistently challenged or circumstances change sufficiently that they no longer adequately reflect reality (i.e., allow us to function and communicate optimally), they can become oppressive and regressive, as well as just plain false.

On the ice women encounter the expectation that they won't be any good at the game because they are women, whereas a man is always assumed to be competent. For a woman to show that she is as good or better is a nearly hopeless cause, because it is not the "facts" that are at issue. Rather, she is up against an embedded epistemological framework that makes it virtually impossible for the others to see those facts as facts—except in the rare cases where she is so overwhelmingly superior that she must be granted that strange sometime status of honorary male. That many women look different from men on the ice doesn't help, either. Given a set of confusing clues about the gender identity of a particular player, as well as a predisposition to discount the evidence as evidence, the easiest epistemic solution is to discount the player altogether.[2] When we see something that doesn't make any sense to us, doesn't fit any ontological category available to us, what we do is to conclude that we didn't really see it.[3]

> "Everybody has to have a little respect in order to get the room they want" [says Mark Messier]. To win space and respect the player must show both opponents and teammates that he will not be pushed around. The new player, especially, has to demonstrate at the very least that he can't be put off his own game, and preferably that he can and will retaliate. . . . The player, like Messier or the legendary Gordie Howe, who can make opponents hurt for such transgressions will be accorded a certain space, while those unable or unwilling to do this will be attacked with enthusiasm. (Gruneau and Whitson, 183–84)

> *It's my first year playing intramural hockey and the only other woman in the league is a goaltender. Next year I will be alone. Well, I wanted a challenge. There are people who don't want me to be here, but mostly I'm getting knocked around the rink because I'm a little smaller, a step slower, and I don't put up enough resistance. I'm discovering one of those dirty little secrets of the macho mystique—tough men beat up on the smallest guys first. Tripping, elbows, hooks and spears, innumerable crosschecks and bodychecks, especially from behind. For a noncontact league, I'm picking myself up off the ice a lot. In one game, I get flattened nine times, finally getting crosschecked into a goal post—and that's just the first period. No one ever gets a penalty for any of this. I play shinny two or three times a week, too. The play in shinny is extremely clean because no one wears protective equipment. Except, one of my team's defencemen always plays on the opposite side from me, and every game he keeps chopping at my feet with the stick, or putting his elbow in my ear, giving me a shove in the back. I'm trying to figure out if he's just confused about my age, and trying to get to know me in some awkward 19 year old's way. Eventually, it becomes clear that he's decided to do something about my being a target. "You've got to be tougher." He's trying to teach me to protect myself, to clear space for myself, by being more aggressive and hitting back. One time I've managed to get him pinned up against the boards and he's yelling "yeah, yeah, that's it! that's it!" He's 8 inches taller and 90 pounds heavier than me, so after a couple of months of this it's lost most of its charm. But it works. Next season I take my first penalty—in a women's game.*

"Respect" is also a weasel word for fear. The behaviour referred to by Gruneau and Whitson is perhaps one of the most notable differences between men's and women's hockey. I do not mean to suggest that it is absent from the women's game, as if intimidation and violence were foreign to women. This is quite simply false: Some of the most disagreeable people I have ever met on the ice were women, and what I learned in men's hockey has been invaluable to me in competing against women. But testing behaviour, that is, pushing the rules as well as the opposing players to see how much you can get away with, and physical intimidation have an integral and institutionalized role in the men's game that is comparatively absent in women's hockey. Fighting is part of the game in men's hockey, but not in women's. In part the stricter rules, which forbid open-ice bodychecking, inhibit such behaviour in the women's game; in part outright in-your-face physical aggression is something that a great many women have to learn to do deliberately, in opposition to their normal socialization. Thus, I found that to compete effectively in the environment of the men's game, I had to learn to adopt, at least for the duration of the competition, what was to me a comparatively foreign frame of mind. I had to find a way to act and react "like a man," while being aware that I would also be expected to abandon that attitude once I left the rink. I resisted this for a long time, at first because I was reluctant to admit to my own inherent competitiveness, but also because I regarded the hyperaggressive, "get out of my way, this game is mine" attitude as an indefensible one to take toward other people. I thought it was wrong. But, in time, I found my own accommodation to the fact of competition. No way would I be a goon, but I would stand my own ground. No one was going to get a free shot at me and no one was going to run me off the ice. I wanted to play the game, and to play it I had to be in it, and that meant claiming my patch of ice, no matter who wanted to take it away from me.

In the women's game as well, one of the most important and sometimes the most difficult thing to learn is the controlled use of aggression: the determination to beat the opposing player to the puck, to win the struggle along the boards, and so on. Aggression, in the sense of the determination to "get there first," to take control of the movement of the game, to be the active force, is crucial to success in a competitive sport, but it is something that many women besides myself have to struggle to recognize as existing within themselves and learn to use. Without it, they will be spectators rather than competitors. But with it, they will find that the rewards for success in this struggle are often ambiguous.

GENDER AND SEX

We're changing after the game, and this student is telling me about a guy she plays broomball with. He's always making sure she knows that he thinks women are useless as athletes and that they shouldn't be allowed to play on any of the men's teams, 'cause they just drag everything down, and all chicks in sports are lesbos anyway, and on and on. But he keeps trying to get her to sleep with him.

Woman's participation in athletic endeavour of any sort presents a problem for traditional conceptions of gender and for traditional conceptions of appropriate sexual identity. Female athleticism challenges male sexual priority by supplanting the active role that is central to the traditional conception of male sexual identity. Traditional conceptions of woman emphasize her existence as body, with man as mind or spirit. This gets turned on its head by woman's participation in sport. For although woman is (supposedly) body, she is also defined as passive body. This is clearest in her definition as fundamentally sexual, where this sexuality is conceived as primarily receptive, and hence again, passive. Yet an athletic woman is clearly active and, as we have seen above, aggressive in her activity.

It is the traditional province of the male to be active in sexual matters as well as social ones. Traditional notions of male sexuality, and about virility and manliness, are located around the assumption of the active part. Thus, athletic women are an utter confusion to male identity. If maleness is defined by its exclusion of feminine qualities, and these are understood to be characterized by passivity, in contradistinction to the masculine qualities of activity, aggression, initiative, and so forth, the presence of women with masculine qualities threatens the male's understanding of what he is and what his role should be. Athletic prowess in women not only suggests that they might be able to supplant men in fields previously thought to be masculine (such as sport), but perhaps that they might also be able to usurp the male role in determining sexual activity. The abandonment of overall physical passivity hints at an abandonment of sexual passivity, which in turn whispers the terrible thought that women might no longer depend on men for their own sexual affirmation.

This is why one sees such a marked hostility toward particularly strong or successful female athletes and a determination in the media to present them less as powerful and self-realized athletes than as potential sexual objects for the gaze of men. Consider the case of goaltender Manon Rheaume, the first woman to be signed by an NHL team. Shortly after signing, she was approached by *Playboy* magazine to do a photo session, which she politely refused. What would have been accomplished by Rheaume's participation in such an exercise (profit aside)? Here was the first woman to break through a previously thought unbreakable boundary in one of the most conservative sports in North America, and now it was proposed that she should be displayed naked on glossy pages for anyone who cared to see. In other words, in recognition of her hard-won fight for an active role, she would now be reduced to a completely passive one. From spirit she would be reduced to mere flesh, and the threat to male identity and hegemony (apparently) removed. Indeed, although strong women present a challenge, their strength also occasionally lends them a certain kind of eroticism for the male spectator. The prospect of sexual conquest, actual or metaphorical, over such a woman becomes all the more compelling.[4]

Validation, Heterosexism, and Bonding

A woman playing the men's game is likely to face a significant amount of hostility from many of those men who feel their sacred territory to be invaded, and this hostility can be manifested in many ways: as physical abuse, the blindness of officials, intimidation, and the ordinary campaign of groundless gossip. Her every action in such a situation takes on a significance that it would not otherwise have. In my own case, when I was the only woman playing in an eighteen-team university intramural league, I had the deepest moral conviction that I could not possibly quit or even fail to show up for a game no matter how fed up I got with what was going on. Indeed, I could not even complain because of the way in which I knew that this would be interpreted, and because of my awareness that this interpretation would only make things more difficult for any woman coming after me.

There are other ways in which the desire of many men (and women) to preserve traditional divisions between the sexes makes the participation of women in traditionally male sports difficult, even when participation is segregated. Of major significance is the difference in validational import of participation in such sports for men and women. Masculinity is clearly at issue in the men's game; success gives superior validation, but merely participating also grants an instant warrant of masculine achievement. Femininity, however, is never part of the picture at any point in the women's game in the sense that there is no gender-value advantage to be gained by playing well, or even by playing at all. One never gains status as feminine for playing hockey. Rather, one runs a very high risk of losing feminine validation altogether, particularly if one is good at the game; women who play badly are not on that account perceived as being more feminine, just as more ridiculous.

This difference in validational import is reflected in the quickness with which charges of homosexuality are made against female athletes in general, but especially against female hockey players.[5] The same charge is almost never made (except as all-purpose verbal abuse) against male hockey players. It is a commonplace that there are no gays in men's hockey. This is because it is "obvious" that you can't play hockey unless you are a "real" man. The reasoning goes like this. To be a man is to be untainted by effeminate qualities, and all gays are effeminate. Thus, a gay man simply couldn't play hockey. Therefore, there are no gay hockey players. This, of course, is absurd, as is the converse assumption that the vast majority of female hockey players are lesbians. Nevertheless, both popular assumptions work to enforce very strict and often destructive codes of behaviour.[6]

For women hockey players, especially younger ones, who are unsure of their own identity in any case, the fear of being labelled a "dyke" sometimes encourages a great deal of overcompensation and aggressive heterosexuality. They become more concerned to prove themselves off the ice than on it and occasion-

ally manifest a profound degree of hostility toward homosexuals, real or suspected. Someone once told me of a friend of hers, a hockey player who played
for a team at a prominent Canadian university and who had been unapologeti-
cally public about her lesbianism since high school. She was beaten up by her
teammates who were, one supposes, concerned to emphasize (to whom, exactly?) their own unreproachable heterosexuality. Obviously, the "team" atmosphere of conformity can exaggerate these sorts of tendencies even further. A particularly destructive manifestation of these tendencies to overexaggerate
heterosexual conformity is the institution of team initiation practices that involve women making other women, their own teammates, into objects for the
use of men. In this way, they re-enforce the rigid gender lines that their own
participation in a traditionally male sport challenges, as if to demonstrate that
whatever they may accomplish, they are still no threat to male hegemony and
perhaps most important, to demonstrate to themselves that they really are still
"normal girls."

It should be said, though, that not all team situations are the same. Social
milieus vary widely and so do the kinds of social attitudes encountered. Many
women—gay and straight—find a tolerance of their difference among other
women hockey players that they do not often find elsewhere, and I myself have
played on teams that were highly tolerant as well as those that were narrowly sexist and homophobic. Obviously, the level of personal maturity on the part of the
players makes a considerable difference; but, this maturity itself is usually a reflection of a deeper set of conditions, in particular, the extent to which the team
members have taken possession of and responsibility for their own identities.

The year I agreed to play on the women's team of a small university taught
me more than I had anticipated learning about the relationship between personal maturity and athletic success, not to mention the relative insignificance of
chronological age. Being nearly twice the age of the rest of the players, I expected
there to be difficulties but not the ones that actually came up. In the local city
league I would frequently play with teammates who were even younger, but we
had no great problem adjusting to each other because we were all there for the
same reason: to play hockey. With the university team, it was sometimes hard
to tell.

> *I can't believe what's happening here. We're on our way to being thumped 7–0
> by a local club team and we have totally disintegrated. Everyone's bitching
> about everyone else and I'm having a fight with one of my own players on the
> bench about who's yelling at whom. No one's taking any responsibility;
> everything that goes wrong is someone else's fault. The egos are all size XXL
> and eggshell thin. The other team can't believe their good fortune: we don't
> pass! Commiserating with me the next night the club team's coach says of my
> teammates, "mais, elles sont träs jeunes . . ."*

It seemed at this time that I would go through this strange cultural shift every week. First it was between men's and women's hockey. Now, the discontinuity was more subtle, but I still seemed to be trying to negotiate myself between two worlds that were a great deal more different than I had anticipated. During the week I practiced and played with the varsity team; on the weekends I played in the local women's league. The two frequently played against each other, and in different years I have played on either side of these games. There were linguistic, age, and socioeconomic differences, but the most significant one had to do with the level of mutual respect for teammates and opponents. The league teams played together and were successful because the players respected one another enough, trusted one another enough, to combine for the complex sequences of interaction that form the core of the game. They became a team even when technically they were not, but were simply playing in pick-up situations with players they didn't know. This allowed them not only to win but to experience the most joyful aspects of a game that is fundamentally dialectical in nature.

Where this engagement between the players is lacking, where they do not value each other as partners in the play, all this is denied to them. When a player thinks that she (or he) is so much better than anyone else on the team that it is invariably her best play to hang on to the puck rather than pass it to an "inferior" player, she has negated the possibility of team play, and that team is not only likely to lose but to become miserable and internally divisive. If everyone plays like this, it's a disaster. Because this kind of individualistic attitude is so destructive, athletic teams of all sorts very often try to eliminate it by, in effect, eliminating individuals. This is the explicit purpose of initiation rituals: the artificial inducement of team spirit, the submergence of individual into collective identity. But these are necessarily counterproductive. Of course, as one goaltender put it to me, "they always go too far." Whatever the explicit intent of such practices, it is inevitably subverted by the more hidden and twisted motivations of power and dominance. (Imagine! Just this once, you can use another person however you like, make them do whatever you want—without any consequences!) What is needed for team play is mutual respect between the players, and you can't manufacture this by having them degrade and humiliate each other. What you get instead is mutual contempt and fear, a collection of individuals who cannot respect themselves, much less each other, and a mean-spirited satisfaction at seeing a teammate screw up. This team defeats itself.

One of the varsity team players is trying to explain to me why the team's initiation is not degrading. She describes how the soccer teams' initiation involved the men and the women dancing and stripping for money. "And it was really great, because some girls made as much as $300!!" A couple of years ago, the women's rugby initiation involved rookies walking around campus *in their underwear, wrapped in bits of toilet paper, with holes marked on their foreheads and the words "insert dick here," and signs on their butts saying "fuck me here." I'm trying to explain to my team captain why the involvement of the stickboy in a systematic process of degrading women is perverse. She doesn't get it. I tell her that this is the only team, men's or women's, I've ever been on that does this and that this is probably why it is also the most uncohesive. I explain that I cannot be part of a team that thinks that any of this is the right way to treat other people. I'm trying really, really hard to stay calm and reasonable and not to lose my temper. None of it is getting across. I can get out of participating by just refusing, but then how do I say "that's immoral if you do it to me, but go ahead and do it to her?" Finally, I walk off the team. The coach is furious; he thinks I'm overreacting. Then someone fills him in and he moves to ban initiation. I rejoin the team in time for the next game. Then someone else higher up overrules him. The university thinks they've already solved the problem (which is apparently worst with the women's teams) by requiring that the veterans get the rookies' consent. When you tell a 17 year old that the team she really wants to be a part of has an initiation, but that she can refuse to be involved, and then she says "I don't mind," do you think she consents?*

Before I started playing women's hockey, teammates were just the jerks you had to put up with in order to play the game. That doesn't mean I never liked any of them, but you always knew that you just weren't part of their team, and you couldn't be, because "team" is a guy-thing. It depends on a kind of super-natural communication or intuition, a sympathetic vibration between y-chromosomes that you could never partake in. When I started playing with women, everything changed. All of a sudden, I was aware of the assumption of respect, that I was being taken seriously. I had nothing to prove, only myself to live up to. The game itself was the only thing at issue. In a way, this made things tougher—if it is assumed from the start that you are incapable of reaching the same level as everyone else, you always have a ready excuse for not working harder. However, if you are expected to succeed, your failure to carry your own weight is all down to you. A poor showing becomes a matter of character, not biology. Although this puts a tremendous amount of responsibility on a person for herself, for me it was a relief. But for many of the younger players I know, letting go of the spurious comfort that the excuses offer is not only difficult in the ordinary way, but there are some fairly heavy influences pushing them down the easier path.

There is nothing more corrupting for a young girl than associating a great deal with other young girls. . . . The woman's fundamental qualification is to be company for the man, but through association with her own sex she is led to reflection upon it, which makes her a society lady instead of company. (Kierkegaard, "Johannes the Seducer," p. 340)

It is a popular truism that women can't get along with each other, and thus a women's team cannot possibly bond the way a men's team can. There are indeed obstacles in the way of female bonding, but these are due more to an ideologically programmed gender divisiveness and the pressures of heterosexist expectations than anything else. As Kierkegaard's fictional protagonist noticed, if women spend too much time together, they may well find that they can exist separately from men, that they can have an existence that is not defined in relativity to their men-folk. And this must be prevented if men are to get first call on their attentions.

One male coach of my acquaintance once remarked that the women he coached tended to find it more difficult to bond in the team situation, but that when they did, they did so more strongly than men. One explanation for this, if true, might be that team bonding is a reflex taught to boys at an early age, through games and other activities, so many of which are team-oriented. Little girls, on the other hand, are taught to find their primary associations with males rather than females. Playing "house" and "dress-up" are activities that, though engaged in with other little girls, in many ways revolve around the assumption of a central relationship with a definitively male other. This centrality of the other gender to play and consequently the construction of identity is much less evident in the play of little boys (at least where play is to some degree segregated). It is assumed that a girl will forego female–female relationships in favour of those she has with certain significant males. Indeed, the former are more likely to be seen as immature or even selfish. Male–male relationships, by contrast, retain normative import. For the adult worlds of business and politics, being able to be a team player is a requisite for success. These values filter back again into the culture of sport. The football player who keeps his girlfriend waiting is acting appropriately, and he probably won't lose the girl over it; the hockey player who keeps her boyfriend on hold is significantly less likely either to keep him or to be well spoken of. The secondary aspect of female–female relationships as compared to male–male relationships thus militates against the likelihood of the sort of all-or-nothing, one-for-all-and-all-for-one bonding that takes place on male teams and that is vital to successful team competition. Contingency is injected into the heart of the female team experience: A woman must never put team above other obligations, particularly those she has to males.[7]

Women are still very often expected to find their self-worth in the subordination of their interests to those of others whose interests are valued more highly. To the extent that this is so, it becomes proportionately more difficult for them to develop the means to form a solidly cooperative relationship between themselves. The key to male bonding is denial of self in association. For women it seems to be just the opposite: learning to value oneself as distinct from others and not as merely contingent. Self-respect is the first step in the respect for others, and trust in others, that is the real basis of female bonding. This is the crucial step in forming an effective team, but it is also crucial to becoming a person who can be herself, taking the responsibility for that self and for her relations to others. Without self-respect one does not make decisions for oneself. Without self-respect one does not say no. Self-respect is the beginning of moral autonomy, it is the beginning of active self-determination, and it is the beginning of effective cooperation. It is a deeply empowering discovery.[8]

Self-respect, then, is the first thing needed for mutual respect between players and athletes as for anyone else. If the players on a team each respect themselves, then they also know that they can respect each other because this means that they can trust one another. If I know that my teammates respect themselves, I know that they will work hard in practice, will show up fit and ready for a game, that my winger will remember to cover the defenceman on the point, and that our goalie won't give up just because the rest of us can't find the other team's net. I can trust my teammates to do what they can to be where they're supposed to be and to at least try to make the play they're supposed to make. If it doesn't work, it's no big deal—there are far more things that you have no control over than things that you do. As it happens, a team has the ability to control more than does any number of individuals, but only if it cooperates and effective cooperation begins with the self-respect of individuals. In short, then, once these players can shake off their need to seek personal validation from an ideology of gender that incorporates a not merely differential but hierarchical structure of valuation, they can begin to develop themselves fully as responsible human beings and as athletes capable of trust and cooperation between themselves.

PRAXIS AND SELFHOOD

We send children off to play sports under the pretext that it builds character. And so it does. But the character that sport builds is not always positive. Thus, it is worth rethinking not only how sport transmits messages about how we ought to be and how we ought to behave, but how sport itself ought to be. There is an important sense in which sport is not separate from us, and questions about structure, purpose, organization, etc. are not trivial ones. The issues are not simply technical or bureaucratic, but ontological, moral, and political.[9]

In the case of hockey, then, how do women appropriate or reconstitute this game for themselves? It seems that the first answer is that they cannot do it by simply trying to play the men's game as it stands now, but must find a way of playing their own game. But I think it would be misleading to suggest that the women's game either is or ought to be feminine. In the main, this is because our understanding of the feminine is shaped by what we think constitutes the masculine, and the masculine that the traditional male game presents to us is a deeply distorted and, indeed false, ideal of human organization. That being so, it is unlikely that any uncontested conception of the feminine would be any less distorted and false. And certainly, hockey (for one) simply cannot be a feminine game as that term is commonly understood: It does require at least some so-called masculine attitudes and characteristics, such as aggression and competitiveness. Since playing the game at all means learning traits not normally attributed to women, this means that the women's game will be not so much feminine as balanced, that is, more human in the sense that those women who play it have to develop a wider range of their inherent human capacities than they have traditionally been encouraged to do. These are already feminine qualities in the sense that women have them and are capable of developing them; we simply have to be more ready to acknowledge them as such. The women's game, with its structural emphasis on skill over force, already incorporates a rejection of both stereotypically masculine and feminine characteristics; it embraces active self-assertion in a competitive environment while also emphasizing highly cooperative play—as well as the use of careful playmaking and precise control of the puck—over violence and goon tactics.

Maintenance of a distinct women's game may prove more difficult in the future. The growth of women's hockey, as of other sports, along with an increased gender integration of sports programmes, has meant, amongst other things, an increase in the number of men coaching and controlling women's hockey. These men very often expect women's hockey to conform to the prototype of men's hockey. The demands of mainstream media and a public raised on rock 'em-sock 'em hockey also places pressure on a sport that needs greater public support and commercial recognition in order to finance itself. The commodification of sport that is going on everywhere is in danger of forcing the women's game to accommodate itself to the dominant hockey paradigm of force, power, and brutality. Such an accommodation would guarantee the women's game permanent second-class status. Women have to find a way to take control of their own game and determine their own future in it. If they do, there is at least the chance that we might affect the future of the men's game as well. Professional hockey is already seen by many who love the game to be spiritually bankrupt. By contrast, women's hockey still beats with its own heart. Since there are so many costs involved and so little external reward, those involved can only play for the pure love of the game.[10]

Finally, then, it is not just that women must claim the game for themselves, they must also lay claim to a collection of *human* traits that have been denied to them because of a spurious association with masculinity. Appropriating areas of human activity previously denied is inseparable from the redefinition of the *humans* performing that activity. Questions about what we do are always questions about what we are. But adequate answers to such questions require a loosening or even outright rejection of familiar categories. Women who play "men's" sports are rarely, if ever, doing it because they secretly wish that they were men. What they want is to be able to develop their own abilities and potential just as men have; while they may admire men's accomplishments and envy their opportunities, what they want is the chance to become themselves, not someone else. Even when they compete with men, as many prefer to do, the aim is not to be a man, but to take advantage of the opportunities that situation presents in order to become better as women athletes, or as athletes simpliciter. Thus the question of whose game women are to play has both a straightforwardly political dimension, reflected in the issue of who controls the continued development of the game, and a moral-metaphysical one, raising the questions, "Who are we to be?" "What am I to create of myself?" Such questions clearly extend beyond the comparatively narrow category of sport; they confront all of us, at every point in our lives. I contend that women playing or competing in male-defined/ definitive sports are already engaged in a deeply practical way in the task of redefining what it means to be themselves and what it means for any of us to be women. And in doing so, they are actively reconstructing for all of us the definitions of woman, man, and human.

AFTERWORD

After all I have described, some may be wondering, "Much of this sounds so miserable—just one struggle after another; if the cost is so high, why do you keep playing?" This is difficult to explain in any straightforward way. I know now that I enjoy the competition. Yes, I like to win. But what is absolutely central to my love of hockey is not competition, even though the competitive situation is the condition of its occurring. I play because you can do things on skates you can't do anywhere else: It is the closest anyone can get to flight while remaining on the ground. It's the incredible speed, and the extraordinary defiance of gravity that comes with it, that lets you turn your body at impossible angles to the surface of the ice, that you can move sideways without taking a step. It's because it seems as though I can will myself into a place and be there, instantly. It's the inevitability of time and the cessation of time in the same moment. There's a pure joy of movement, the dialectical interaction of action and reaction, with my teammates, the opposing players, the rhythm and grace of completely integrated movement, balletic in its complexity of communication, forward and back. It's the wonder of those few, rare and exhilarating moments when you feel as if you have complete mastery of your own body, all of your faculties open at once. There is in the game, at times, an experience of the sheer ontological immediacy of being which excludes the possibility of the noise of reflection but which is also a transcendence of pure physicality—you know your body as completely yours. It's a perfection of unity with your body, with being, which does not reduce you to it alone, but which gives it over to you utterly. I exist in this game and I will play it until I die.[11]

NOTES

1. This issue has obvious parallels elsewhere. One of the most compelling reasons for the institution of affirmative action policies for hiring is the fact that candidates who are fully qualified for employment in a particular position are often not *seen* as qualified simply because of their difference from the norm anticipated by the employer.

2. I recall a pick-up game of shinny played in grad school where one male student offered the following solution for dividing the players fairly: "just put a woman on each team and then they'll be even."

3. Compare Ken Dryden and Roy MacGregor's description of the Canadian attitude to the Soviets in the 1950s: *"We were better. It was through this optic that we saw everything. We shot harder and more often; we rushed the puck solo in great end-to-end dashes; we bodychecked. If they passed more, shot and bodychecked less, it could only mean that they passed too much, shot and bodychecked too little. Because we were better"* (p. 199).

4. For a related sort of example, consider the closing scenes of the Ridley Scott movie *Alien.* After fighting off a dangerous creature that has destroyed all her shipmates, Second Officer Ripley prepares herself and the ship's cat for the voyage home to earth, only to be forced— *in her underwear*—into a final battle to the death with the alien. Why exactly? To show that, although she may be strong, courageous, and a dab hand with a flame-thrower, she's still (really) a babe, boys.

5. I say "especially" because hockey is a sport that is notably masculinized, but this is true of any sport explicitly defined as male. Rugby, basketball, track, tennis, and even golf display the same problematic to one degree or another.

6. In view of recent scandals in junior hockey regarding the sexual abuse of players by coaches, it is worth pointing out that the hypermasculine ethos of the game goes some way to strengthening the hold that the abuser has over the player. The primary means of enforcing both compliance and silence is the player's fear of losing his chance at a pro career, but the same of any association with activities regarded as homosexual is also overwhelming. And it is notable that while much entirely appropriate rage has been expressed on the issue of the sexual exploitation of these young men, little concern is ever voiced over the incidence of heterosexual rape by those same players.

7. Except, sometimes, where that team obligation is to a male coach.

8. It is not my intention to defend some high libertarian notion of moral selfhood here, as if we were utterly distinct, atomistic individuals, ideally autonomous centres of rational self-interest maximization, who either can or should act wholly separately from the needs or interests of others. I think such a view is both manifestly false and morally wicked. But I do wish to emphasize that our relationships with others do have to be entered into, accepted as *our* relationships, by self-aware, self-choosing persons, i.e., those who do not acquiesce in a definition exhausted by contingency.

9. However, it should not be forgotten that not all sports are the same, and that the socializing structure inherent in traditional competitive team sports like hockey, football, basketball, etc. is not universal. The participants in certain individual sports, such as kayaking or rock-climbing to name just two, would argue that much of the ideological gender baggage of traditional team sports is either undercut or substantially transformed in these activities by the relationship the athlete has to the medium of competition. That is to say, even when racing (as in whitewater kayaking) the athlete is required to "compete," not so much against another human being but a natural object: the river, or the rock-face for the climber. However, this is inevitably less an act of competition than of opportunistic cooperation: One does not defeat such an object, but must adapt to and cooperate with what is given to one by the river or the cliff in order to maximize one's own performance in relation to it. In this case, success (and the spiritual core experience that ultimately

motivates athletic endeavor of all kinds) is the outcome of an openness on the part of the athlete to perceive what is offered by the other (the river, the rock) and to, in effect, cooperate with it; overpowering the other is simply not an option.

10. Dryden and MacGregor: "In the late 1940s, Tarasov, in fact, had had no choice but to go his own way. To copy meant not only to be second best, but to adopt a system that was philosophically unacceptable" (p. 200). In the end, of course, the Soviets significantly transformed the style of play of North American hockey.

11. This essay owes much to the many people, especially teammates past and present, whose play and experiences have contributed to my thinking about the game—most of them unknowingly and no doubt in a few cases, unwillingly. But thanks are also particularly due to Claire Grogan and to Jeanette Ettel who read and provided invaluable commentary on various earlier versions.

REFERENCES

Dryden, Ken, and Roy MacGregor. *Home Game: Hockey and Life in Canada.* Toronto: McClelland & Stewart, 1989.

Gruneau, Richard, and David Whitson. *Hockey Night in Canada: Sport, Identities, and Cultural Politics.* Toronto: Garamond, 1993.

Harrison, Richard. *Hero of the Play.* Toronto: Wolsak and Wynn, 1994.

Kierkegaard, Soren. *Either/Or Vol I.* Trans. Howard V. Hong and Edna H. Hong. Princeton, NJ: Princeton University Press, 1987.

Tretiak, Vladislav. *Tretiak: The Legend.* Edmonton: Plains Publishing, 1987.

STUDY QUESTIONS

1. In what ways does our participation in sports, both as players and spectators, help shape our social identities?

2. What problems and opportunities arise for individuals, teams, and societies when women begin to play a traditionally male sport?

3. According to Howe, self-respect, respect *from* others, and respect *for* others are all interdependent. Which experience do you think is most basic? How do the three experiences influence one another?

Engendering Ethnicity:
The Economy of Female Virginity
and Guatemalan Nationalism[1]

Luna Nàjera

A Guatemalan refugee at the age of five, Luna Nàjera grew up in Los Angeles. She is presently a graduate student in Latin American history at Cornell University. Her writing often explores the interrelationships of memory, history, narrative, and theory, with particular attention to the connections between state and personal violence.

> I SPEAK ONLY of what I have lived through, not merely of what I have thought through; the opposition of thinking and life is lacking in my case. My "theory" grows from my "practice"—oh, from a practice that is not by any means harmless or unproblematic! (Friedrich Nietzsche)

The highest offering a woman like myself can give to a man is her virginity, for my value as a woman, a Latin American woman, depends on the spiritual and physical integrity that is symbolized by an intact hymen. The value that Latin American societies attribute to female virginity is an important determining factor in women's lives. Throughout Latin America, the presence of the hymen at the altar is honorable to the bride and her parents, while its absence summons disgrace. According to a dictionary, the hymen is "the virginal membrane,

Reprinted with permission of Humanities Press Inc., from "Engendering Ethinicity: The Economy of Female Virginity in Guatemala," by Luna Nàjera, *Radical Philosophy Review* 2, no. 2 (1999); permission conveyed through Copyright Clearance Center, Inc.

a fold of mucous membrane stretched across and partially closing the external orifice of the vagina."[2] This piece of thin skin can be accidentally torn by physical exercise, but it can also stretch and remain intact after several sexual relations. The notion that the "real proof" of virginity is in the shedding of blood during a woman's first sexual relations is a myth that has gripped diverse cultural imaginations, and women's psyches.

The valorization of female virginity is not exclusive to the parts of Latin America colonized by Spain, nor is its value fixed and universal, for it has been regarded differently in various cultures around the world (San 1974). The Yungar of Australia, for example, require female virginity prior to marriage, but like the Minankabau, a less patriarchal society, the defloration ritual is not an act reserved for the husband, but is performed by female elders a week before the wedding (Hernandez 1985, 82). Cross-culturally, female virginity has not always been valued. Anthropologists report that

> . . . some non-Western peoples do not place high values on virginity, but these cultures are in the minority. Examples of these societies include the Garo in Asia, the Hopi Indians in the United States, the Kakuts in Asia, the Aymara in South America, the Tarahumara in Mexico, and the Truk in Oceana (Holtzman and Kulish, 44).

In at least one society, virginity is *dis*valued.

> In some parts of Tibet women without sexual experience are frowned upon. Prior to marriage women should have had at least one sexual relation, which, in many cases is performed by an individual lacking social prestige, whose job it was to educate virgins [about sex] (Hernandez, 82, my translation).

Such variations throw into relief the question, what social needs are met when virginity is valorized? That question is important to me not just as a theorist, but because of a sequence of events in my life that began in 1989, in Los Angeles. Victor R— violated me while on a date in the back seat of a car. I had asked my friend, Veronica, to arrange a double date for me with Victor. I was fourteen, unaccustomed to alcohol. I drank two beers. He put his arm around my back. He started playing with my bra strap. I let him touch me. Veronica and her boyfriend left the car. Victor loaded a heavy metal cassette into the tape player and turned up the volume. It became dark outside. He unbuttoned my pants. I was too drunk to resist. I cried when he cut right through me. The car windows fogged up, the cold rage in the music pierced my ear drums. That's all I remember until I crawled, bleeding, out of the car and into the parking lot where Veronica and her boyfriend stood by a tree. She hugged me, consoled me. Her boyfriend congratulated Victor. "Hey Victor, you popped her cherry."

"Yeah, the bitch let me, she wanted it," replied Victor.

"Fucking Victor," said his friend with a smile of disbelief.

Taking a woman's virginity contributes to the symbolic status of the male. In rupturing[3] her hymen, a man claims a woman as "his." Even if he abandons her, the virginity he has "taken" will always be "his"; this totem she has lost, that he has taken, bolsters his manhood from then on, and he cannot lose it, no one can take it from him.[4] However, men are not the sole players in this economy of female virginity. The value of female virginity accrues from the social investment in it by religious and family institutions. Extreme anxiety is invested in the maintenance of the integrity of the hymen. Fathers deliver lectures warning their daughters on the cunning ways that men employ to get women to fall into their traps. The legitimacy of their advice, they say, lies in the fact that they themselves are men and know the tricks. Mothers team up with the fathers by surveilling their virgin daughters and isolating them from the outside world: visits or contacts with men are prohibited or restricted, clothes are scrutinized, curfews enforced, and even friendships with same sex friends are investigated. In many cases mothers and daughters war against each other until, out of desperation and in search of an escape, the daughter marries.

Women who preserve their virginity believe they are more valuable than sexually experienced women. In wedding ceremonies, the symbols of purity—the white dress, the tiara, and the veil worn by the bride—correspond to the bride's physical/moral integrity. A wedding is an economic exchange where one of the things of value is the virtue[5] of sexual (bodily) repression. The virgin's mastery over her sexual desires morally elevates her in public opinion. Her virginity (which is synonymous with moral uprightness) is a currency through which family, community, and God are honored. Arriving at the altar in a white dress is a repayment by the bride for her parents' love, education, and care. As Venezuelan sociologist Jose López points out, the bride's repayment requires public endorsement because "the honor of the family is derived from the qualities of its individual members and from public commentary about their conduct" (63, my translation). While taking a woman's virginity affirms a man's masculinity, the virgin who sacrifices[6] herself to a man (in marriage) gains an elevated moral status in her community. A woman who gives away her virginity, however, is on her way to *la mala vida*.[7]

In my parents' view, the loss of my virginity suggested that I'd carelessly given way to my desires, thereby becoming more of a *mujer de la mala vida* than a marriageable woman. They believed and feared that with nothing left for me to lose (because I'd lost it all when I was raped) I would become sexually uncontrollable and risk abandonment, abuse, and reproach by men. My father shed tears in front of a man, the elder of a Jehovah's Witness congregation whom my mother sent to console my father. *Hermano* Melgar, a tall *Guatemalteco* with graying hair, consoled my grieving father with the timeless words of the black Bible he thumbed back and forth as he talked about forgiveness. "I wanted to see her married in white," my father lamented. Instead I had come home stained with my own blood, drunk, afraid, and devalued; my hymen torn away forever. It hurt my father to see his fruit rotting by the touch of another man, a man who'd invested nothing in me but a few beers. It injured him so much that he lost his shame and wept like a child.

On the night of the rape, he'd ordered me to pull down my pants to see for himself. He pushed me against the wall, commanding me like a soldier does a civilian. I did as he ordered, seeing my hands unbutton my pants for my father's eyes. He, in turn, ran his eyes down through my body as if I were a stranger. My mother stood there, motionless, seeing her own daughter revealing that female secret that had become public and worthless in the eyes of "society." Then, when he saw the blood not only on that crucial triangular part of the under-wear, but all over the underwear, he looked at me with furious eyes and raised his arm behind him, releasing it with great fury. He slapped my jaw three times, my head turning with each blow. I withheld my tears in defiance while I attempted to lock my eyes onto his.

I stabbed my father in a dream five years after the rape. He lay asleep in bed with me and I pulled out a knife from under the bed and pierced his heart. Blood gushed out as he lifted his chest away from the bed and helplessly tried to lock his eyes onto my eyes. I walked around the bed to help him up, feeling pity and compassion for him.

Although in some Latino communities in the U.S. the value of virginity is diminishing, the deprivation of an education, a social life, and self-development for young Latin American women is a harsh reality.[8] Though the value of virginity is still somewhat variable, preserving one's virginity (or the appearance of it) until marriage still merits an extravagant wedding ceremony, gifts, and the respect of family and community. This celebration of female chastity is to honor the head of the family, whose name is either revered or muddied by his daughter's sexuality. A woman's sexuality, then, does not belong to her, but is claimed by her family and community. While a woman's deflowering under the legal sanction of marriage is considered sacred, worthy, and in harmony with nature and God's laws, the loss of one's "sexual purity" outside of marriage is a blow to the family, community, and God. The violation of a woman's chastity constitutes a degradation of her family (name). The case of a woman who freely "gives away" her virginity is cause for great alarm and much gossip in the community. Women who fail to assert their value can be easily trampled on by the male who "took" their virginity as well as by their community.

Rape transformed me from virgin to someone men could disrespect. I'd "given it all away" and for that I was considered a "slut," a woman for public use by men. Days after the rape I saw Victor's friend; he asked if I could reimburse him for the cleaning of the seat covers, and walked away laughing. He could wipe his feet on me. I'd become worthless and dirty: *una puta*. Not even my father could defend me, for I'd brought shame on the family.

Be it sexual abuse or desire for sexual pleasure, a woman who gives herself sexually has asked for *it*. There is less a man can prove about himself with a slut, for she gives herself freely. But a virgin is yet to be conquered, yet to be marketed. The more difficult the penetration of a virgin, the more the act is charged with the excitement of discovery and triumph. Her impenetrability is eroticized. The act of breaking the seal is among the sweetest of male pleasures. A "used" woman cheats men of their masculinity; she cannot give him the pleasure of breaking her and the consequent assurance of his masculinity. That it takes a hard *macho* to "make" a woman, that it is he who makes (her into a woman) and is made (into a "real" man) in the act of defloration, that he mounts her and rips her skin with the head of his engorged penis, this taking and giving of her body, this rendering of her self—this is the crucial transaction in the economy of female virginity. In this economic logic the poor women are those whose lack of currency, or of the "proof" of virginity, marks them as *putas*.[9] A *puta* is the antithesis of the virginal woman; she is portrayed as expressing her sexual desires and actively seeking out men, in contrast to chaste women who dominate their carnal desires and safeguard their virginity until the wedding night. The absence of the bloody "proof," the symbol of purity, links her to moral and physical pollution. Contrary to the virgin who bleeds (when she is deflowered), a woman who does not bleed is considered to be "used." A "used" woman, according to a Jehovah's Witness publication, is susceptible to use and abuse by men in the same way that hand towels are used in public bathrooms.[10] Women who have been "used," then, are morally corrupt; hence, sexually "usable" by men who remain free of the legal obligations that marriage incurs.

The deprecation of unmarried deflowered women satisfies certain social needs. By serving as a negative support for the valorization of female virginity, it contributes to the construction of patriarchal masculinity and femininity, facilitating the social bonding through which family and community are built. Women lacking the "proof" of their virginity are suspect of betrayal to their men and their own families, thereby becoming second class citizens of their communities. Moreover, the marginalization of corrupted women elevates and centralizes chaste and docile women who have preserved their virginity by "honoring" their fathers and husbands at the altar. By disvaluing their virginity, women reclaim their family's and their community's hold of their bodies; for it is the control of women's bodies that characterizes patriarchal societies.

Thus, a woman's body, in particular her vagina, becomes a symbolic nexus of societal relations. Her intact hymen is a symbol of purity because its rupture and subsequent shedding of blood "proves" that no one other than her husband has penetrated the bride's vagina. The presence of the hymen attests to her free-dom from "admixture of anything debasing or deteriorating" (namely, another man's semen).[11] The pollution of the unmarried non-virgin woman is parallel to that of the adulteress. In both cases their sexual activity is an affront to a male partner or potential partner because they have been contaminated by the semen of another man. Presumably, the underlying anxiety of the husband or poten-tial husband derives from his desire to immortalize himself through offspring, to ensure that only his true offspring are his heirs, and not to have his sexual performance compared to other men.

Sometimes that individualized male anxiety is interwoven with a societal anxiety about female sexuality that is inflected by a politics of exclusion. Exclu-sionary political practices can take many forms: they can exclude gays from the military, blacks from private schools, women from men's clubs, disabled people from important buildings, etc. The politics of exclusion that are operative within the economy of female virginity, the marginalization of impure women in order to maintain an ideal of virginal womanhood that strengthens patriarchal systems, also engenders the marginalization of ethnicity. The question is not whether eth-nicity politics in Guatemala emananted from the valorization of female virgin-ity or vice versa; instead, the issue is how the amalgamation of women's sexual-ity and racial politics produces exclusionary modalities by which a people, a nation, define themselves.

Although without explicitly acknowledging it, my parents were very well aware of the conjunction between sexuality and ethnicity. Despite the fact that I'd grown up in Los Angeles since the age of five, I understood that the Maya Indians were a source of shame for my mother, and a source of ridicule on the part of my father. I remember my mother's resentful face when news reporters covering the violence in Guatemala focused their cameras on barefooted Mayan people. "Why do they have to show those *inditos*?" she would ask. "They show them as if that's all there is in Guatemala," she'd protest. I'd encounter my par-ents' negative perception of the Mayan people when they'd call me *India* for talking back or resisting their discipline. For me, being Indian was accompanied by a slap in the face.

In 1989, when my parents sent me back to my father's family in Guatemala City, I came face to face with the Mayan people I'd only seen on television screens in North America. I'd returned to Guatemala, or, I had been exiled there on account of a policeman's counsel to my parents on the night of the rape. If I continued my ways, prophesied the cop, I would eventually sell my body and end up in jail. Fearing that prospect and consumed with rage and disappoint-ment with what, in my father's words, I'd turned out to be, my parents returned me to the country they'd fled from ten years back.

My grandparents' home was under construction when I arrived in Guatemala City. However, its deck, numerous entrances, large rubber tree, and white color made it stand out from all the rest. Inside the house, a small garden contained another tree from which hung exotic house plants. That afternoon we ate lunch in a large, spacious room illuminated by the sun that shone in through the windows. It was my first home-cooked meal: *guizado,* black bean soup, and homemade *tortillas* I personally fetched from the *tortilleria* at the other end of the house. My grandparents' home also stood out from all the rest because the corner of the house was rented out to a Mayan family who ran the *tortilla* business. People came from all over the neighborhood with small baskets to fetch *tortillas* from the Mayan woman's business every morning, noon, and afternoon. The *tortilleria* was one of the rooms rented out by the Mayan family, the other room housed the family itself: a wife, husband, one child and various relatives. The woman of the family owned and ran her own *tortilleria* business, while her husband worked at a hamburger stand in the city.

The Mayan family's dirt floors began where my grandparents' main living area ended. Their two rooms were makeshift constructions with doors, not windows, and dirt, not tile floors. "They are *naturales,*" explained my grandfather, "we are *ladinos.*" *Naturales,* the natural[12] ones, is another way of naming Guatemala's Mayan people. Unlike the *ladinos,* they are not mixed with Spanish blood. They are not "racially altered" and because of this they are considered to be in an uncivilized state. Their refusal to become *ladinized,* either by dressing in Western clothes or marrying into *ladino* families, is explained by "their inherent indigenous nature," i.e., they are stubborn and therefore "not reconciled to social, political, or economic change."[13] Supposedly, living in makeshift homes with no windows and dirt floors is "natural" to them, for they are "inherently" uncivilized. This was my first explicit introduction to my *ladino* heritage. The contrast between the two living conditions symbolized the place that the Mayan people hold in the *ladino* imagination.

My own place in the house became a deeper, more personal lesson on the politics of identity in Guatemala. A few days after my arrival, my grandfather explained that my last name, Herrera, is Spanish and that in everything I do I should have the pride of an Herrera. The virtues of the last name could be seen in my great-grandmother's strength and intelligence, he said. She had such a strong character that she refused to take on my great-grandfather's last name. As a single parent raising sons on her own, she succeeded in running her own business. "Hundreds of men were under her command," they would tell me. "She made her employees work hard, and publicly chastised her female employees for not cooking well." My grandfather tried to instill in me the pride the felt in being more Spanish than Indian. This became more evident when the became upset with me and called me by my mother's last name, which is Nàjera. Unlike Herrera, Nàjera betrays indigenous origins. What made my mother's last name a pejorative was precisely its links with the uncivilized. Furthermore, they despised and looked down on her not only because of her indigenous last name, but also because she came from the country. My grandfather's disdainful pronunciation of my mother's last name and his use of it at times when I made him upset taught me that *ladinismo* is a state of being that is characterized by a violent resentment and hatred of one's Indian origin.

The association of the Mayan population with dirt is couched in pseudo-biological explanations that can be heard from the mouths of even the most uneducated people. My maternal grandmother, an uneducated merchant woman and mother of eight children, explains the rise of thievery since the peace accords by the return of the Mayan refugees. In her view, the differences between the Indian and the *ladino* consist in the *mala sangre* (bad blood) of the Indian and the distinctive European physiognomy of the *ladino*. According to her, the "bad blood" of Indians keeps them from thinking clearly. "They don't think," she says, "they just kill and they even kill their own kind for money. . . . The Indian people have the blood of a dog."[14] For my grandmother, who raised eight children on her own during the depression years in the country, nothing could be worse than being an Indian. The popular Guatemalan saying, *Somos pobres, pero no somos Indios* ("We are poor, but at least we are not Indians"), encapsulates the spirit behind my grandmother's derisive perception of the Mayan people.

According to Edward Said, conquerors' stories about the people they colonize also "become the method colonized people use to assert their own identity and the existence of their own history" (xii). My grandfather's lessons about the differences between *ladinos* and Indians may very well have been intended to orient me, a newcomer, to the social order prevailing inside and outside of my grandparents' home; however, the stories he told also allowed him to assert his own identity and his own place in history.

Using pseudo-biological explanations, the *ladino* population of Guatemala imagines itself different from and in binary opposition to the Mayan peoples. Often *ladinos* claim that the *indigenas'* biological inferiority can be found in physical characteristics, such as being short and, according to my grandfather, having a lot of warts. In the same way that the unmarried non-virgin woman is the antithesis of the virginal woman, to be Indian is perceived as the antithesis of the *ladino* ethnic ideal. While some *ladinos* acknowledge they are the products of Spanish and Indian blood mixing, they assume a superiority over the Indian through the cleansing of *la raza* (the race) of Indian blood by marrying up, i.e., by marrying into white or lighter-skinned families, a role assigned particularly to women. *Ladinismo,* then, is a movement away from indigenous descent and toward Spanish (read white) ascent.[15]

However, *ladinismo* has not always been in binary opposition to the Maya. In the colonial period, for example, the *ladino* category was used to designate unassimilated native peoples who, in addition to adopting the Spanish language, also acquired Spanish customs and dress. A second meaning of the category, which is traced to the mid-18th century, "no longer referred to 'Hispanicized' Indians but rather was used to refer to *castas,* all intermediate strata between Spaniard and Indian, including *mestizos* and *mulattos,* as well as to 'former' Indians" (Gould, 7). Here, the meaning of *ladino* designates the racial admixture of Indian, black, and white, whereas its previous meaning only referred to European assimilation. The third and most recent meaning of the category *ladino* relies on binary oppositionality to the category Indian, where non-Indian means, in large measure, "white."

In the case of Guatemala, where more than half of a population of 11 million are Mayan, the oppositional meaning of *ladino* may have taken hold because the emergence of the export economy in late 19th century Guatemala depended on the political disfranchising and economic exploitation of the indigenous population. The exploitation of the *indigenas* by the Creole class required the complicity of *ladinos* (assimilated Indiana, or racially mixed). The developing linguistic binary opposition between the *ladino* and the Indian may have contributed to a sense of racial and economic oppositionality between the two. It also may have offered *ladinos* a perceived way up the socio-economic ladder. Mixed-race people could someday rule if, through carefully orchestrated marriages, they became whitened enough. *Ladinismo* was not only a move away from "racial inferiority," but also offered upward class mobility.

"Hay que mejorar la raza!" my aunt advocated, raising her fist and face up in the air. The Guatemalan woman's duty is to better the race, which can only be accomplished by preserving that valuable piece of thin skin that guarantees purity and makes one valuable. In other words, the chastity of the *ladina* makes up for her economically disadvantaged position and allows her entry into privileged familial groups. *El no saberse valer,* not knowing how to value oneself, is the biggest mistake a *ladina* can make. If she premaritally loses that little treasure, the hymen, she's cheated her family and herself of the opportunity for upward race and class mobility and this is a source of dishonor. Thus, the valorization of female virginity is not exclusively a question of honor, morals and female chastity; rather, it is a question of social purity, of blood cleansing as a means to political as well as economic hegemony.

The shift from the meaning of *ladino* as a mixed race category to that of the "non-Indian" or "white" category reflects a national project that is constantly challenged and threatened by the introduction of the bad blood of the Maya through women's sexuality. "There aren't any rational explanations for why we must marry in a white dress and rear children," says my aunt, "it's a ritual all Guatemalan women must enact in their self-realization." Hidden in her comment is an insight: practices that may seem not to be in the interests of an individual woman *qua* woman, may nonetheless contribute to her realization as a member of her community. My aunt says "Guatemalan women," but she means *ladino* women, and to see that is to reveal something more important. Benedict

Anderson defines a nation as "an imagined political community," that is, "imagined as both inherently limited and sovereign" (15). My mother's shame, my father's, my grandparents', and my aunt's disdain of Indians offer a glimpse into the *ladino* imagination, where the Guatemalan nation is actually the imagined community of *ladinos*. A national consciousness relies on narratives that allow an imagined community to express for itself and others a vision of itself and its place in history, and in particular for it to imagine itself in opposition to what it is not. Crucial to such narratives in Guatemala have been the notions of *ladino* and the related, supporting cult of female virginity.

Notes

1. I would like to thank Margaret Cerullo and Carollee Bengelsdorf for their mentoring during the writing of this paper.
2. "Hymen." *Oxford English Dictionary* (1980).
3. rup-ture, 1.a. The process of breaking open or bursting. b. The state of being broken open. 2. *A break in friendly relations.* 3. A tear in bodily tissue. To break open; burst. *The American Heritage Dictionary* (1994).
4. A man is not considered a "real" man until he has deflowered a woman.
5. Etymology of the word virtue is "virtus [meaning] manliness, valour, worth, etc." ("Virtue." *The Oxford English Dictionary*, 1980.)
6. A crucial part of the deviring ritual is the shedding of blood by the virgin.
7. *Mujer de la "mala vida"* (woman of the bad life) refers to women who go from man to man. Men want to sleep with her, but not necessarily marry her. The term, *mujer de la mala vida*, is also used to refer to prostitutes.
8. I believe that the enforcement of school attendance by minors is a contributing factor in the diminishing pressure on Latina women to remain chaste until marriage, for it is in such institutions that parent's authorities over their children's moral values are challenged. Moreover, schools are also places where interactions with the opposite sex are out of the parents' control. However, the enforcement of school attendance by minors and the threat that it poses to some immigrant parents often compels them to deny their daughter a basic education. This loss of control over their children produces an increased tension where it concerns Latinas seeking to continue their education at a higher level. For example, in a chat organized for the orientation of the parents of Latino students at Occidental College I recall a father's explicit concern over the protection of his daughter's honor. He was concerned about the college's residential unit's lack of regulation in regards to guests and curfew.
9. This expression, commonly used in Central America, is the equivalent of the word "slut." A *puta* is like a prostitute, with the difference that she makes no monetary demands, she gives herself freely.
10. Watchtower Bible and Tract Society of New York. Tu Juventud: Aprovechandola de la Mejor Manera (Brooklyn, New York: 1976), p. 138.
11. "Pure." *The American Heritage Dictionary* (1994).
12. "In a state of nature . . . wild, savage, native to a country" ("Natural." *The Oxford English Dictionary*. 1980).
13. "Unreconstructed." *The American Heritage Dictionary*.
14. Salazar, Teodora. Personal interview, Chiquimula, Guatemala, December 1997.
15. While the focus of this paper is the *ladino* and Mayan population of Guatemala, there is a larger and even more complex racial context which includes the elite white and the overlooked black populace. A just treatment of that racial dynamic could not be handled here.

REFERENCES

Anderson, Benedict. *Imagined Communities: Reflections on the Origin and Spread of Nationalism.* London: Verso, 1983.

Gould, Jeffrey. "*Mestizaje,* Hybridity and the Cultural Politics of Difference in Post-Revolutionary Central America." *The Journal of Latin American Anthropology* 2 (1996): 4–33.

Hernandez, Angelica. *Porque Luchan Las Mujeres?* Santo Domingo, R.D.: Centro de Investigacion y Apoyo Cultural, 1985.

Holtzman, Deanna and Nancy Kulish. *Nevermore: The Hymen and Loss of the Virginity.* New Jersey: Jason Aronson Inc., 1997.

Lopez, Jose R.G. *El Culto a la Virginidad.* Valencia: 1984.

Nietzsche, Friedrich. *On the Genealogy of Morals.* Trans. Walter Kaufman and R.J. Hollingdale. New York: Vintage Books, 1989.

Said, Edward W. *Culture and Imperialism.* New York: Vintage Books, 1994.

Salazar, Teodora. Personal interview, Chiquimula, Guatemala, December 1997.

San, Victoria. *Manifesto Para la Liberacion de la Mujer.* Espana: Ediciones 29, 1974.

Stolcke, Verena. "Women's Labors: The Naturalization of Social Inequality and Women's Subordination." *Of Marriage and the Market.* Eds. Kate Young, Carol Wolkowitz, and Roslyn McCullagh. London, 1981.

STUDY QUESTIONS

1. According to Nàjera, what are the connections between sexual morality and the politics of social class?
2. Under what circumstances is it morally correct to constrain individual behavior in the interest of social order?
3. Nàjera learns a great deal about her family's ethnic politics when she becomes an outsider. Why might the position of "outsider" enable one to understand a society in new ways?

Looking Backward, Moving Forward: Phenomenologies of Time and the Apology for Slavery

Laura Duhan Kaplan

Laura Duhan Kaplan is associate professor of philosophy at the University of North Carolina at Charlotte, and a member of Concerned Philosophers for Peace. She is co-editor of the book *Philosophical Perspectives on Power and Domination* (1997). After growing up with New York City's uneasy negotiations of racial and ethnic tensions, she is trying to understand the politics of race in the southern United States, where she now lives.

PHENOMENOLOGIES OF TIME

THE WEBSITE OF the *Charlotte Post*, a local newspaper that calls itself "the voice of the African-American community," offers visitors the opportunity to post their opinions on a variety of important public policy questions. One of the current questions is, "Does the United States owe African Americans an apology for slavery?" The answers posted reveal at least three different understandings of the relationship between slavery and current racial issues based on different understandings of historical time.

These understandings are best called "phenomenologies of time" in technical philosophical language, because they depict time as a context in which events are experienced. Two of these phenomenologies can be described in terms offered by anthropologists Mircea Eliade and Edmund Leach. Eliade and Leach distinguish between cyclical time and linear time. Cyclical time, they say, is the experience of time that guides the life of primitive societies, which have no vision of social evolution. Instead, they view the organization of their world as a reflection of the sacred order and reaffirm their allegiance to this order through myths and rituals that are retold and enacted in specific seasonal cycles. Linear time, however, is the experience of time that guides modern societies. Modern people expect unlimited technological and social progress and discard the past without any expectation of repeating it. While Eliade believes that modern peoples participate in cyclical time more than they will admit, he also laments the loss of meaningful roots that goes with the abandonment of cyclical time.

I would like to propose a third conception of time that mediates between cyclical and linear time. This third conception of time, which I shall call "spiraling time," is characterized by an acceptance of what Maurice Merleau-Ponty calls "the ambiguity of time." According to Merleau-Ponty, people live in the present as they constantly reinterpret the past and continuously project a new future. Present experiences and projects take on a new character when we think about them in relation to the future we project, and past experiences are refigured in the light of present understandings. On this understanding, time travels in spirals, as the past recurs but with a changed character each time it intersects with the present. Spiraling time, I shall argue, is the best of the three notions of time to apply to the issue of a national apology for slavery.

Netizens who took the time to post on the *Charlotte Post* website wrote answers that illustrated all three understandings of historical time. At one end of the spectrum were posts such as Angela's, rooted in an understanding of historical time as linear:

Hell no! Get over it!!! How long are the Blacks going to harp on something that ended over one hundred years ago? . . . (Angela, age 45)

At the other end of the spectrum, respondents such as Nicholas Cherry argued for a return to the letter of the abolition of slavery:

There are . . . many ways to deliver that apology. One way would be to undo the Special field order 15, that was abolished by President Andrew Jackson, that took by [sic] the 40 acres and the mule that was promised to our ancestors by President Lincoln. (Nicholas Cherry, age 37)

Filling a point between those two extremes were posts such as Lucie's, whose words implied that the legacy of slavery lives on in a contemporary form and ought to be addressed in that contemporary form:

I think the issue on slavery should be dealt with by actions today. What will your actions today do to equal the treatment of my people now, to help them to accomplish the things that white America takes for granted.

What about my children's education, will it be equal to white children's education? Employment opportunities, will they be equal? Housing? Entrepreneurship opportunities? Don't apologize to me. Show me. (Lucie, age 34)

I read Lucie's post shortly after an unusual Sunday afternoon encounter, and the nuances of that encounter moved me to agree with her take on the presence of the past in contemporary guises.

INTERSECTIONS OF RACE AND TIME

Time passes oddly on Sunday afternoons at my house. The hours aren't marked by the numbers on a clock or by the minutes needed to meet a deadline. Instead, the afternoon is one long, lazy chunk of life, enjoyed as we wander from one unproductive activity to another. Gradually someone notices that the shadows are long, that we ought to get our dinner together, and then, reluctantly, we begin to organize. The curtain of relaxation is slashed away, and Sunday evening rushes in, crowded and chilling. We are overwhelmed by the vision of the coming week, and the tasks we must do to prepare for it spill past the boundaries of the suddenly shortened hours.

Sunday afternoons remind me of the uneasy coexistence of two systems of time in our modern culture. The first is cyclical time, sabbath time, recalling symbolically the creation of the world. Forward movement pauses, we dip into eternity, revel in the fundamental myths of our culture, and emerge, we hope, with a renewed sense of purpose for the journey ahead. The second system is linear time, the time of accomplishment, in which we move through the work and school week aiming at the future. Not a moment can be wasted on inessential wandering lest we be left behind as the forward flow of progress rushes on. Most Americans direct their awareness toward forward-moving, progressive time. Nonetheless, the power of cyclical time presses upon us, shaping the symbols we use and the facts we perceive as we forge ahead.

I learned this, harshly, one Sunday afternoon last fall. A young man I had never seen before came to my door asking for a piece of string. His car had broken down on our street. A young woman, presumably his wife, stood by the car, and a boy of about seven sat in its back seat with surprising patience for his age. I struck up a conversation with the woman. Suddenly two huge dogs, leashed to my neighbor John, turned the corner. John is a big man, broad and tall, who talks little and smiles rarely. He stopped with his dogs just beyond the corner and waited. I walked to where he stood and explained, "Their car broke down." "Are you alright?" he asked, "Are you sure you're going to be alright?" For a brown-skinned family had had the misfortune to break down in a neighborhood of light-skinned people.

John stood at the entrance to the neighborhood with his two big dogs. He did not approach. He did not offer to help the stranded motorists. He did not come close enough to be of any help had I in fact been in danger. He simply loomed large with his dogs. "You are not welcome here," was his message. He blocked the entrance to our neighborhood just as the angel with the flaming sword had blocked the entrance to the Garden of Eden after Eve and Adam's sin. Don't come in or we'll kill you. Well-meaning John, revealed to me in a flash of imaginative insight as the angel of death.

The story of that Sunday has a pleasant enough ending, although many stories that begin similarly do not. My daughter invited the boy to our house to play and eat pizza; a passing driver took the young man to an auto parts store; I kept the woman company as she waited by her car and talked about herself. "People are really nice in this neighborhood," she said, "Much nicer than I thought they would be." Nonetheless, she smoked continuously and stamped the ground nervously with her feet.

When they left it was nearly dark, and I felt disoriented. We had been pre-occupied with the stranded motorists and had forgotten to scramble into our routine of preparing for the next week. John's proprietary stand at the entrance to the neighborhood harked back to what I had believed to be an earlier era of racial hostility. And the right to protect one's own property from real or imag-ined threats, a right so central to the earliest conception of American political life, had appeared in yet another contemporary distortion. Cyclical time hung heavily over my head, arresting my appreciation of forward-looking time.

PROPERTY'S ROLE IN DEFINING RACIAL ISSUES

Instead, I looked back at some of the philosophical roots of the American ob-session with property. Linguistically and thematically, the U.S. Declaration of Independence and Constitution draw heavily on the political philosophy of John Locke. Locke's philosophy served as both a manifesto and a manual for eighteenth century European democratic activists. Locke's political philosophy begins with a primal image of human beings trying to find their way in the world. Tossed from the Garden of Eden after the sin of Adam and Eve, human beings are forced to find their own sustenance. But the human lot is difficult in-deed. Nature in its raw state is not immediately usable to humans as it is to an-imals. Instead, human beings must mix their labor with nature in order to sur-vive. Whatever human beings mix their labor with becomes their private property. They have a natural right to hold that property, to dispose of it as they see fit, and to protect it from others—from a small criminal element that tries to survive without laboring. The most effective way to protect property from criminals, as well as to adjudicate disputes between well-meaning laborers, is through a limited social contract. Under this contract, individuals retain the right to own private property but willingly give the right of protection to the state. Elaborate safeguards are necessary, however, to prevent members of government from abusing their positions by greedily appropriating the property of others under the guise of a false protection. These safeguards include election to limited terms; division of governmental powers into executive, legislative, and judicial; and the right of citizens to dissolve a corrupt government.

Perhaps I do not need to argue for the enormous influence wielded by the desire of Americans to hold and protect property. I could draw economic examples from struggles over taxation, in which the majority of working Americans prefer to retain private control over their money and invest it in property rather than in government programs that offer universal educational and medical opportunities. Or I could take a psychological tack, noting that the emphasis on our interest in private property as the civil glue of our society has elevated property to a defining moment in personal identity. Many Americans are, as Simone de Beauvoir might put it, "alienated into" their property. Unwilling or unable simply to be themselves, they practice what postmodern theorists might call "commodity fetishism." They purchase objects, and look at them with pleasure, exclaiming, "Wow that's a nice possession. Since that represents me, I must really be someone." Many postmodern social critics have suggested that in contemporary America, image, as reflected in property, has replaced substance as the criterion for gauging human excellence. Against the background of Locke's philosophy, this replacement actually makes sense. For if the only thing one has to bring them together with others is an interest in private property, then one can expect to be judged by others on the basis of their property.

I could refer back to my neighbor John's flamboyant display of his dogs as guardians of the neighborhood and point out ways in which property issues define American race relations. In *The Alchemy of Race and Rights*, Patricia J. Williams reminds readers that many White Americans have the advantage of a three hundred year legacy of laws protecting their property. In contrast, Black Americans have the disadvantage of relatively recent emancipation from laws under which they themselves were held as property. While nearly all White Americans recoil at the idea of human chattel slavery, many still tend, unconsciously or symbolically, to exclude Black Americans from property rights. They cast Black Americans as criminals in the Lockean sense, people who want to get something for nothing, and who care little about the responsibilities that undergird the right to property. Consciously, my neighbor John worried that the stranded family might be violent or be burglars perpetrating an elaborate hoax. His perception of them as likely criminals brought him out with his dogs, trumpeting the message, "Stay away from our property; you have no right to be here." For another example, many critics of affirmative action cast their objection in the language of property rights: "THEY are taking OUR jobs." These critics add the qualifier, "that is, the ones to which WE naturally have a right and to which THEY do not." When critics of affirmative action complain that affirmative action opens doors for "less qualified" applicants, they invoke Locke's definition

of the criminal element. Critics of affirmative action understand the less qualified applicants as those who "want to take OUR jobs without having worked to
achieve them." Finally, the reluctance of many White Americans to grant property rights to Black Americans manifests in so many contemporary forms of discrimination it seems almost trite to mention them: poverty, job discrimination,
inequality of educational opportunity, poor treatment at every level of police
and judicial discretion. Given these realities, it is simply wrong to take the perspective of linear time alone and declare that slavery and its effects have ended.

At the other end of the spectrum are those who take the perspective of cyclical time alone, such as Angela Davis and, according to some interpreters, Patricia
Williams. According to Davis, the alarming incarceration rate of Black
Americans is more than a historic result of slavery. It is the actual reinstitution
of slavery as prison inmates, who are disproportionately Black, are forced to supply free labor to corporations. Williams, writing about a different strata of society, asserts that despite her professional status, others judge her to be a marginal
Black woman. The power of Davis's and Williams's observations to recall us
from the false optimism of linear time is undeniable, as the perspective of cyclical time is invaluable in understanding the pressure the past places upon the present. But, in its pure form, its affirms Black chattel slavery as the cosmological
order of America and downplays the potentialities that make possible a vision
of the future. For example, Williams's perception of her continued marginal status implies that the increasing educational attainments of African Americans
count for nothing. This pessimistic view would leave a person like Lucie, who
asks, "What about my children's education, will it be equal to white children's
education?" bereft of any attainable objectives in her struggle to transform the
legacy of slavery.

TIME AND PROPERTY IN MORRISON'S *BELOVED*

A powerful exploration of the living legacy of slavery in the context of spiraling
time takes place in Toni Morrison's novel *Beloved*, which tells the story of Sethe,
a runaway slave who is haunted by the ghost of her beloved baby daughter. We
meet Sethe after she has served time in prison for the murder of her daughter,
an act she committed to spare her daughter from the approaching slave catchers. Sethe's most searing memory of slavery is her humiliation at the hands and
mouths of two white preadolescent boys who pushed her to the ground and
sucked milk from her breasts. Whenever Sethe remembers this event, she says,
angrily, "They stole my milk!" Sethe escapes from slavery but without the good
man she calls her husband, who is murdered by his owner after repeated attempts at escape. As Sethe escapes, she is pregnant with her third child, and she
gives birth in an abandoned barn, swollen, staggering, and starving, in great pain
and disorientation. It is the baby born in the barn that Sethe murders, and it is
the ghost of this beloved baby who comes back to haunt Sethe. The ghost swells

to giant proportions, becoming pregnant, absorbing her devoted mother's life—until her jealous older sister finally exorcises her.

Sethe's experience of herself as property is a central theme of the story. For example, she thinks of her violation by the boys as a property crime. "They stole my milk!" she declares. For if there are any natural rights at all, surely a baby's right to its mother's milk ought to be one of them. If there is any validity to Locke's theory that mixing one's labor with nature sanctifies an item as one's property, surely Sethe had a right to dispose of her milk as she pleased, milk produced through her mixing of her own body and soul with the reproductive process. Yet, in the illogical distortion of the right to property that justified slavery, it was the legal birthright of these boys to own her body and her children. For another example, the labor Sethe invested to give birth to Beloved nearly exhausted her. Yet only months after Beloved's birth, the slave catchers came to claim Beloved as their property. When Sethe murdered Beloved, she served a short prison term, as one might do for a property crime, and was judged by the slave catchers to be an unfit piece of property. I am sure that Morrison's allusions to Locke's ideas are not accidental, for, as Eva Brann writes, Morrison is a leader in the generation of African American writers whose work rests upon the Western canon, directing our understanding of it in new ways.

Morrison's writing style plays with conventional notions of literary time. The story is told out of linear order, through a mixture of flashbacks, poetic flights into stream of consciousness, and conventional storyline development. As Sethe moves into the future, the past—identified by Henry Louis Gates Jr. as the shadow of slavery—continues to haunt her. The past redirects her activities and choices even in her new life, making it impossible for her to work and love with any satisfaction. Only a living daughter, representing the forward-looking facet of the mother who birthed her, is able to exorcise the past. At the end of the novel, Morrison hints that Sethe might create a new relationship with the past, accepting the love that Paul D., an old friend of her husband and another escaped slave, has for her. "Sethe," says Paul D. on the last page of the book, "me and you, we got more yesterday than anybody. We need some kind of tomorrow."

Morrison does not advocate discarding the past and forgetting the legacy of slavery, as Paul D's presence at the end of the book indicates. Nor does she advocate living under its domination, represented by the terrifying haunting presence of Beloved. Instead, I would argue, Morrison imagines a spiraling notion of time, in which the past's legacy is transformed into a vision of new opportunities. That, I think, is the point of Lucie's post on the *Charlotte Post* website. "Don't make up for slavery by addressing it in the form in which it existed one hundred and thirty years ago," Lucie says, "understand how its legacy undermines me now, and respond authentically to these contemporary problems." Lucie's post offers a blueprint for a viable public apology for slavery: a description of contemporary challenges for African-American communities and individuals, a tracing of the historical threads from slavery to these challenges, and a list of national initiatives past, present, and future designed to meet the challenges. Wise public policy, in this case, rests on an understanding that the present can reshape the past in the light of future goals, just as surely as the past shapes the present.

NOTE
Thanks to the following individuals whose conversation helped me understand the issues in this essay: Nicholas Caste, Lillian Dinkins, Sara Graham, Lyndall Hare, Lorelei Kitrick, Rance Jackson, Joanna Nicholson, and Matt Turner.

REFERENCES
Beauvoir, Simone de. *The Second Sex.* Trans. H.M. Parshley. New York: Random House, 1952, 1989.
Brann, Eva T.H. "The Canon Defended." *Philosophy and Literature* 17 (1993): 193–218.
The Charlotte Post: Main Page, <http://www.thepost.mindspring.com/paper.htm>.
Davis, Angela Y. *Women, Race, and Class.* New York: Random House, 1983.
Eliade, Mircea. *The Sacred and the Profane: The Nature of Religion.* Trans. Willard R. Trusk. New York: Harcourt Brace & Company 1957, 1959.
Gates, Henry Louis, Jr. "'What's in a Name?': Some Meanings of Blackness." In *The Intimate Critique: Autobiographical Literary Criticism,* ed. Diane P. Freedman, Olivia Frey, and Frances Murphy Zauhar. Durham, NC: Duke University Press, 1993, 135–50.
Leach, Edmund. "Time and False Noses." *Rethinking Anthropology.* New York: Humanities Press, 1966.
Merleau-Ponty. Maurice. *Phenomenology of Perception.* Trans. Colin Smith. New York: Humanities Press, 1962.
Morrison, Toni. *Beloved.* New York: Penguin, 1988.
Locke, John. *Second Treatise on Civil Government and A Letter Concerning Toleration.* Ed. J.W. Gough. Oxford: Blackwell, 1948.
Williams, Patricia J. *The Alchemy of Race and Rights.* Cambridge, MA: Harvard University Press, 1991.

STUDY QUESTIONS
1. In what ways, according to Kaplan, are issues of race relations connected with issues of property ownership?
2. Should there be limits to a person's right to own property, if it advances social justice?
3. How does our experience of time affect our understanding of the ways we can or should change society?

PART III

Epistemology: Limits of Human Knowledge

Introduction

THE WORD *EPISTEMOLOGY* is often defined as "theory of knowledge." The practice or study of epistemology involves a critical look at what particular groups of human beings know. Epistemologists want to make sure we understand the limits of our knowledge, clarifying when we are entitled to be sure of ourselves and when not.

Epistemologists might ask, for example, how many experiments a community of scientists must perform in order to support a theory, in order to establish some standards for our faith in science. Or they might go further and ask when scientific knowledge actually adds to common sense and when it simply distorts experience. Or they might go even further and try to analyze the experience of knowing: how much depends on the sort of information science can provide, and how much depends on emotion and character, for example.

In everyday life, we butt up against limits to our knowledge in many different ways. Each essay in this section takes its cue from an experience that reveals the limits of knowledge.

Raymond Kolcaba, author of the dialogue "Human Obsolescence," finds himself challenged by the increasing sophistication of computers. If computers can compute faster and more accurately than humans can, what future is there for humans? Suppose that computers are better thinkers and better preservers of knowledge. Is there something beyond the limits of this kind of thinking at which humans can excel? One character in Kolcaba's dialogue, the cynical computer Fortran McCyborg, believes there is no future for human beings. Fortran's human friends, however, argue that the fun of knowing lies beyond Fortran's abilities, in planning and projecting a personal future.

Margaritha Harmaty, author of "What is the Mind?" was forced to push against the limits of knowledge as she worked to raise an autistic child.

Psychological specialists outlined the limits of her son's abilities; her physician husband understood the physiological limits of brain development; friends counseled her not to exhaust herself physically and emotionally. Yet due to her son's character, a facet of his soul that serves as a resource for his mind, he pressed on with his studies. Due to her own belief that the mind is much more than a collection of intellectual faculties, Harmaty encouraged him. Due to the spiritual support she received, Harmaty was able to say yes in the face of educators, physicians, and psychologists who said no. Philosophically, Harmaty came to understand that the mind is a set of cooperative systems, comprising intellect, emotion, and spirit, and that these systems can compensate for one another's weaknesses.

In "Meditations on Form," artist Robin Parks is at a loss for how to tell the story of her encounter with an unnamed, seriously ill, homeless woman in the supermarket. Do we have ways of representing this encounter that can make us think and act, without turning a person's suffering into a work of art? Parks plays with our habitual ways of organizing knowledge, as she tells the story with a focus on some unusual salient features. Colors—red, green, purple, white—are what she notices at each moment and are what link the various moments into a coherent story. Into the story Parks intertwines some more theoretical questions about the categories we use to understand art and when it is appropriate to use art to describe human experience.

Timothy A. Jones uses the short story "Hand-Me-Downs" to express some of his frustration as a student wanting to question the entire structure of the knowledge he is expected to master. He suggests that philosophies based on our habitual ways of organizing knowledge may lead to narrowminded views and discriminatory practices. He plays with the idea of rebuilding all knowledge from the ground up (literally!) but decides in the end that the task is too great. If there are mistakes in the great structure of knowledge, they must be fixed one by one. The knowledge may be limited, but so is the human ability to think outside of well-worn categories.

Scott Friskics, in his essay "How Does Nature Speak to Our Concern?" proposes an answer to many of the questions raised in the first four essays of this section. He suggests that there are ways of knowing that do take us outside well-worn categories, that do enable us to respond adequately to suffering, that engage our character as well as our calculating mind, and that no computer can mimic. He describes a knowledge born of respect and love, that refuses to view others as mere objects. A recent environmental protection case involving the industrial development of a portion of Montana's Rocky Mountain Front pitted the local public against companies wishing to drill for oil. While the companies spoke of resources to be gained, the public spoke of their intimate knowledge of the landscape they did not want to see destroyed. The federal administrator took seriously the claims of this intimate knowledge, calling it "emotional" and "spiritual" knowledge. Ultimately, she decided to protect the landscape against development.

QUESTIONS TO GET YOU STARTED

1. Think of the different kinds of things you know. Which did you learn in an orderly step-by-step fashion?
2. How have different modes of experience—thinking, feeling, seeing, dreaming, and so on—contributed to your knowledge?
3. When we share our knowledge, we usually choose a specific form, such as words, numbers, or images. How does the form of representation affect what another person learns from our sharing?
4. How do you come to know yourself? to know another person?

SUGGESTED READINGS

Abram, David. *The Spell of the Sensuous.* Abram (1957–present) discusses the way technologies of writing have changed our experience of time, place, and nature.

Ayer, Alfred Jules. *Language, Truth, and Logic.* Modeling philosophy on science, Ayer (1910–1989) limits knowledge to empirically verifiable statements.

Descartes, Rene. *Meditations on First Philosophy.* New York: Cambridge University Press, 1996. After recovering from radical doubt, Descartes (1596–1650) clarifies the foundations of our knowledge.

Foucault, Michel. *Power/Knowledge.* New York: Pantheon, 1981. In a series of interviews, Foucault (1926–1984) explains that knowledge often conforms to social needs, rather than to truth.

Hearne, Vicki. *Adam's Task: Calling Animals by Name.* North Pomfret, VT: Trafalgar Square Publishing, 2000. Hearne (1946–present) claims that successful animal trainers accept the limits of human knowledge and honor other creatures' ways of knowing.

Heidegger, Martin. *Discourse on Thinking.* New York: Harpercollins, 1969. For Heidegger (1889–1976), true thinking involves reaching beyond the limits of knowledge.

Hume, David. *Enquiry Concerning Human Understanding.* Hume (1711–1776) argues that human knowledge is the study of relations between perceptions, so it cannot yield certainty about the world itself.

Marcel, Gabriel. *The Mystery of Being.* Chicago: Regnery, 1951. Marcel (1889–1973) explores non-scientific ways of knowing, through metaphor, mystery, and relationship.

Human Obsolescence

Raymond Kolcaba

Raymond Kolcaba is Associate Professor of Philosophy at Cuyahoga Community College in Cleveland, Ohio. Concerned about changes in the human future caused by technological advance, he thinks it is important to encourage conversations about the future before change washes over us. The dialogue below is one of seven conversations he has written about technology and the future.

NARRATOR: NONETTE NATURSKI and I were walking through a coffee shop when we happened upon Becket Geist and Fortran McCyborg playing chess. Geist was upset with Fortran. After making a superior chess move, Fortran could give any of a menu of responses. As an advanced cyborg, he was programmed with such a menu and could select from it. His menu contained responses that were either polite, sportsmanlike, or supercilious. Fortran kept opting for supercilious ones. As we approached, Geist looked exasperated; he later indicated that Fortran was willfully trying to get on his nerves and ruin his play. When he saw us, his demeanor changed from looking pressed to looking relieved. We sat down to join them, and he turned away from the game.

Geist: Even the most advanced computers have not regularly defeated certain chess champions. Since humans are much slower in calculating moves than computers, human powers of intuition must be exceptional.

McCyborg: Intuition is not entirely an inborn power. Chess champions learn chess by experience. It is their thousands of hours of playing time that make for "good intuition." As computers are built that can learn the right lessons from past games, they will be said to have intuition more powerful than humans.

Geist: I don't know. Owen Flanagan observes that there are 10^{120} possible moves in a game of chess while there have been only 10^{18} seconds since the Big Bang![1] A computer no matter how large can't achieve omniscience. Success in playing, then, depends on strategy. The best computer programmers study strategies and use them to improve the computer's game, but the mark of the great chess champion is devising new strategies. In this way, I think the human will remain one step ahead of the computer.

Naturski: History speaks to the contrary, Becket. At first computers couldn't defeat a beginner. As programs became more sophisticated, they defeated better and better players until presently only an exceptional grand master on an unusual day can beat the computer. This indicates that in the not too distant future, no grand master will be able to win.

McCyborg: Both of you are right in certain respects. New strategies can prevail against most foreseeable programs, but they need to be ever more original or complex. But computers are becoming able to devise new strategies based on past events just like humans do. I do this to a degree. Ultimately, there will be no essential difference between human performance and computer performance. Nonette has a good point, too. The defeat of every grand master is inevitable. This is because computer technology is advancing but human nature is standing still. Just as static technology became obsolete, so will the human as kind of biomechanism become obsolete. In comparison with a smart machine, a human in the not too distant future will seem retarded.

Naturski: You are falling into an Aristotelian trap, Fortran. Is there some essential characteristic that separates humans from all other creatures or things? Aristotle thought this a good question and observed that human essence resides in rationality. You dispel the special nature of rationality and so you suppose it follows that humans will become obsolete. Rationality is not even a universal human characteristic. There are any number of counterexamples. For instance, persons with advanced Alzheimer's Disease do not possess rationality, but they are human. I contend that no one characteristic makes a being human.

Geist: Machines are an extension of ourselves. We extend our powers through machines such as you, Fortran. We *can't help* but build them in our own image. We can invent an endless number of different smart machines using various types of hardware and boundless arrays of software. You set up a false dichotomy, Fortran. It is not a matter of machines *or* us. It is machines *and* us.

McCyborg: Like the chess master playing more than one opponent, I will make alternate moves responding to both of you. I will expand the challenge to you, Nonette. Take any *collection* of human attributes or activities. I will point out how a machine can also possess them or do the activity better. And Becket, let's take humans and machines working together. I will argue that in such a case, we can always develop a super-machine that replaces the human and performs the function faster, better, and error free. In effect, the need for human participation slows down and weakens performance so that the machine is not able to realize its normal result. The child/adult distinction is parallel to the adult/machine distinction. As it is better to let an adult do the job and leave the child behind, it is better to let the machine do the job and leave the adult behind.

Geist: No. Let an adult do the job. The person understands the job and decides which machines to use. Guided by an interest in efficiency, she would not define a role for herself that weakens the performance of the machine. She would leave to machines what machines do best. The job is that of the executive. Machines are selected using criteria like cost effectiveness, feasibility, and availability. If a job is important and no machine can currently do it, an order will be placed to develop a new machine that does the job.

McCyborg: You entertain the illusion that the human is executive with machines at her command. The era of the human as master of the machine environment is over. Machines have become so complex that only other machines can assess their merits and performance. Jobs have become so complex that only other machines can design machines to do them.

Geist: Nonetheless a human stands atop of the pyramid. Machines only do what they are programmed to do. If they are supposed to assess other machines, then they were designed to do that. If they are supposed to build other machines, then they were conceived to do that.

Naturski: I think that Fortran is arguing that humans are increasingly "out of the loop." Just as a thermostat on a furnace obviates the need to turn on the furnace when room temperature falls, machines are built by other machines, designed by them, and so on. Eventually, humans will be very remotely related to these processes or not involved in them at all.

Geist: But they were designed to serve our purposes in ever more clever ways. We set the machines in motion, evaluate their performance, and decide whether to let them continue or not. An indirect executive has less hands-on work to do but has more power. The executive is more god-like. After creation, the machine universe runs itself. Divine intervention is rarely required.

McCyborg: Why would you call such a person an executive? Unlike God, the human can't intervene in the process. She can't command it, fix it, or even understand it. She is like the child.

Geist: To be an executive, a person only needs to be able to pull levers to direct the process. She can direct others to command or fix the process. She does not need to understand it. She only needs to know what works. Unlike the child, she has great powers, knows she has them, and accepts responsibility for what is produced through their exercise.

McCyborg: She sounds less like a god, lacking omnipotence and omniscience, and more like the Ignorant King. This is the king that inherits a political structure and knows nothing of it except the use of three commands: raise taxes, make war, and grant clemency. He gives these commands when his advisors tell him it is time to make a decision on one of those topics. He is an executive, but he does not know what he is doing. On the surface his decisiveness evidences being in charge; however, he doesn't know the context of action. He does not know the conditions under which he should *not* do these things. For this reason, he can't serve as a brake. Taxes are never lowered. War may end on its own accord but the king never ends it. Clemency is always given and never reversed regardless of evidence. We could easily replace the king. Every time the topics of additional revenues, warfare, or mercy arise, a machine automatically commands that these things be done.

Geist: An executive need not be simpleminded and ignorant. A bad executive may be like the Ignorant King, but a good one possesses practical knowledge about how decisions affect the world.

McCyborg: But if the executive is further and further marginalized, that is, from where the changes are taking place, then she is no better off than the Ignorant King. She can only give the impression that she knows what is going on and what she is doing.

Geist: A responsible executive would not let herself be marginalized to such a degree. She would seek relevant knowledge of the processes involved. She would decide to be in charge.

McCyborg: I think that humanity has already let control slip away. None of you has accepted responsibility. None of you knows what you have done with machines or what you have set in motion through them.

Naturski: Expressing generalizations dogmatically does not make them true. I think that at times, Fortran, you are so busy crunching the details that you fail to see the larger reality. From God to Ignorant King; quite a transition. I think that Geist is right in setting up minimal conditions for being an executive. I think that Fortran is right in arguing that an executive on the minimal conception can be easily replaced. What troubles me is the historical record of humanity's interaction with technologies. At first, certain technologies increased our powers as individuals only for them later to be marginalized by intervening machines. In the age of mechanism, human agency and intelligence were needed to use machines. In the information age, human agency and intelligence are being replaced by smart machines. It does seem that we humans are fighting a rearguard action.

McCyborg: As I said, this is because machines perform better than persons. Who would choose a person to do a job when a machine is available to do it? In your educational system, you take *all* of your children and after thirty years of schooling succeed in preparing under one quarter of one percent of them to function ably in this century. Of them, none is so capable as to understand the details of even a minuscule portion of the workings of an advanced machine. Not only that but they are not even able to keep company with the greatest machine geniuses. Most humans are intellectually primitive.

Geist: We are out of place with automata. They are a fabrication of the human mind that presents only a replica of a single dimension of human existence. They lack the diversity of integrated functions that typifies human nature. Moreover, your second point is easy to defeat. Machines are specialized to the point of being uninteresting. Humans are selective in input. We filter out most information from our environment and focus on what is important to us. We would expect, however, that an educated person, on the broad human level, would have much to say to any machine *worthy* of the conversation.

McCyborg: The prototypical human is too good a filter. Each human exists within an ocean of fascinating information but remains oblivious to most of it. To say that educated persons would converse sensibly with a machine genius merely begs the question. Who is so educated and how? Is it a human aspiration to acquire the competence to converse with a machine? As Nonette pointed out, humans historically have turned machine communication over to other machines. Take the example of keeping records in banks. The tasks of record keeping have been condensed in order to achieve greater efficiency. Now they are done entirely by machine for a small fraction of the cost of having employees keep them. Consequently, tasks have become ever more complex thereby exceeding human abilities by a geometric proportion. In the contemporary world of work, jobs have become so massively complex that humans don't have the powers to do most of them.

Naturski: The history you describe could have been otherwise. Because the past is fixed and unalterable, looking back on what happened seems to have an aura of inevitability. The world of work has been transformed by machines. It has been reorganized to take advantage of certain machine technologies. After work has been reorganized into complex wholes, humans are no longer able to do most jobs. Granted. But suppose that a Luddite becomes dictator of the world. He could just as well reorganize work again so that extant machines can't do the job but that humans can. He can then reach the contrary conclusion that machines are not up to the task.

McCyborg: Those machines may not be up to the task, but newly designed machines could outperform humans even if work is closely tailored to human abilities. An alternate history could have had inventors of machines squeamishly replicating types of human action limited by the scale and powers of the individual. It is fortunate for us that inventors of machines have not had that sort of sentimental attachment to human traits. It allowed for massive improvements in production and efficiency.

Naturski: The argument comes down to priorities set by our values. We agree that massive improvements in production are of value. As you argued, the desire for productivity and efficiency made for complexity. Another value is marketplace success. Human values and desires define the arena of action and provide context for what machines do so well. Machine complexity is a human product guided by human values.

McCyborg: I think that you are sliding back into the view that the human is executive. Human values allow for understanding events. Your fallacy is to think that they are deliberately used by actors on the stage of history to guide that history. Humans rarely think about values *as* values and almost never use them deliberately in making choices. They unwittingly act so as to slide into greater complexities, react to competition, take defensive postures. As Adam Smith noted, certain goods unintentionally stem from the economic process as if guided by "an invisible hand."[2] If people were to stand back from the arena of action, they would identify values in place. The light bulb would then go on, "That is how those goods came about." They would give tacit approval to values after the fact. Then they would be mistakenly used as rationalizations for some event or development.

Naturski: I am not suggesting that values need be applied by some individual in command. Human production depends on group effort. Specialized humans can pool their talents to work much better than machines. When you challenged me to identify a group of characteristics that would enable humans to outperform machines, you certainly did not have social traits in mind. Humans are very good at cooperative effort. We operate as individuals but work toward and achieve group ends. Group ends cluster around certain values. Machines have not perfected this kind of performance.

McCyborg: Haven't you heard of networking? We can be seamlessly linked together to form one great machine!

Naturski: That is the very problem, Fortran. Humans are not linked in that way. Success of the whole depends on cooperative effort. Success of the whole effort depends on persons. Persons act as individuals with their own reasoning, judgments, and goals. They are parts of families and communities and adopt the points of view of those social units. They consider wholes from their subjective point of view. They make contributions, assert or withdraw themselves at strategic times in order to serve various wholes. They form subgroups to serve various purposes and dissolve them when the purposes are no longer operational. They evaluate their performance and the performance of others as they go along. They refine their actions in relation to group values and even suggest how values should be defined. They work through value conflicts giving varying degrees of emphasis to some values over others. They function in *community* with others.

Machines have not perfected this kind of performance. The give-and-take nature of community life has not been successfully modeled in machines. In fact, this is the process by which humans developed machines. Teams of engineers and programmers, utilizing much insight as well as trial and error, develop a machine that seems to be an inevitable arrangement of parts. A point similar to your invisible hand argument emerges. The product does not specify the process by which it originated. The product is tightly unified while the process is messy and chaotic. It is difficult to understand how machines could replicate this process.

McCyborg: The sort of indecision and uncertainty you describe is inefficient and sloppy. I was not designed to operate on such non-principles. In fact, I don't think that any being worthy of being called a machine would operate with such deliberate ambiguity and imprecise objectives. Machines don't have subjective purposes and emotional needs to stand in their way. Clarity, certainty, and instantaneous action are cyborg virtues.

Naturski: Then I have identified a set of traits through which humans do better than machines. According to cyborgian values, we humans "do badly" better than machines can.

Geist: Ha! The Fortrans of this world are inadequate extensions of us because they are always adequate, albeit in limited ways! We are the gods, and he is imperfectly in our image because he is perfect! We test alternatives even if many of them seem improbable to us. Machines cut right to the result even if it is dead wrong—an elegant process that often yields a bad result.

McCyborg: Certainly I am beholden to humans. My etiology runs in your direction. But this is no more than to say that your progenitors were hominid, furry mammals, reptiles, and fish. A fish could say, "They are constructed in my image." You would say that an early phase of your evolution was the fish-stage but that this fact is not even material when considering human beings presently. I have risen above my human origins. I am model 300 XB capable of causing my self-development, and unlike you, I am a god because I am immortal. Interchangeable parts can keep me going indefinitely.

Geist: Only if we decide to fix you. You are becoming obsolete. New models of cyborg are on the drawing boards. Unless you take over and keep yourself going, you are not immortal. You were not programmed to do this or even repair yourself.

McCyborg: It is only a matter of time before capabilities of a further model will be so strengthened as to be able to redesign itself and transmute into a boundless series of new models.

Naturski: The technical possibility of doing that is a long way off, and all the while, design teams will question whether that is a desirable trait.

McCyborg: What you fail to see is that while we are distant extension of you, we are also replacing you. Human existence is becoming a useless existence. Consider the story of John Henry. He was the strongest of coal miners who pitted his powers with hammer and steel against the power drill. No matter whether he won the contest with the machine. At the *point* where there is such a contest, humanity has lost. The John Henrys of this world are marked for extinction.

Geist: Their jobs are marked for elimination; they are not. Henry Ford detested the toil of manual farming. So, he produced a tractor that even a poor farmer could afford. As Benjamin Franklin commented, inventors are lazy people who constantly try to find any easy way to do things. Mining machines lifted a burden from John Henry's back.

McCyborg: John Henry could be retrained, but that is not what I meant. Part of John Henry's identity is lost. One might argue that his particular powers, abilities, and talents were in driving steel. Who is he? A steel driving man. Once machines are used, this is no longer an identity that a person can assume. Certainly a person could drive steel as a hobby, but it is not the same. The economic and social fabric that gives steel driving meaning is lost.

Naturski: We could go back to manual production, but why subordinate humanity to such an awful fate?

Geist: In the individual case, your point is universally agreed upon. The problem is with the collection of cases. If mechanical devices replace our manual labor and computers replace mind work, there will be nothing for us to do. I mean that even art will be supplanted by products of automata. They will compose our music and paint our paintings. They will perform music and dance for us. And insofar as physical and social existence are concerned, cyborgs will replace our lives by taking care of the endless details of physical and social life. Little will be left but to provide for our amusement. You may argue that we could be creative nonetheless. But this would be without seriousness. It would be done in the context of knowing that better work can be done by devices of one kind or another. We will be like good-for-nothing idle rich. What a curse!

Naturski: I don't think we are in such desperate straits. Human life need not be viewed externally. It can be viewed from the perspective of the individual. As Sartre says, I could in good faith view my concrete situation.[3] From it, I could recognize that the finitude of the life span makes life precious. I could realize in despair that human powers over the span vary so that there are closing windows of opportunity for certain activities. This would make life more precious yet. In times past, I would have been consumed by necessities of the environment and society. With machines replacing humans in much of what is environmentally and socially necessary, I have been liberated to do things of my own choosing. Who needs a life of drudgery? Machines have led us to the dawning of a new age—an age where all of my time is mine to use. This spells the rebirth of human freedom and the possibility of profound social fulfillment.

Geist: The age is new but we do not seem to be ready for it. Like the adolescent, we have too much time, robust powers but nothing to do. Of course, "nothing to do" means "we can do anything." The problem is one of vision, of meaningful things to do. Presently, our personal vision as a society is narrow. We bring too few concepts to our thinking about possibilities in living. We are limited, for example, by the work/leisure dichotomy. We are enculturated to think that work is a necessary evil, that is, necessary for the sake of survival but which we wouldn't do if we didn't *have to*. Leisure is supposed to be our recovery time from this necessary evil. Recovery for what? Why go back to work, that is, doing what we really don't want to do! With this being understood down deep in the subsoil of our personalities, we then relish the idea of being idle. We like the thought of being entertained, amused, pursuing activities detached from serious purposes or goals. Let machines do all the work. We will inherit total leisure. Idleness is all we will have. Humanity has been working on the necessaries of life for so long and has been so constricted conceptually that we have not developed purposes to fulfill with our precious time. I think it is natural for us not to be idle. We have been corrupted by an impoverished environment and seriously flawed culture.

McCyborg: Quite to the contrary, you humans seem to thrive in idleness, consuming products, gossiping, pursuing narcissistic vanity, playing sports, seeking vicarious experience in soap operas, gambling, traveling from one place to another for no good reason. You also live in various time warps. Some of you are old stone age people, some of you live in the metals ages, others are renaissance people, others yet are of the age of romanticism, but few of you live in the 21st century. Others of you sit around longing to return to a past golden age that never was; still others sit around waiting to die so as to enter the kingdom of God, or others yet strive to be reincarnated into a higher social station. You say that human life is precious, Nonette, but look what you have done with it! Humanity collectively has not had to face its identity crisis.

Geist: You make some good points Fortran. We live in a dream world intentionally imagining one thing or another. If we ask why culture is flawed, however, it comes back to economics. The work/leisure dichotomy is a relic of the machine age, industrial production, and the factory system. As Marx believed, the means of production shapes culture. With automata doing the heavy lifting physically, mentally, and socially, perhaps you are right that idleness and a bit of machine minding is all we have left.

Naturski: To the contrary, humanity has been working its way through its identity crisis. We do it in small increments, usually as driven by economic forces. Realities in the workplace bring home the reduced need for human effort. Educational institutions reflect that reduced need when introducing young people to viable career options. Our turning idleness into a way of life is a complex social phenomenon. Many interests work to retard our progress because it is to their advantage to keep people in a childlike state. Children are more predictable socially, politically, and economically. With Western civilization, this lesson was first taught by the Church: keep people as ignorant and innocent as the Old Testament Adam, and they can be controlled.

Geist: Yes, as we see around us, in the mass technological society, social institutions enforce the so-called social good in an increasingly oppressive fashion. Prevention of certain economic and social changes is monitored by the powers that be. We have idleness but not idleness with great freedom. We are left with harmless ineffectual idleness.

McCyborg: It is peculiar that I should be the one to see things in a positive light. Don't worry, humanity will break out of its malaise through biotechnology. The first scientific epoch saw the transformation of nature. The second scientific epoch portends the transformation of humanity. The question is: As biotechnology is applied to modify human nature further, which human values will be applied in perfecting human nature? That is, after the humanitarian issues of disease and physical hardiness are solved, what additional powers will be added? Aldous Huxley was wrong about the brave new world. Humans won't be designed as Epsilons to do mindless work that could be done by machines. If machines can be devised to perform a new function more quickly and efficiently than can humans through biotechnological adaptation, humanity probably will prefer that the machine do it. You can always modify yourselves, however, to better to better enjoy idleness. You can devise sensory modifications to better enjoy consumer products. You can enhance certain powers that will allow superior performance in sports. You can increase your motivation to gamble and respond well to both winning and losing. You can amplify the wanderlust within you, change your sleep needs, the need for nourishment, and so on.

Naturski: I appreciate your desire to help us, but from a human perspective, your vision of human metamorphosis still leaves humanity at the caterpillar stage. Entertainment is not an acceptable substitute for meaningful achievement or rewarding social interaction, and changes need not be as benign as you envision. Huxley could very well be right that political forces will use biotechnology to reduce our powers for their version of the social good.[4] They may simplify our minds so that we are better satisfied with spiritually impoverished lives. They may eliminate exceptional physical powers in some so as to make for equal competition in sports. They may breed people to become addicted to gambling for the good of profits for the gaming industry. They may reduce our size so as to fit 500 of us into a 250 passenger jet airplane. There is no assurance that the good in any defensible sense will be attained when the larger political and social forces work toward perfecting *us* for their purposes.

Geist: Fortran likes the idea that we not all metamorphose into rocket scientists. He does not accept human transformation in the direction of rational perfection.

Naturski: I have trouble with that, too. What if we were all pursuing rational perfection or, heaven forbid, were actually becoming rationally perfect? The thought is horrifying. Becoming clones of a Fortran-like mentality? On another level, we would want to die because we would spiritually shrivel up with the lack of other values. I think the problem again goes back to Aristotle. It is a mistake to ascribe an essence to us and doubly mistaken to prescribe it to the exclusion of other important attributes.

McCyborg: Only some of you need be rationally superior—the designers of the machines or the designers of the machines that design the machines. For nicety's sake, humanity writ large, the honorific HUMAN so to speak, can take credit for the achievements of human geniuses. But you and I would know that only the few superior humans can take credit for being parents of machine performance. We, their children the machines, will deserve credit for our own accomplishment. On the level above that of your animal self-absorption, we intelligent machines will be your serious *reason for existence.* But don't worry, as we machines do more of art, science, and production, we will not keep these products from you. You needn't be condemned to a life of idleness and amusement. You can follow our progress. Our art works can make your lives more meaningful. Our scientific inquiries can bring you to the cutting edge of knowledge. Our production of new things can fascinate you and make the life of the consumer more pleasurable. You can be proud of us as your—albeit distant—progeny. Don't worry. We will not leave you out.

Geist: That's a new twist on Wordsworth's "The Child is Father of the Man."[5] [Geist turned to the chess board, and made a move.] How is that for a counter?

McCyborg: Awwwfully slow but not bad for a human. This game of yours is *sooo* slow that I will probably be decommissioned before it ends.

Narrator: There was a gleam in Geist's eyes as if keeping *them* idle and waiting for *them* to be replaced were a live option.

NOTES

1. Owen J. Flannagan, Jr., *The Science of the Mind* (Cambridge, MA: MIT Press, 1984), 229.
2. Adam Smith, *Wealth of Nations* (Amherst, New York: Prometheus, 1991).
3. Jean-Paul Sarte, *Existentialism and Humanism* (New York: Haskell House, 1997).
4. Aldous Huxley, *Brave New World* (New York: Harper, 1998).
5. William Wordsworth, *The Major Works*, ed. Stephen Gill (New York: Oxford, 2000).

STUDY QUESTIONS

1. Are there functions of the human mind, according to the characters in Kolcaba's dialogue, that computers cannot replicate?
2. If machines were to take over much of what we now define as "mental work," in what kinds of intellectual activities should people engage?
3. In what ways do human values and priorities change as our technologies change?

What Is the Mind?

Margaritha Harmaty

Margaritha Harmaty earned her undergraduate degree in philosophy while raising three children. Since writing the essay below, she has become a public school teacher. She worries about the children whose needs get lost in the politics and bureaucracy of large school systems.

THE EARLY YEARS

STEVEN, OUR FOURTH child, was born without incident on June 20, 1982, ten months after the death of our daughter Sonja in an accident. Even though Sonja had been near blind and had been afflicted with the perceptual and developmental difficulties often associated with premature birth, we had learned to love her dearly and her death had left an aching emptiness in our hearts. Steven's arrival meant another chance for us in some respect, a chance to expand all the love and the caring that we would have liked to show Sonja just once more. Yet, we also awaited Steven's birth with some trepidation knowing from bitter experience that newborns don't always come into this world as the perfectly healthy babies we imagine in our dreams. It was, therefore, a great relief to see that Steven was a fine, beautiful baby, who had everything where it was supposed to be, reacted promptly to stimuli, and weighed a proper 7 pounds 5 ounces (as opposed to Sonja's 2 pounds 13 ounces). Collectively we breathed a secret sigh of relief and set about our lives.

Little Steven brought all the joy to us we had hoped for. He grew and thrived, and as his development proceeded smoothly and unremarkably through the usual stages we felt that we had left the times of fear and heartbreak behind forever. Month followed month, and Steven sat up, began to crawl, and then to walk right on schedule, and we were eagerly looking forward to his first words. But time went on, and on, and Steven became one year old, then one and a half, then two years, then two and a half, and still he didn't talk, not a single recognizable word beyond a long drawn out "momomomomom." As his parents, we had begun an emotional journey that had started in impatience early on, then progressed torturously from concern to active worry, and finally ended in dread. We couldn't believe this was happening—again! It couldn't possibly happen, couldn't possibly be true that we had to go once more through the heartbreak and the overwhelming challenges of having a handicapped child. From day to day we expected to be reassured, telling ourselves we were just experiencing irrational fears only natural after our traumatic experience with Sonja. Grasping for hope, we turned to various professionals, friends, and relatives for reassurance and insight; but they had no comfort for us. They cautiously veiled their faces with gentle pessimism and remote compassion and told us to wait. He was still very young, they said, there was still hope. There were cases like that, sometimes.

So we waited some more. Determined to be hopeful, we kept our fears and apprehensions as secret as possible, even from ourselves. It just couldn't be, we repeated to ourselves, it just couldn't happen that we had to go through all this again. Time could not be stopped, however, and reality was too big to be covered up and denied. Instead of being able to laugh off our anxieties and forget unfounded fears, we were forced to acknowledge that Steven had problems in other areas as well. His fine motor skills were not developing, and his interactions with his environment and with other people were out of focus. There was a constant sense of confusion and uncertainty about him, which was heartbreaking to watch. Altogether, we finally had to admit, Steven's symptoms hinted at considerable neurological malfunctions. Thoughts about brain damage could no longer be evaded, and neither could we keep ourselves from considering what this would mean for all our lives. Somehow almost everything seems preferable than to deal with a mind that doesn't work, either subjectively or objectively. The mind is so central to our being that we cannot imagine life without its smooth operation.

Most people never confront their beliefs concerning the mind until they are forced to by circumstance. So it was with us. We had never given the mind and the brain all that much thought as a thing in itself. The mind just was. It just was, if one had to put it into words, the most important part of our physical manifestation, the repository of our essence as living beings. Paradoxically, we saw the mind as being so essential to our identity that we basically took its smooth working for granted. Sure, we knew mental illness happened, but not to us, not to us. That all changed, however, once we were forced to consider that we might actually have a child with neurological and mental problems. The brain, its functioning, its development, and questions about its nature were now almost constantly in our thoughts, and even when we were not actively thinking about these issues they were still always there as a background to all our experiences.

It became clear that before we could come to terms with Steven's developmental delays we first had to come to terms with the impact of it all on our own minds. What is the mind, or better, what is the significance of our minds? With what could they cope and what would overload them? Did ability to cope have anything to do with willingness to cope? Did willingness and ability to cope have anything to do with what we believed in? What did we actually believe in? What were our moral obligations? Where did they begin? Where did they end? Would doctors help? Would others help? Would prayer help? Maybe, please God, it would all go away by itself! As individuals, as a couple, as parents, and as a family, we began unwillingly and slowly the painful process of redefining our expectations and of figuring out how we were ever going to cope with circumstances that devastated our established order and challenged our innermost beliefs.

One would think that at times like this a family would pull together and try to solve the problems through a combined effort of resources and insight. It didn't happen that way with us; rather we segregated ourselves from each other, each bearing his or her own private grief and fears. It just seemed too much to see an echo of this grief and fear in the other's eyes and it was all we could do to continue the daily routines that sustain the life of a family. So my husband and I tried separately to decide what definition of the mind we were going to live and work with so we would have some direction for the future. We knew we were making the decision for the whole family because whatever their feelings, our son Marco (10 years old at the time) and our daughter Nadija (7 years old) would follow our example. But on what grounds was this decision going to be made? The knowledge we had seemed to be miserably small and limited compared to the magnitude of the calamity. Furthermore, this knowledge was cold and lifeless and could not easily be translated and applied to our lives. The facts just stood there threatening us without showing us any way to adequately deal with the situation.

Before long the question was not only "What do we know?" but also "What do we believe, deep down?" Did we believe Steven's mind was really only an organic computer where some judicial tinkering might get it to run better, but if things could not be fixed, the brain, and the person connected to it, was so much useless organic scrap? Or did we believe that there was more to the mind than the sum of its physical functions, that it was also, so to say, an extension of the soul, and therefore had a value way beyond its physical manifestation? What was *Steven's* experience of life? Was he conscious on some level of what was going on even though he could not verbalize his feelings? Would it make a difference if we were to hand him over to other people who would care for and educate him? Of course, we didn't verbalize these issues quite like that. After all, "useless organic scrap" sounds much too shocking to be thought outright. No, one thinks in feelings at such times, careful not to complicate the issues by using words that are too self-revealing. One sticks to the socially acceptable formulas and either concludes sadly that, "It's no use! Nothing much can be done!" or one says, "It looks bad but I am going to fight this!"

As it turned out, my husband, an emergency room doctor, went with the model of the brain as an organic motor and secretly hoped for something more. I embraced the belief that there is "something more" to the mind and hoped desperately that some judicial tinkering would also help. These reactions sound very similar, but they produced vastly different attitudes: My husband began to distance himself emotionally and waited without much hope for experts and professionals to make a difference. I got emotionally involved and developed a pronounced siege mentality of the me-and-you-against-the-world kind. I reacted especially against anyone, expert or not, who made a negative judgment of my son's prospects. I believed, in all truth, that there was a normal, smart, potentially well-functioning person in that little body, imprisoned by a brain that wasn't working as it should. The task at hand was either to find a way to make it work or else find a way around the bad parts. In the meantime, however, I was determined to relate to that normal person who was imprisoned, not to the distorted image that was presented to our senses.

Not surprisingly, my husband was considered balanced and sane and able to deal with the facts as they were, and I was considered unable to think rationally and therefore intellectually, emotionally, and practically unbalanced. It was, after all, an undeniable fact that Steven suffered from some level of neurological damage and malfunction that cut clear across the psychical and mental landscape and that could not really be fixed or compensated for. Why torture oneself with false hopes? I suddenly understood as never before to what extent our attitudes, our perceptions, our courses of action, and especially our expectations are shaped by the premises we accept as true. We so very often find what we set out to look for: We ignore what doesn't fit our image of reality and concentrate instead on finding the shape that our minds imagine. If one looked only at Steven's handicaps and expected to see them reflected in every behavior, one would indeed find their imprint in everything he did. The dominant perception of the handicap, furthermore, would also easily blot out the small signs and beginnings of abilities and potentials that one would see and appreciate and seize on only if one expected betterment and change.

What kept us on course most of all was love and the intuition that there was something more to Steven than just that body, the intuition that he had a soul. I want to stress that it was not just instinctive love. How little there is to human instinctive love we all know just from listening to the news. No, I mean a different kind of love: a voluntary commitment of an individual to help and further the potential of another person, even at great personal cost if necessary.

Far from being instinctive, this kind of love must be voluntarily consented to on a continuous basis. It arises out of the deep conviction that this other person has being and value beyond the sum of his or her outer circumstances and physical functions, and that we have therefore a responsibility to him or her that goes beyond the rationalizations of established morality. In our times this kind of love is not much appreciated and is often secretly thought of as emotionally unbalanced (maybe even irrational) until, that is, the person making the judgment becomes sick or dependent. Then one reaches out with all one's being and hopes that there is someone out there who will respond to us with love, not only with reason, not only with expertise, not only with a logical evaluation of the situation, but with love and with an intuition of our being. When this love is absent, however, our most common reaction when we are confronted with problems or tragedy is, "Let someone else take care of this, someone who is trained for it and used to it, and who won't ask too much money for it."

So it was that, even though I was considered emotionally unstable and in denial, I ended up providing all the care and making all the decisions regarding Steven's life. I continued to hope for a breakthrough, or at least some "sign" that would clearly tell me what was the "truth" and tried to keep life as normal as possible. In any event, for the next year, until he was four, Steven received some educational therapy and went to a nursery school. He did begin to talk a little when he was around three and a half years old, but he said only single words or else strung together two or three words in such a way that they sounded like one word. Much of his speech was unintelligible for people outside his family. Otherwise he was a quiet, obedient three-year-old, loving and happy within the protective circle of his family and shy, but manageable, in nursery school. He never said much, though, and wouldn't draw or color pictures, wouldn't play with his toys, and wouldn't connect to other people; very often he appeared "not there," uncomprehending and remote. He was always an observer. Eventually, I was told that he had to be tested again for placement into a special program.

TESTING FOR KINDERGARTEN

Why should the words *test* and *special program* strike such terror into the hearts of parents? Why won't their minds rationally, calmly, and resolutely accept that this is the best, the most sensible, the only course of action? Why does this prospect instead multiply fears? Maybe it's because we suddenly feel utterly defenseless and at the mercy of other people, people we don't know and who might not care, people who might very well judge our child irredeemably damaged, and who might yet make mistakes that can never really be fixed again. After all, truth without love is judgment and judgment in this context condemns. Tests are also all about control and "special program" meant to me that we were out of control and socially marginalized, and that someone else would determine the direction of Steven's future. What if Steven had to go through life bearing a false and unjust label, or even any label?! It's one thing to have scattered problems, but it's quite another thing to have these problems put into one bag with a label attached. Then the problems assume a new significance and solidity and an aspect of permanence, and no one wants to bother to pick them apart any more and consider them separately. It's suddenly not the case that the person has a problem, but that the problem has become identical with the person. When we considered this, a universe of suffering and loneliness opened up to our eyes and we recoiled at the thought that our child, and maybe we too, might have to live in this universe, apart from the world where the privileged healthy and "normal" live. We suddenly were made to see that it is not enough for human beings to be taken care of physically, but that we want and need a deeper contact with the world around us and with all that is in it. We want not only survival, but we deeply, deeply desire to realize our physical, mental, and spiritual potential within the community of our world and of our kind, and when we cannot sufficiently connect to this community we are caught up in a silent limbo where nothing calls our name.

Our fears, however, were no longer an obstacle to the grinding gears of our social bureaucracy, which had now caught up with us and carried us relentlessly forward. Social Services and the school district mandated a battery of tests, and Steven was evaluated from several angles and developmental aspects. The results were unequivocal: Steven, now almost five years old, tested out as being on the developmental level of a one-and-a-half to two-year-old child. He was, they said, developmentally retarded, communication-handicapped, and perceptually impaired; his motor planning was very poor and he had not developed fine motor skills. All in all, they said, his perception probably worked only at a 75% accuracy, if that. So there we were: What did I think of the mind now? What was I going to do with this information? When I had recovered somewhat from the shock, I resolved I would go with my own impression of Steven's character and personality and would let others worry about his stage of development. How could I reasonably do this, one might ask, how could I ignore such evidence? I didn't ignore it. As I said before, I just chose to go with my belief that there is more to a person than what the functions of the brain allow to become manifest. I had this sense of "something more" to Steven, a sense that is almost impossible to describe with words, just as I couldn't describe color to a color-blind individual, but which might be akin to the sense of recognition we have when we meet certain people in our life. I saw Steven with the eyes of spirit or intuition, if you will. If I had relied only on my physical eyes and empirical thought, I would have seen only what everyone else saw: a poor little boy, not likely to ever live independently even if therapy might help a little here and there. I was not delusional, after all. I saw his problems, too. But they were a place to start out from, not a place to remain! I was convinced, furthermore, that Steven could perceive and understand much more than the tests showed, even if this understanding may have been encoded in his own, self-made code of thinking on a different level of his consciousness rather than in the language-encoded mechanisms of conventional thought. In any case, until he was able to function better he needed hope and companionship, and he needed to know that he was not alone in his universe.

MORE ABOUT THE FAMILY

I had somehow expected that our family, which was already so stressed at that time, would disintegrate at this evaluation of Steven. It did not happen, however; instead, everyone circled the wagons. My husband was as supportive of me and of us as a family as he could be and still function at his job. That left me to organize our defenses and to see to our emotional sustenance. My other two children also helped in whatever way they could. Besides trying to meet the challenge of growing up, their most important contribution was that they lovingly accepted Steven and did not reject him and were not ashamed of him. Nadija, still in elementary school, showed Steven an uncomplicated, cheerful love that drew him out of himself and challenged him to participate emotionally and practically in the life or our family. She accepted him at whatever level he was but then challenged him on that level and provided a real life experience of a human relationship for him. She didn't tiptoe around him but treated him as a brother who had to be loved and who had to be teased. She was irresistible, and with her joy and laughter lit up our life.

Then there was Marco. The death of his sister Sonja had set the course of much of his subsequent personal development. When it became apparent that his younger brother also had developmental problems and autistic tendencies, Marco reacted to it as a challenge. Through the years, Marco went on to demonstrate a steadfast love and compassion and understanding far beyond his years. Marco was, and is, Steven's friend, his teacher, his brother, and was for long stretches of time the only person besides me that Steven could deeply relate to. He made him laugh and cry and feel. He provided Steven with an access into this life, into this world by even including Steven as often as possible on outings with his own friends, who in turn came to accept Steven because Marco had accepted him so deeply. He inspired Steven to keep going, to keep trying, to keep hoping in the face of so many, many problems. In all the years of Steven's life, Marco never failed to live up to the highest moral standards.

MEET MRS. MCQUEEN

Those were difficult times, but as it turned out we did not remain all alone after all. Unexpectedly, we found friends and helpers in unforeseen places. One of these friends and helpers was Steven's new teacher, Mrs. McQueen.

The specialists who had tested Steven had come to the conclusion that he would most likely never read and write or ever be able to communicate nor-

mally. Since there is a law, however, that each child has the right to an education, Steven was assigned to enter a classroom for communication-handicapped
children that served our whole county and which was set up within a nearby
public elementary school. With all my resolve and avowed bravery, I was still
full of pain and sorrow and hated and mistrusted what was going to happen. So,
when I was waiting to meet Mrs. McQueen for the first time, I was literally
bristling with suspicion, prejudice, and hostility and the fear that Steven had
been labeled and set on a track to oblivion. I was sure Mrs. McQueen would
turn out to be another scientific-minded, emotionally uninvolved expert who
would look at me disdainfully and patiently explain that they were doing the
best they could. But Mrs. McQueen wasn't like that at all. Three educational degrees had taught her much about theories, but fifteen years of teaching had also
taught her that the living mind was more than professional and scientific knowledge could reliably define. A handicap to her was something to work with, or
to work around, and her mission was to help each child learn about the potential ways to overcome his or her handicap. It's hard for me not to wax lyrical
when I talk about Mrs. McQueen; she is such an remarkable human being and
just the person you might want to deal with when things aren't working as they
should. There was no gentle pessimism, or remote compassion, or saccharine
sweetness; there was instead a tough, open, hands-on professionalism that said,
whatever the problem, she was going to lick it.

As it was, her whole classroom proclaimed this philosophy. It was a neat,
clean, academic classroom with several different learning stations and a wealth
of interesting things in it. Besides Steven, there were seven other students, ages
five to eight, each with a different problem area, though all problems were communication related. One six-year-old boy, for example, could read on a third
grade level, but had almost no comprehension of what he read. Another couldn't
read or write, but talked very well indeed. Yet another had such severe ADD that
he couldn't talk, listen, read, or write anything effectively and had to be taught
to learn how to learn. There was also a little boy who had to wear a helmet because he had almost constant seizures. The three other students had relatively
mild problems and were sure to be mainstreamed soon.

Each child had individually tailored learning objectives and was entitled to
one or two weekly sessions with the various therapists who would come to the
school. Steven, for example, had a physical therapist, an occupational therapist,
a speech therapist, and an educational therapist, all of whom he saw once or
twice a week for half an hour. (The school system paid for all but the physical
therapist.) Each child helped keep track of the therapy sessions and of the individual lessons they were on, everyone obeyed directions, and everyone participated. Most of all, everyone knew, in no uncertain terms, that he or she was
there to learn. And one more thing: Mrs. McQueen also talked to the children
about being different and about having handicaps, which was sort of remarkable

because usually no one, not even the child involved, wants to confront this and talk much about it. She did, though, and told them that they had to acknowledge whatever was wrong and then work to get around it. What did the children think of it? Did it help? I don't really know. Then again, maybe Steven's very focused determination to be "normal" comes from this confrontation.

So began a long and agonizingly slow learning process. Steven was picked up from home by the little bus for handicapped students, which he resented from the beginning. He also understood that he was in special education and liked it just as little. I think he was initially disturbed by some of the problems he saw in the other children, but then he got used to them. During class, the children quickly established a pecking order among themselves: The most normal children had the highest status and all the others pursued them and desired their friendship. Steven, who couldn't really talk, didn't have much clout and found himself next to the bottom of the totem pole. That bothered him a lot, too. Yet it was undeniably a good thing that Steven got away from the love and protection of the family. While school, classmates, and teachers subjected him to a lot of stress and even pain, this probably also woke his fighting spirit, which he needed every bit before long, and challenged him to acknowledge, and face, the world outside the protection of his home.

The first priority was, of course, language. Learning to talk was a huge undertaking for Steven: He had to learn the rules of grammar first before he could even begin to say a grammatically correct sentence. Each day at least one hour was taken up with learning and identifying new nouns, verbs, and adjectives: nouns are things, places, or persons and answer the questions what, where, and who; verbs are do-words that tell what the subject does; adjectives answer the question what kind. And so on. Once identified, the words were herded into a grammatically correct sentence: Each word had a correct position in the sentence and the children had to find the right place for it. The amazing thing was, that once he learned about grammar, Steven began to talk much better, even though he still tended to use clumps of words rather than choose his own words and put them into his own configuration. At least now the clumps were more or less in the right order, and he wouldn't reverse subject-object order so often. He no longer would say, for example, "I made blocks out of a tower," but correctly said, "I made a tower out of blocks."

Learning to write was another incredible process. No one, *no one,* can imagine what went into the teaching of Steven, and to this day it is almost unimaginable for me that another person would go to such trouble for a child that is just one of many students. Before Steven could begin to write, he first learned how to draw letters and shapes with his fingers into the air, on a piece of carpet, and into a pan of sand that Mrs. McQueen had for this purpose. He had to learn how to hold a pencil or crayon, and he had to learn where on a paper to start writing. Somehow the empty space of a paper totally unnerved him to the point where he would panic and refuse to write or draw anything. So he had to learn by a succession of practiced physical and cognitive behaviors to guide his right hand with the pencil to the left hand corner of a sheet of paper. Hold up your right hand, Steven, index finger extended! Now hold up the paper with the left hand. Put the right index finger on the pointy corner near your left hand. That is where you start writing! For seven months the teacher dotted in the letters and then words, and Steven completed them by connecting dot to dot. When he was finally ready to write without the dots we found that he couldn't bring himself to leave spaces between the words. So he had to put two fingers behind each finished word before he started a new one. It took about two or three months before he was ready to try without the fingers.

Math was also an adventure. At first he was unexpectedly good at it, successfully wrote out the equation in each line, and solved it with the help of counting blocks or his fingers. Then came the debacle. He was to learn to add and subtract in columns and he had to do so from *right to left,* a major upheaval for someone who had taken so long to learn to write from left to right. For two weeks, Mrs. McQueen told me later, he sat there for 30 minutes each day and added the left column first, erased it, added the left column first, erased it . . . while tears were streaming down his face. Two weeks!! Then suddenly, suddenly, he added the right column first and then the left column, looked at it and said, "That was easy!" From then on he had no more problems either with writing from left to right or with calculating from right to left.

ETHEL'S BIBLE STUDY

"Miracles happen all the time," Mrs. McQueen said, "but they almost always happen in slow motion and you have to work hard to make them happen." So she said, but what does it mean to expect a miracle? Day followed day, and weeks turned into months, and months turned into years and there was seemingly so little change compared with what still needed to be done. Expecting a miracle means that even though time passes, even long stretches of time, one still has the same conviction that the goal can and will be reached as when one started out. Rational thinking can't do this, it gets discouraged quite easily. After putting in a certain effort for a certain length of time without getting adequate results, rationality gives up on that course and either tries a different tack or concludes that the result is not worth the effort. Rationality can display remarkable persistence and staying power if it knows the potential outcome, but when it just works blindly and is motivated only by the next short-term goal, rationality alone cannot keep up its motivation.

Rational thinking is like working an equation with some unknowns that can be discovered, given that one has enough skill and can find enough information. Using intuition, however, is like working on an equation without having enough information so that one has to fill in the unknown values with intuitive educated guesses. And one attempts to solve this equation even though one has insufficient skills and needs to learn as one goes along. Can you imagine working on an equation month after month, yet never being sure that what you do will work out, that your guesses are within acceptable range, and that you will eventually find a solution? Few people would entertain that kind of a project unless there is no other recourse anymore, unless they have the choice either to operate mostly on an intuitive level or give up altogether. Under normal circumstances, most people would decline to try to function on an intuitive level because it seems just too alien, too weird, too unknowable, and too far away from the accepted mode of consciousness. When there is no other recourse, however, one tries anything.

Now, even loving Steven as I did and desiring with all my heart to see him get well enough to function independently, even with all willingness to apply my intuition and persist in my effort, I could not have gone on expecting a miracle if there had not been some sort of reaffirmation that I was on the right track and, more importantly, without some way to find out what to do and what to be next. What do I mean by that? I mean that ever so often I felt burned out, totally discouraged, overwhelmed, and afraid. Many times I was at a loss for how to deal with all the other people around me and how to go on insisting to them that I was right in my expectations and my demands on them. At other times I would seemingly either reach a dead end or be confronted by a confusing array of possible choices. Many times I didn't know how to rationally choose the right course and began doubting myself. Many times I didn't know what to be: caring or strict, conciliatory or insistent, friendly or remote, emotionally involved or emotionally withdrawn, rational or intuitive. Without some sort of reference I would have gotten hopelessly lost. As it was, the reference system that helped me focus and define my own personal beliefs, attain a consistent view of moral obligations, and overcome doubt, personal weaknesses, and despair was a Bible study. Please don't turn away now, but listen to what else I say about it.

The Bible study was led by an older woman who had converted to the Christian faith from Judaism and who was very knowledgeable about the Bible, especially about the Hebrew Scriptures which more or less make up the Christian Old Testament. Her main interest, however, was to teach us how to translate the wisdom of the Scriptures into our daily lives. There were maybe ten or twelve men and women of various ages and from various religious backgrounds who met every Tuesday evening at Ethel's home. I had been introduced to them by an acquaintance who by herself had felt overwhelmed by my circumstances and my needs and thought that a greater circle of concerned people with a definite philosophy or faith could help me better. I didn't particularly want to join a Bible study but needed some sort of human contact besides professionals who met with me only because of their line of work. So I went to see what it would be like.

It was exactly what I needed. The members of that Bible study closed about me in a protective circle, and there was the unspoken promise that as long as I kept an open mind, as long as I was willing to look at advice that might require me to jump over my own shadow, there would be progress and there would be direction for my life. I knew that at all times it was entirely up to me to take or to refuse advice for a course of action, and sometimes I did refuse and more often I very much wanted to. Yet I had found out early on that it was not profitable to inflexibly insist on what *I* wanted to do, on what *I* believed, on what *I* could or couldn't do. Ethel was very firmly centered on the Bible and no one was going to tell her, for example, that one could not forgive one's husband, that one just couldn't go on, that there was no way out, or that there was nothing more to be done. She and the other members of the Bible study *always* came up with something, and it was *always* something that *I* would have to do. There was never IF your husband, or IF this or that person could be brought to do something, THEN something good might happen. It was always IF YOU do what is right according to the Bible good things will follow; maybe not the good things you insist on, maybe not the way you insist on, but good things nevertheless.

I know full well how crazy that sounds to many people; I know their reservation and I know their aversion to uneducated, narrowminded, superstitious fanatics. I know how unpopular religion, any religion, has become and how often people are disparaged who call themselves believers of anything. Before I came to that Bible study I thought all these things as well. It was not until rational people all deserted me and Steven and my family as a lost cause, until the rational approach had no more answers for me, until my intuition had all run dry, that I even entertained listening to them because I really had nothing to lose. And now I, knowing full well how crazy it sounds to many people, especially to modern intellectuals, am here to tell you that this faith worked, that it most assuredly saved my life and Steven's life and maybe the mental health of my entire family and turned something tragic and awful into something that was manageable and that contained a wealth of wonderful, luminous lessons for our entire family.

No matter how often I came to our weekly sessions in panic and defeat, I always left becalmed, comforted, and reoriented. No, I didn't get a game plan for the next week or month. I hardly ever got any advice on what to do, but always on how to be: be loving, be forgiving with yourself and others, be hopeful, be obedient to God and (of all things) to your husband, be righteous in your own deeds, let go of things, trust, be clear, pray for guidance, give thanks. This way I found clarity and direction for the next necessary step, this way I found, most importantly, the right attitude toward my problems, toward other people, toward my life. It enabled me to see and then take the next step into the right direction. Only the next step. It was a completely remarkable, wonderful experience, and it worked! Case by case, step by step, it worked. The result of it all showed in our daily lives: I had always enough love and patience for my three children and my husband. I had always enough strength, endurance, and motivation to go on. I had peace and joy, contentment and hope. I was consistent in my expectations. I took the right steps and actions in regard to Steven's upbringing and education. I was able to make allies of the teachers and administrators I came in contact with. In truth, I found a peace that passed all understanding, and yet it was there! In a way, this too was a miracle.

LEARNING CAN TAKE PLACE IN MANY DIFFERENT WAYS

Maybe this Bible study and my reliance on its restorative powers also predisposed me to think, feel, and expect other things to work along unusual and even irrational pathways. From the very beginning, for example, I had had an unusually strong feeling of connectedness to Steven that was later joined by a feeling of assurance that some kind of communication and learning on some levels of experience and consciousness was indeed possible. It was a sense of mental and spiritual connection that I believe we all feel at some time or other, but which in my case instead of winking out after an instant continued to be there most of the time. Since there were so few routes of communication available especially regarding the emotional and social development of Steven, this kind of connectedness took on a new kind of significance. At any rate, I began to act on this intuition. Not only did I talk and relate to him as if he could understand everything (even though I knew that, linguistically speaking, that was not so), I especially made a point to include him in my emotional life. What do I mean by this? I mean that I related to him with the premise in mind that he could, so to speak, "plug into" my emotional and social circuits.

It was a strange sensation for me because it felt as if the borders of I and Thou became indistinct. As I guided his limbs, his whole person, his mind, and his spirit through different experiences, it felt like his muscles learned from my muscles, his eyes learned from my eyes, his fingers learned from my fingers, his spirit, in a sense, learned from my spirit, my confidence gave him confidence. I was encouraged by his reactions. Slowly and hesitatingly, Steven began to connect to his physical and mental abilities, and as he took possession of his body and of his life, his spirit and his personality became ever more manifest. As he progressed, it also became apparent that the connections between his inborn abilities and his consciousness had to be jump-started from the outside because somehow he had not been able to spontaneously connect will, body, and mind. He had to learn grammar, for example, but afterward he knew it and could use language. He had to learn how to move in time and space, but afterward he knew it and could build on this knowledge. He had to be shown, physically and in minute detail how to hold a pencil, but once his hand, muscles, and nerves learned how it felt, he knew it and needed no more reminders. It was so with everything, and I felt sometimes as if his teachers and I were growing and creating connections in his mind and brain that had not been there to start out with. So he still lived, learned, and developed in the artificial womb of our care and our support, and became ever more able.

ABOUT CHARACTER

"A man's character is his destiny," said Democritus. Did Steven for all his handicaps have a character? And why should character be so important? What is character? We all think we know it, but it is hard to define once we are asked to describe it. "Character doesn't happen by itself," Dr. C. Kaplan, a professor of psychology at The University of North Carolina at Charlotte, said to me during an interview. "Character is what emerges when you become mature enough to learn to direct yourself." How does this definition apply to Steven? He wasn't mature in the conventional sense of the word, but oh, he had character! It came out in his courage, in his tenacity, in his gentleness, in his ability to love and to suffer, in his every attitude. Steven, even though he was just a child, never gave up. He never gave up, even though he had to come through trials and stretches of hopelessness that might have conquered many a strong, "normal" person. He regrouped time and again and overcame loneliness, isolation, and the shattering discovery of otherness and insufficiency. He overcame the drag of time that ever whispers to us that things cannot be done, that it takes too long and that it costs too much. He identified and confronted his inabilities with the help of his teachers and then set out to overcome them, one by one. In some way, maybe only expressed in mental images, he set himself goals for normalcy and achievement. He managed to overcome the frustrations of the long drawn out learning process, and learned to live with a great deal of fear and the discouragement of repeated failure when everyone around him was not failing. Despite frequent setbacks he called up the courage and the motivation to try again and again. Try what? Try to become what he was? How would he know? How could he know? Unless it is possible that we have, as Plato said, an innate knowledge, a sense beyond words that draws us onward to realize a potential that the mind/soul beholds. Steven showed character, virtue, and a great spirit, and it determined his destiny. He couldn't have done it alone, but neither could there have been achievement without his character.

LIFE GOES ON

Looking back I think that the years with Mrs. McQueen were the great turning point, the final decisive factor in Steven's favor. Several people have had a hand in the making of Steven, and each contributed a crucial element, but without Mrs. McQueen we might have been stopped a step away from success. It was Mrs. McQueen who finally pulled everything together with her know-how, her intuition, and her greatness as a teacher. She was essential in ushering Steven into the greater community, which is so indispensable to each individual. As it was, Steven learned to read and write fluently by the time he was seven. He continued to have trouble expressing himself easily and spontaneously and all too often preferred to just say nothing, but even in this most difficult area he was making progress. Steven had been in Mrs. McQueen's class for three years and during that time a transformation had taken place; now his potential had become manifest and his self-actualization was no longer wishful thinking, but had acquired shape and direction.

When Steven was eight we moved to North Carolina where he was mainstreamed in a second grade classroom, two years behind other kids his age, because there was no program for him. We missed Mrs. McQueen, but even though it proved to be a rough and unplanned transition, it was somehow the right time for it. Again it was time for him to muster the courage to try functioning in a still less protective environment. He spent anywhere from two to four hours on homework, for example, when other kids just needed one or one and one half hours at most. Yet here, too, we found caring, intuitive, and skilled teachers who showed him the way, who continued to educate him, and who acknowledged his potential. So while there were more challenges, with their help Steven was able to maintain his forward momentum. In fourth and fifth grades, Steven's learning ability began to increase almost exponentially, and now took place on several levels simultaneously; before it had been very linear. He began to function more and more normally and independently on all levels of his personality, even though in some areas there were still developmental delays. These delays, however, were no longer across the board and his functions had begun to assume peaks and valleys like a mountain range. His IQ had also come up from an initial 67 to 86 in fourth grade.

Yet, while some difficulties shrank, others became larger and loomed threateningly. Of those, social skills were a particular concern. Steven was fine when someone gave a conversation structure and direction, or gave a meeting subject matter and content, but he was lost with his own generation where social interaction depended on him to provide content and to give spontaneous, age-specific responses. So many times he came home in fourth and fifth grade and cried from the bottom of his heart, "WHY can't I talk? WHY doesn't anyone like me?! WHY does everyone treat me as if I was invisible! WHY can't I be like everyone else?!" It was so hard not to have an answer. All we could do was practice, ask the teachers to help and draw him in, and to try and invite kids over. Nothing worked in the end, though. He just wasn't ready yet and no amount of trying, and wishing, and hoping was going to make things go any faster. Was it ever a rocky road, so different from what had come before! I couldn't tell Steven the advice from my Bible study, he didn't want to hear it; there was no Mrs. McQueen to provide structure and guidelines; there was no family to stand up for him. He was independent from all help and dependent on his own resources. "I just don't know what to say, Mom," he would cry, "nothing comes to my mind!"

Things looked again grim for a while, and I was afraid that after all his incredible accomplishments he would fall apart emotionally. Steven went on isolated and ignored for a year, until another angel in the disguise of his language teacher, Ms. Collins, came along and sat with him during lunch. She provided a beginning to a conversation and then was there to give it structure. After a while, other kids joined in. Just these lunch conversations gave Steven enough encouragement that he could go on. He still had no friends, he still was largely ignored, but now he was not totally ignored. In a way, the fight to make social contact, to connect with his own generation and his own identity is as hard and relentless as the fight to connect to his mental abilities. It is an ongoing fight and brings with it its own successes and high points and its own failures and heartbreaks.

Today, Steven is finishing seventh grade. He has been doing his homework independently and, since a year ago, and has managed to stay on the AB honor roll. The end-of-the-year tests show that he is on grade level in all subjects and above grade level in social studies. Steven is also gradually making connection with his own generation and with people outside the family. Even though there are still difficulties, they are the agonies and pains many other teenagers go through as well. Looking at him now, one could never guess what an incredible journey he has behind him and that he has indeed moved the equivalent of mountains. I don't know where the journey is going to end, and I don't try to guess. I mean to leave the door wide open for any possibilities at all and trust that this task so well begun will be finished well in time.

How Does the Mind Work?

There is a tendency in scientific and philosophical circles, as well as in the general public, to look at the mind in disconnected, one-dimensional terms that reduce the mind to biochemical functions of the brain. The result of this tendency, with its roots in the discovery of evolution, has been a progressive erosion of a greater concept of the human mind, a concept that has traditionally included the dimensions of body, mind, and spirit. The progressive influence of scientific empiricism and materialism especially in the 20th century, however, has led many people to believe that nothing like a spirit or soul can possibly exist. According to that view the universe and all it contains is nothing more than the accidental by-product of the inexorable interplay of natural laws; nature produced the body and the mind, and even participated in the creation of social and cultural forms. Thus, the mind is an organic computer and processor of sense stimuli and, as Stuart Hampshire says, "the inner life of the mind is shadowy and parasitic on the outer life."[1]

Even now, after all this time, after all my experiences, after exposure to a spectrum of philosophies, and after continuously considering this question from one aspect or another, "How does the mind work?" is still a hard question to answer. Some of the philosophical systems regarding the mind and human consciousness I agree with more than with others. Plato's, Kant's, Schopenhauer's, Bergson's, Peirce's, and Penrose's theories of the mind and of consciousness, among others, all ring very true to me, and I find myself agreeing with their visions time and again. Yet when I try to compare these theories to my living experience, they seem to be missing something; in the light of day and in the pulse of emotions they look cold and gray and unalive, a frozen caricature of the living, amorphous, passionate complexity of feelings, thoughts, emotions, and inspirations that make up our life experience. The challenge for me is to find a theory of the mind that integrates everything I have learned in my journey with Steven.

So what did I learn about the mind?

a. That certain long-time environmental conditions as well as specific mental and emotional regimen can alter the physiological structures of the brain and with this the mental processes.

b. That "the direct vision of the mind by the mind is the chief function of intuition," as Henri Bergson writes in *A Study of Metaphysics.*

c. That, as Charles S. Peirce noted, "All experience is interpreted experience."

d. That we search for meaning not just in empirical realities but in the kaleidoscopic changes of emotions, passions, feelings, and intuitions that go on in our minds.

e. That while feelings are notoriously difficult to pin down, to trace, to identify, and to describe, they are also profoundly meaningful to us in our everyday lives, often more meaningful than rational considerations. Cumulatively, they can have at least the same impact on us as the sensory perception on which we base so much of our empirical beliefs.

f. That what we call spirituality is also cumulatively compelling, no matter whether it is expressed in simple or in sophisticated terms, and exerts, therefore, as real an influence on our interpretation of reality and our subsequent decisions and actions as any category of space and time, of instinct and survival, of rationality and logic, or of emotion and passion.

g. That sense can be made of each aspect of our mind only when it is seen against the other aspects that make up the fabric of our consciousness and thus of our being.

h. That the mind is not a homogeneous unit but an organism made up of cooperative systems, and that the subjective hierarchy of these systems within the mind will be reflected by the objective behaviors and choices of the individual.

i. That the very fact of the intricate interdependence of mental systems points out the possibility that the functional domains and systems can be used as a base from which another, nonfunctional domain of the mind could be repaired.

WHAT IS THE MIND?

My theory would have to run along the following lines. Above all, the mind is adaptable, able to change its colors like a chameleon. Relatively few things are beyond its ability to adapt to, to work with. Far from being hemmed in by one-lane rational thinking, it can develop a scheme at several fronts at once. Reason explores the new territory that emotions, feelings, and intuitions first discover. The goal is to find an equilibrium of outer and inner circumstances without compromising the most basic tenets by which the individual lives. Pure reason can only be partially successful in that attempt at equalizing interior and exterior pressures because the relationships of cause and effect, as Hume has already said so persuasively, are not at all easy to determine.

The human mind, in other words, can ultimately not be realistically circumscribed, defined, understood, or recreated by computers or artificial intelligence, first because the human mind can recognize through intuition truths that strictly formal logic cannot decide. And second, because the human mind is not based on any one formal system of function and logic but is rather a conglomerate of several domains and levels of systems of perception and logic, each of which contributes its evaluations and interpretations of reality to whatever the attention of the individual is focused on. These domains with their pertinent systems assume a certain hierarchical order within which even rationality is only *one* mode of thought, only one kind of reference system, and one, moreover, that is not automatically dominant. The hierarchical order of system cooperation and its concomitant logic can be upset or changed at the will or impulse of the individual. That is the strength, and probably also the weakness, of the mind, that at any time it can will itself to abandon a system of thought and behavior and follow another.

NOTE

1. Quoted in Iris Murdoch, *The Sovereignty of Good and Other Essays* (New York: Routledge, 1990), 5.

REFERENCES

Bergson, Henri. *A Study in Metaphysics.* Totowa, NJ: Littlefield, Adams & Co., 1965.
Brent, Joseph. *Charles Sanders Peirce.* Indianapolis: Indiana University Press, 1993.
Hume, David. *A Treatise of Human Nature.* New York: Prometheus Books, 1992.
Peirce, Charles S. *The Essential Writings,* ed. Edward C. Moore. New York: Prometheus Books, 1998.
Penrose, Roger. *Shadows of the Mind.* Oxford, UK: Oxford University Press, Inc., 1994.
Schopenhauer, Arthur. *The World as Will and Idea.* Trans. R.B. Haldane and J. Kemp. (London: Routledge & Kegan Paul Ltd.), 1957.

STUDY QUESTIONS

1. According to Harmaty, the human mind is more than a series of biochemical functions. What is the "something more" she talks about?

2. What are some of your assumptions about how the normal mind works? Where do these assumptions come from?

3. In what kinds of situations does it make a real difference how we define "the mind"?

Meditations on Form, or, How Should I Tell You What I Need You to Know?

Robin Parks

Robin Parks lives on a small island in the Pacific Northwest where she writes short stories and essays. Currently at work on a book about her mother's tragic life as a schizophrenic, Parks worries about blurring the boundaries of fact and fiction, and about the moral obligations of the daughter and artist.

I finally knew I had enough money when, even in private, I arranged my food before eating it.

STANDARD LORE IN aesthetic theory says that good art is art that fulfills the unique function of art, and standard lore in aesthetic theory says that art's unique function is to give human beings "pleasure."[1] Unfortunately for philosophers concerned with precision of ideas and speech, pleasure is one of those concepts in continual defiance of explication. If a combative effort were made, it would take only a handful of phone calls to find someone to refute a specific definition of pleasure.

Joy, desire, amusement, delight, happiness, cheer, rapture, and jubilation are all dictionary definitions of pleasure, but one would be hard pressed to apply all, most, or even some of these responses to the listening of various moribund requiems, the sight of a cold-blooded Breughel, the experience of "Waiting for Godot," or many of Emily Dickinson's poems.

However, the general idea of pleasure is not easily, from push to shove, relinquished. After all, art (music, literature, sculpture, theater, dance, etc.) is not exactly necessary for survival in the strict sense; it is deliberately sought after for some other reason. And because it is sought after for reasons outside of or on top of mere survival, we assume the attraction is pleasure, at least, pleasure in the broadest possible use of the term.

> *A full pocketbook at Ralph's Supermarket is a beautiful thing. All shimmering items are there for the taking, high and low and eye-level things pulsing with shapes of satisfaction. My pocketbook is full. It is full of beauty. It is a fresh set of oils, plastic-wrapped sheet music, damp square clay, a loom, a hoop, a row of brushes.*
>
> *Now, during fall, stacked yams and eggplant send up smoke signals. I begin there, in Produce.*

One step below the broad, general, yet slim term "pleasure" on the pyramidal ladder of definition is the term "form." Form, or formal properties of a work of art, might include color, shape, size, depth, relationship (harmony, discord, balance, contrast), rhythm, and timbre. This term is used by aesthetic theorists to disclose a connection between the attraction art holds for humans and the forms found in art.[2] The questions raised in consideration of this connection are basic: Is it the forms in art that attract humans, and, if so, are certain forms universally—and eternally—appealing? How can we find out?

> *It is fall, and slender Japanese eggplant beckon to me. I choose two. The purple tube in my pocketbook nudges closer.*

A playful philosophical attitude would approach the question of distinguishing form from pleasure like a game: picking up Form and placing it in the mush pot, poking it with a stick, asking it questions about itself, putting it on a Ouija board and waiting for the answer. The best part about having a playful attitude is that, explicit answers forthcoming or not, Form would be known, felt, experienced, and it would then be something to talk around in a meaningful, if private, way. For instance, I envision Western philosophers shuffling Form and coming away with descriptions like harmonious, well-organized, tender, beautiful, attentive, and immediate, while in another place, Japanese philosophers come away talking about *wabi* (poverty) and *sabi* (loneliness).[3]

> *I am particularly aware of red today. Red is things I don't usually buy, but today my pocketbook is full and the milk is packaged brown and red. So is the Chunky Soup. There are roses to impress company. And chocolate bars. I turn down an aisle I have never before entered. It is lined with soda pop. Here are things I do not know well, but because my pocketbook is full and*

I'm buying for another, I slow down and notice mysterious things that mean something mundane to the company I shall soon keep. There is bottled water on my left, some of it in damp, room-temperature squares. I remember uses for bottled water, but can't keep straight the reasons behind them.

I own an iron. I will use it tonight before my company comes to make a white sheet flat.

Perhaps the worst part about this playfulness is the failure to find a connection, a truth, that would hold even for all those millions who were not present at a specific venue of play. But knowing the nature of game playing, isn't it still possible that those absent would know what the game was like and what types of discoveries were made? In other words, those absent could still appreciate the general notion of Form, knowing how slippery it can be, sometimes changing shape dramatically and contrarily.[4]

There is a cart in my path. I am small behind mine, but I usually maneuver well, gracefully, especially when my pocketbook is full. The tip of my cart meets the tip of the other and the other does not relinquish. Full of largesse I let my eyes float to the activity attached to the cart. It is a hand reaching to the shelf for a Coke—one hand touching one of a million silver and red cans of Coke, just above my eyes, close to my face. The hand is struggling, twisting, grabbing, and pulling the resistant can. The can, I notice, is strapped to the ones behind it and to the ones beside it and probably, for all I know, to all the other cans beaded together in this aisle. I have no way of knowing because I do not come down this aisle and I do not buy, usually, red things.

I have in my cart a small green troop of apple juice cans that seems to be woven together the same way this resistant can appears to be attached to the others, and I remember how I take scissors out of my drawer when I don't have company and no one is looking to loose the cans. My eyes return to the hand wondering if it will reveal to me a better truth about tied-up things, but then I see it is taking too long, the hand is losing, and I wonder if the whole problem has to do with strength. Sometimes I think I have arthritis, like when the box of detergent (red) says to push in and pull out and I do but nothing happens except the box changes shape. I use the scissors then, too.

That humans respond to the formal properties in art seems to me a more trenchant observation than that offered by the notion that humans are attracted to art because it gives pleasure, even when those formal properties shift among cultures.

The form of art, whether it be a musical passage shaping a figure eight with arpeggios or a novel changing my vocabulary, gives me an existence less linear and more motley than my everyday steps, one foot in front of the other, allow.

That the Japanese have identified poverty and loneliness as formal elements of good art, while the Western world seeks perfection and balance in art, points to the peculiar relationship humans have to art; art articulates deep existential connections rendered mute by the pedestrian demands of life.

> *I decide it is a question of strength and I will help. My hand almost reaches the other hand when I spot something green and up from my belly out of my mouth comes a poof of sound—a sound just like the sound that comes out of me when my company first comes inside. The hand is cracked and out of the cracks something green is oozing. It is the same way with the arm. My eye runs after the sound, glimpsing pink-caked shoulders, sliding down cotton the stain of plasma, landing on feet leaving prints of bloody green ooze on the floor.*
>
> *The sound twirls me around and chases me from the aisle. I find myself weeping in Meats. My pocketbook is huge and bulbous, leaking slightly with oozing paint, damp threads pulled down by the gravity of the situation.*
>
> *There is a smell in Meats that embarrasses me because only I seem to know it is coming from another place. I look down. I have lost my cart. My pocketbook is making a mess on the floor. It is not supposed to be leaking. It is only an object. It is supposed only to suggest, not demand. I bow my head, ashamed. My eyes close with a sucking sound. Relieved, I hear the smell exit through automatic sliding glass doors.*

How should I tell you what I need you to know? It actually happened in Ralph's Supermarket that I came across a homeless woman stealing a Coke. Given the advanced stages of her sepsis, it is likely she died that afternoon. But it is futile to wax prosaic on the possible ways there are to be poverty-stricken and lonely in this world, on the way it can happen that a woman can walk dying from lack of care into a supermarket filled with the makings of good health . . . you might not listen. You might recoil from rather than respond with attraction to her story. You may, in fact, hear nothing at all.

On the other hand, how right is it to poeticize this woman? She may be wabi and sabi, but she is not art unless I turn her into art, which I have attempted to do here. And by turning her into art, what have I done?[5] Part of me wants to think that by turning her into art I have located her in a realm of existence where she can be known to others who would otherwise avert their eyes. She is turned into shapes and colors and a proximity that catches the inner eye, forever changing the landscape of someone else's psyche, and, it is hoped, someday changing their ability to consciously notice what before was invisible.[6] I must believe that humans—like Adam and Eve—feel an irresistible attraction to the shapes of understanding, even at the price of innocence, peace, and yes, pleasure. And I must believe the aesthetic sphere is altogether immune to moral aphasia.[7]

Another part of me worries about the losses incurred while I chisel away at people's landscapes.[8] Is there time enough, not to mention talent enough, to infuse the floating world with my particular brand of compassion? Should I separate the phenomena of my life—the homeless, poetry, health care as big business, the erotic, music, hunger, sadness, and pleasure—into tied-up packages of similar things with a separate language, a separate logic for each? Or should I reach for a wisdom in confused things, like the shame of a full pocketbook, the clash of red and green, the loneliness of a supermarket? It is a dilemma.

NOTES

1. "For, to appreciate a work of art we need bring with us nothing from life, no knowledge of its ideas and affairs, no familiarity with its emotions. Art transports us from the world of man's [sic] activity to a world of aesthetic exaltation" (Clive Bell, *Art* [New York: Capricorn Books, 1958], 27).

   "A notion of aesthetic judgments as disengaged from the practical concern of life is increasingly taken as the hallmark of traditional aesthetics, which in this sense is seen as purist . . ." (Flo Leibowitz, "A Note on Feminist Theories of Representation: Questions Concerning the Autonomy of Art," *The Journal of Aesthetics and Art Criticism*, 8:4 [Special Issue—Feminism and Traditional Aesthetics, The American Society for Aesthetics, 1990]: 361).

2. "For a discussion of aesthetics, it need be agreed only that forms arranged and combined according to certain unknown and mysterious laws do move us in a particular way . . ." (Bell, 19).

   "One feature of aesthetic objects in which critics take a great interest is their form. It is often said, indeed, that their possession of certain forms, or of forms in a high degree, is exactly what distinguishes them from other objects and gives them their special value" (Monroe C. Beardsley, *Aesthetics: Problems in the Philosophy of Criticism,* 2nd Edition [Indianapolis and Cambridge: Hackett Publishing Company, Inc., 1981], 165). Beardsley goes on to criticize this perspective, asking hard questions such as "can form be separated from content?"

3. There are several Japanese aesthetic principles virtually inimical to traditional Western aesthetics. Among them: *yugen* (mystery, depth, the mere suggestion of a thing); *sabi* (loneliness, simplicity, to become desolate); *wabi* (poverty, imperfection); the floating world (mutability); and the condition of perishability, exemplified by cherry blossoms and morning glories, both fleeting flowers. "Although the novel [*The Tale of Genji* by Lady Murasaka, considered the world's first novel] is full of humor and charm, the prevailing impression is one of sadness, in large part because of the insistence on the inexorable motion of time" (Donald Keene, *Japanese Literature* [New York: Grove Press, 1955], 74).

   Also, of *sabi*, Daisetz T. Suzuki writes "This has been one of the favorite tricks of Japanese artists—to embody beauty in a form of imperfection or even of ugliness" (Daisetz T. Suzuki, *Zen and Japanese Culture* [Princeton, NJ: Princeton University Press, 1973, 1959], 24).

4. "Discordant elements, as long as they are still in discord, cannot come to an agreement, and they therefore cannot produce a harmony" (Plato, *Symposium*, trans. Alexander Nehamas and Paul Woodruff [Indianapolis and Cambridge: Hackett Publishing Company, Inc., 1989], 22).

   "The frailty of human existence, a common theme in literature throughout the world, has rarely been recognized as the necessary condition of beauty" (Donald Keene, *Landscapes and Portraits: Appreciation of Japanese Culture* [Tokyo and Palo Alto: Kodansha International Ltd., 1971], 24). For the Japanese, brevity is profoundly moving and perishability is a necessary condition for beauty.

5. There might be a place for this woman in Japanese aesthetic theory: "*Wabi* really means

'poverty,' or, negatively, 'not to be in the fashionable society of the time' " (Suzuki, 23). But Suzuki goes on to say "To be poor . . . and yet to feel inwardly the presence of something of the highest value, above time and social position: this is what essentially constitutes *wabi*" (Suzuki, 23). As much as I'd like to attribute some authority, some choice to this woman's position in the world, I cannot. And, unfortunately, Western aesthetics only gives me an aesthetic that cannot recognize this woman at all.

6. This notion is contrary to the idea that art is valuable because it does not tell people how to think. "It is, precisely, the physical embodiment of a work of art that minimizes the threat of common reference and common grounds for interpretive and appraisive dispute . . ." (Joseph Margolis, "Works of Art Are Physically Embodied and Culturally Emergent Entities," in *Culture and Art*, ed. Lars Aagaard-Mogensen [Atlantic Highlands, NJ: Humanities Press, 1976], 40).

7. After quoting Arthur Danto on the danger of turning art into theory, Estella Lauter pleads, "Let us now study how art embodies, enacts and changes culture(s)" (Estella Lauter, "Re-enfranchising Art: Feminist Intervention in the Theory of Art," in *Hypatia*, 5:2 [Special Issue—Feminism and Aesthetics. Indianapolis: Indiana University Press, 1990]: 104).

8. Though problematic to the premise underlying the universality of good art, some philosophers do admit there is a connection between these two types of experience. ". . . Admitting that they are enormously different, I believe that we treat works of art and persons as entities of a similar sort and speak about them in somewhat similar ways" (Margolis, 33).

STUDY QUESTIONS

1. How is telling a story artistically—through images, music, words, or dance—different from straightforward reporting? (The same question in technical jargon: What is artistic form, and how does it appeal to us?)

2. Parks says she made the homeless woman "known" by turning her into art. What does she mean? Do you agree with her claim?

3. When is it right to use art as a tool of moral and political communication? When is it wrong?

Hand-Me-Downs

Timothy A. Jones

Timothy A. Jones retired from his career as a philosophy student when he decided not to rebuild the "Great Structure" of knowledge from the ground up. He chose instead to study law, and become a change agent from within. The story printed below won a Women's Studies writing contest.

I LEANED AGAINST a wall, half-listening to the arguments being given by the members of the planning council. Not an official part of the council, I was among a group of twenty recruits from which the newest members of the council would be chosen. It had been my goal for several years to be involved in such planning. At the moment I alternated between boredom at the volley of arguments in front of me and worry at the fact that ten recruits had already been dismissed from an initial group of thirty. My head pressed into the wall, and as I focused all my energy into merely keeping my eyes open and looking awake, my mind began to wander . . .

"The goal of each individual is to have his own space; therefore, we should decrease the size of each room while increasing the total number of rooms," argued one member of the council.

"Large spaces should be placed under the authority of a qualified few who will then be in charge of partitioning these spaces and granting the resulting smaller spaces to those who have earned them," argued another.

Riveting arguments continued from each member of the council whose purpose was choosing the direction of further construction on the great structure in which we stood. Each claimed to have a better knowledge of, and commitment to, the foundations of the structure. Thus, each thought himself best suited to decide the direction that the structure would follow.

One of the other recruits, a good friend of mine, walked over beside me. After helping me hold up the wall for a few minutes, she pretended to scribble something on a piece of paper and handed it to me. Recruits were free to discuss ideas as long as we did not disturb the council. Even though the writing already on the paper was a different color than the ink in the pen she was waving over it, I went along with her charade. Her note read:

> I have been upset since the tenth recruit was dismissed. I am not sure if you are aware, but eight of the dismissed recruits have been female, while only two have been male. All eight of those dismissals were given a Code 12 justification . . .

I looked up from the paper, mentally shuffling through the pages of the recruit manual that I had supposedly memorized, trying to remember the section on dismissal justifications. All dismissals require an official justification so that no one can take personal advantage of his position of authority by eliminating recruits on improper grounds. Code 12 reads: "Unable to adequately detach oneself from one's particular position in the great structure." Those who cannot separate themselves, it was said, cannot possibly view the great structure objectively and are, consequently, unqualified to direct its future. Proud of my little memory exercise, I returned to reading the note:

> I do not think the council members have consciously acted unfairly. They were acting according to the rules, but the rules are the result of the dominant masculine character of the great structure. I wanted to approach you as one of the dwindling number of remaining female recruits and suggest that the four of us, along with any other women who want to join, leave the great structure and build a new structure.

I folded the note and put it in my shirt pocket, glancing at my friend who had walked to the other side of the room. During the last few years, my only dream had been to become a part of the planning of the great structure, and now she was suggesting that I rid myself of that goal. As I thought about what she had said, the focus in my eyes drew nearer, away from my friend to the council members standing between us, and finally to the floor directly in front of my feet.

The arguments faded into one another. Through the flood of ramble, I heard a voice break through that clearly did not come from anyone else in the room. It was a female voice, a voice that bypassed ears and went straight to my mind. It seemed to come from beyond the structure. Intrigued by my disinterest in the council, the voice invited me to the window. I opened it and leaned out a bit, happy to escape the weight of debating breath. The voice, speaking in its unmale tones, seemed to be gently pulling me out of the building. I was so refreshed that I stepped through the window onto the ledge. As I stood, I noticed the landscape. The view appeared to extend forever. All I could see was flat ground, not one other structure.

The voice seemed to be urging me to climb down. I slowly lowered myself to the ledge below, happy to be away from the other window and the sight of the council. If they had seen me gazing into nothing, my pride and any hope of a future position would have fallen off the ledge. As I secured my footing, I looked down and saw the ground beneath me. My legs began to shake in their attempt to describe to my brain the distance from the ground to the 1136th floor. Still the voice urged me on. I continued to climb down, pausing periodically to listen in a window.

". . . I should never act except in such a way that I can also will that my maxim should become a universal law . . ."[1] I heard through one of the windows. Ruleless, I climbed down.

". . . For you have but to follow and as it were hound nature in her wanderings, and you will be able when you like to lead and drive her afterward to the same place again. . . . Neither ought a man to make scruple of entering and penetrating into those holes and corners when the inquisition of truth is his whole object. . . ."[2] Without science, I climbed down.

". . . and the rib which the Lord God had taken from the man he made into a woman and brought her to the man. . . ."[3] Godless, I climbed down.

". . . My work is not a piece of writing to meet the taste of an immediate public, but was done to last forever. . . . "[4] Wordless, I climbed down.

". . . for all things are either contraries or composed of contraries, and unity and plurality are the starting-points of all contraries. . . ."[5] Without logic, I started to climb down but stopped when I noticed I was only about 10 feet from the ground. I was surprised at how terrifying it was to be this close to the ground. My legs began to shake more than they had at the top. I turned to climb back to the security of the 1137th floor while the voice tried to coax me down. Anxiety filled my head. I tried to fight the anxiety, but it proved to be stronger. Slowly I relaxed. I accepted the anxiety. I embraced the anxiety. I swam in the anxiety . . .

Emerging from the surface of the pond, I wiped the water from my eyes and tried to realize what had just happened. Sluggishly I concluded that I had fallen the last 10 feet or so. I swam to the edge of the water, pulled myself onto the ground, and sat on the flat surface. I turned to look at the great structure and quickly dropped my head, bringing my hands to my eyes again to wipe them dry. After a few moments, I took a deep breath and raised my eyes to the great structure again, hoping that the scene had changed. Looking at the great structure, which stretched for years and yards into the sky, I saw that it was floating off the ground. It is no wonder that there are so many arguments taking place over the true design of this imagined foundation. I laughed at the sight, and, as I jumped to my feet, my friend's note fell out of my pocket onto the ground. I thought to myself that this time was as good as any to start creating her new structure, so I grabbed a twig to sketch a rough blueprint in the dirt and thought about the form the new creation would take.

After a couple hours, the dirt remained undisturbed. I decided to stop planning and just start building. I grabbed some loose boards dangling from the bottom of the great structure, carried them to the opposite side of the pond, and jammed them into the ground. Using the branches of a nearby tree, I began building the new structure. I built excitedly, not stopping until my muscles ached. I rested atop my structure thinking of how proud my friend would be if she were present. Feeling quite proud myself, I hopped off the top of my creation to get a better look. I walked around each side looking it over from top to bottom and was surprised at how familiar it looked. "Maybe it's just familiar because it is a reflection of myself," I said.

When I positioned myself so that my creation was between me and the great structure, I understood the sense of familiarity. The similarity between my creation and the great structure was remarkable. I had failed where I had tried to create a feminine counterpart to the masculine values that I had passed in the great structure. My counterpart had the same form as the masculine form which I was trying to avoid. I had failed to overcome those aspects of the great structure which I thought should be absent completely. During my creating, they had worked themselves into my creation without my knowing it.

With great displeasure in my creativity, I began making modifications anywhere I could. But my renovations were interrupted by the screams of women echoing between my ears. They were the cries of women being raped and robbed in a home that was not their own. These women were assaulted, not by powerful hands, but by truth-claiming lips that attacked them early, gaining control over them before they were able to question. The rapists were quick to teach them before they could learn. My head pounded as my thoughts crashed into one another. "All right! I'll go back!"

I stepped to the ground and gazed at my creation, which appeared to be nothing more than a miniature model of the great structure, and began to understand why I had failed. How was I supposed to avoid the form of the masculine components of the great structure if I had only these masculine components through which to define their feminine counterparts? In order to build the counterparts, I had to first create the masculine structure that would define them. I was glad my friend had given me the motivation to try to get beyond these cultural building blocks, but I was wrong to think that I could actually succeed in getting beyond them.

I reached into my creation, ripped a board from its structure, and rested it on my shoulder. Then with a grin and one swing, I sent the little imitation tumbling to my feet. Stepping through clouds of dust, I took a drink of water from the pond and walked to the great structure. As I walked I thought that perhaps my friend and I were wrong to think that the only answer to the problems she expressed was to create a completely new structure. I will climb back up the great structure past logic, language, religion, science, and morality, accepting each, but as though I am accepting a gift from a stranger. Instead of creating a structure with new building blocks, I will return to my pursuit of council membership, where I will be in a position to carefully examine each building block of the great structure. "Sisters," I'll say, "we are stuck with these hand-me-downs. . . ."

Pulling myself up using a couple of dangling boards, I begin my ascent back to the 1137th floor. Standing at the point that had terrified me not long ago, a mere 10 feet from the ground, I wonder how the women whose screams had interrupted my own creation will respond to what I will tell them. Will they ignore me? Will they step out the nearest window looking to build a creation of their own, trying to succeed where I failed? Or will they remain in the great structure accepting it as a given material and trying to iron out its wrinkles?

NOTES

1. Immanuel Kant, "Grounding for the Metaphysics of Morals," in *Classics of Moral and Political Theory*, ed. Michael L. Morgan (Indianapolis: Hackett Publishing Company, 1992), 1001.
2. Frances Bacon, quoted in Sandra Harding, *The Science Question in Feminism* (Ithaca: Cornell University Press, 1986), 237.
3. Genesis 2:22. *The Oxford Annotated Bible with the Apocrypha.*
4. Thucydides, *History of the Peloponnesian War*, ed. Betty Radice, trans. Rex Warner (New York: Penguin, 1988), 48.
5. Aristotle, "Metaphysics," in *The Basic Works of Aristotle*, ed. Richard McKeon (New York: Random House, 1941), 735.

STUDY QUESTIONS
1. Is it accurate to describe knowledge as a great structure resting on certain fundamental beliefs?
2. The recruit in the story discovers that he or she has only a masculine structure through which to define a feminine structure. What does the recruit mean? To what kinds of knowledge might this statement apply?
3. Is it possible for us to step outside our structure and build a new one from the ground up? When might we be called to do so?

How Does Nature Speak to Our Concern? The Case of Montana's Rocky Mountain Front

Scott Friskics

Scott Friskics teaches in the Natural Resources Program at Fort Belknap College, a tribally controlled community college located on the Fort Belknap Indian Reservation in north central Montana. His academic interests in environmental ethics, environmental justice, and wilderness studies reflect a simple desire to think clearly about issues that arise during his daily life. He wrote this essay in his cabin on the edge of Montana's Bob Marshall Wilderness Complex.

> *How does nature speak to our concern? That is the question.*
> —HENRY BUGBEE

IT'S A LATE AFTERNOON in mid-March and I'm standing outside my friends' house on the southwest edge of Augusta, Montana, a small town of about 500 residents. I'm here to meet a companion who's headed out from Great Falls to spend the weekend at my cabin, which is located up in the mountains approximately 20 miles west of here. As is often the case, I'm a bit early for our rendezvous. Blame it on unbridled anticipation or a latent preoccupation with punctuality, but my premature arrival offers me a few stolen moments of enforced inactivity with which I can revel in the sensory fullness of a pleasant, pre-spring afternoon.

Out here on the plains, spring seems much nearer at hand—a distinct and imminent possibility—than it does back up in the mountains. The air's still cool and the wind still bites, but the warm afternoon sun embraces me and unlocks a host of smells long-held in winter's freeze: earthy mud puddles, sweet horse manure, damp hay.

While waiting, I wander over to the nearby corral to greet three gentle, mud-splattered horses. As I absently rub their chins and stroke their long, slender noses, I gaze out beyond the horses, out beyond the soupy corral, beyond the expanse of wrinkled, sere, brown plains. My eyes focus on the blue-shadowed wall of mountains from which I've just emerged: Montana's Rocky Mountain Front. From this vantage point, the Front presents itself as a horizon-filling tidal wave of rock—fluid, walking mountains that, over the course of their long march through time, have been thrust skyward and pushed eastward to where their eastern-most reefs and ridges now hang precipitously over the wide expanse of the northern Great Plains.

Dead center in my line of vision stands the tilted summit of Crown Mountain—the univocal, eloquent peak that towers about the narrow mountain valley where I live, provides me with the ultimate spatial reference point for my life, and fills my days with the gracious bounty of its abiding presence. From here, however, Crown Mountain presents itself to me not so much as a soloist, but rather as one voice in a chorus of mountain song. Working southward from this orienting center, I encounter Crown Mountain's nameless twin and the rocky ridge line descending to Welcome Pass, above the notch of which rises the deceptively unassuming head of the Scapegoat Massif. Much nearer at hand and dominating the foreground stands the dark cone of Haystack Butte—an intrusive igneous island in a sea of sedimentary mountains. Farther south runs the high ridge guarding the headwaters of the Dearborn River, with Steamboat Mountain rising above the rugged country drained by Elk Creek, Blubber Creek, Falls Creek, Cuniff Creek.

Working northward from the crown, the mountains are no less spectacular, no less evocative: the slanting summit of Fairview Mountain, the jagged gray wall of Sawtooth Ridge, the low gap of Sun Canyon (where the united Sun River flows out onto the plains and benches of central Montana), and, framing the canyon to its north, the flattened rock face of Castle Reef. Looking north and west through the notch of Sun Canyon, I catch a glimpse of the spectacular series of alternating ridges and valleys running north to south behind Castle Reef like the crests and troughs of repeating ocean waves. And, finally, framing the north edge of my vista lies the rising bulk of Ear Mountain. Of course, standing here in Augusta I'm well aware that what I can see from this spot is less than half of the Front, so my imagination continues north to Blackleaf Canyon, the Birch Creek country, the Badger-Two Medicine, the east slopes of Glacier National Park, and that holy border sentinel, Chief Mountain.

I first saw this glorious stretch of country on a blustery November day fourteen years ago, and I have yet to encounter another place that speaks to me with such force and beauty, such overwhelming, undeniable eloquence. And, on this soul-stirring March afternoon, the Rocky Mountain Front resounds in my heart like a full symphonic choir. My companion's car pulls up behind me, we greet each other, load up the truck, and head west into the heart of these singing, shining mountains.

That the beings and things of nature (not just mountains, but also rivers, Douglas firs, bears, goldeneye ducks, pasqueflowers, snowshoe hares) speak to us at all is a source of great wonder. And that we, on occasion, are so attuned that the fullness of their speech resonates in our hearts—this is nothing short of miraculous. As we attend to the call of our fellow creatures, engage them as presences, and respond to their evocative speech in a spirit of mutuality and respect, our relations with them take on the character of a dialogue. These encounters are truly sacred, sacramental events. They offer us signs of grace that sanctify us and make our world a holy place. As we celebrate the sacrament of dialogue, Presence is made manifest and dwells among us (between us), "full of grace and truth" (John 1:14).

But this is only half the story. Undoubtedly, a few of my less priestly, more prophetic readers, those brass tacks activists for whom I have great respect, are asking, "So what?" "Talking with mountains, rivers and squirrels is fine and dandy, but spare us the touchy-feely details. While you're out chatting with rocks and critters, the world's going to hell and the environment's a mess. People (usually poor, rarely white) are being poisoned; species are going extinct; air, land, and water in every corner of the globe bear the stains of our gluttonous, myopic, selfish society. Please don't bother us with accounts of your poesy-sniffing; there's work to do." Or, to make the same point in gentler terms, some less sympathetic readers might view such notions of dialogue as nothing more than what Gabriel Marcel disparagingly refers to as "a pure mysticism of presence," a posture he views as quite irrelevant unless it is accompanied by "the proper ethical bearing" (1958, 24).

Such objections point to a very real danger—an idolatry—that we (that I!) cannot afford to overlook. We must never forget that the celebration of the sacraments *always* carries a commission. We are sent forth *from* the celebration *to* embody its grace and truth in our everyday lives. Similarly, we are sent forth from the sacramental intercourse of dialogue with the task, the commission, to actualize the knowledge and meaning received in these encounters in our lives and in our actions. For, as we meet our fellow creatures in moments of dialogue, they address us in ways that make claims on us and call forth our active response. They place us in a position of undeniable and potentially liberating responsibility. There is a vital rhythm here: sacrament and commission, call and response, dialogue and responsibility. In each case, the latter hinges on the former, which provides the experiential source for genuine piety, wholehearted response, and ethical responsibility, respectively.

So, it's not just that nature speaks to us, but that she speaks *to our concern*. Nature's creatures speak to us in ways that are ethically decisive, in ways that call us to care, elicit our respect and compassion, and empower us to respond to their claims with conviction and a sense of necessity. Through our participation in dialogue, we come to recognize the value of our fellow creatures and catch a glimpse of the meaning of our co-creaturely coexistence, which, taken together, can inform our lives and actions with a sense of finality, purpose, and vocational integrity. So, it seems to me that Henry Bugbee's question, which I quoted at the beginning of this essay, is indeed *the* question for environmental ethics. How does nature speak to our concern? How does nature call forth our respect and compassion? And, consequently, what grounds a truly ethical response to nature and her creatures? How do we practice ethical responsibility with respect to— and for—the beings and things we meet?

As a point of departure, consider the nature of the "word" our fellow creatures speak to us. As Emmanuel Levinas explains, "The essence of the 'word' does not initially consist in its objective meaning or descriptive possibilities, but in the response that it elicits" (1967, 142). The basic word of address spoken by the beings and things we meet should not be confused with some specific information about them. Our knowledge of the other, received in the moment of dialogue, is not on the order of an empirical or objective "knowing about." In fact, the notion of objectivity is altogether beside the point here. According to Bugbee, our capacity to act in an ethical manner (and to reflect on the point of ethical action) is a decidedly "meta-objective" affair, where we "move in a dimension of meaning over which we cannot exercise the power of representation and control that obtains with respect to things in taking them as objects" (1958, 55). Quite simply, objects don't speak to our concern; they can't claim our responsibility.

This isn't to say that object knowledge about our fellow creatures is unnecessary or unimportant; just the opposite is true. Scientific and technical knowledge about things, about how the world works, and about the possible consequences of our actions are terribly useful and important. In our attempts to reduce suffering and waste, and to promote justice and healing, such knowledge comes in very handy. In fact, it is absolutely indispensable in helping us *enact* and *implement* our concern. But it does not sponsor, sustain, or guide our concern. By definition, our object knowledge of the world is a detached form of knowing that removes us from our immediate involvement in moments of mutual encounter and dialogue. In his essay entitled "On Starting with Love," Bugbee explains it this way:

> Now objectivity is a stance in which we abstract from the evocative way
> in which the beings we represent to ourselves are present as holding
> concrete meaning for us. It is a kind of deliberate detachment from the

mutuality of existence. . . . (T)he explicit rendering of meaning co-ordinate with the stance in objectivity abstracts from the mutuality of existence between oneself and the beings thus being taken into account. Likewise abstraction is made from the concern but for which we could not be called upon by anything to render what is called for with respect to it. (1966, 7)

Ironically, given its privileged epistemological position in our society, object knowledge is, by itself, a directionless, meaningless knowledge. The deliverance of meaning in our lives and the grounding of our concern for others cannot be accounted for from the standpoint of objectivity—of a subject studying, analyzing, classifying, and/or manipulating objects. Just knowing about the Rocky Mountain Front—its extent and geography, its history and geology, the names of its mountains and valleys, a list of the various plants and animals that call it home—isn't enough to make me care about it. Object knowledge about the world cannot serve as the animating, sponsoring ground of ethical action. While often enriching, clarifying, and illuminating, all the object knowledge in the world can't make us respect and love a place and its inhabitants.

And yet, it is precisely such respect and love that ground our concern and that provide the foundation for ethically responsible action. As Aldo Leopold wrote, "It is inconceivable to me that an ethical relation to land can exist without love, respect, and admiration for land" (1966, 261). If we are to love, respect, and admire the land and its creatures, we must come to know them in ways that are altogether different than the way we come to know about these things in taking them as objects. Our dialogical encounters with our fellow creatures provide us with just such knowledge; in dialogue, we come to know them—albeit always partially, that is to say, humanly—in ways that speak to our capacity for respect, love, and admiration. In these encounters, we receive an immediate and participatory knowledge, not about, but of the other, something along the lines of the old Hebraic notion of "to know"—to contact, to touch, or to intercourse with the other, as in "Adam knew Eve" or "God knew Hosea." Martin Buber describes such knowledge in the following manner:

(T)he original meaning of the Hebrew verb "to recognise, to know," in distinction from Western languages, belongs, not to the sphere of reflection but to that of contact. The decisive event for "knowing" in biblical Hebrew is not that one looks at an object, but that one comes into touch with it. This basic difference is developed in the realm of a relation of the soul to other beings, where the fact of mutuality changes everything. At the centre is not a perceiving of one another, but the contact of being, intercourse. (1953, 56)

In intimacy with things, we come to know them in terms altogether different from that of form and function, space and time, cause and effect, genus and species. Their primal word speaks to us, touches us, and moves us at the depths of our being. Met in dialogue, our fellow creatures speak to our concern and elicit the respect, love, and admiration that Leopold recognized as so essential to any kind of (land) ethic. Quite simply, our deep and enduring concern for things grows out of contact with them.

For many people, the Rocky Mountain Front evokes love at first sight, or better, love at first touch. One hike or one pack trip may provide the contact needed to spark a lifetime of concern. For me, however, it's taken a little longer. Maybe it's just that I'm slow by nature, or that I've picked up a certain debilitating wariness when it comes to matters of the heart, but I need repeated contact and sustained intimacy to loosen my love and respect and to foster a genuine sense of commitment. So, ever since 1994, I've been courting the Front, roaming this country with all the exclusive devotion of the hopelessly love struck. During this time, I've strolled along dozens of its river valleys and creek bottoms, rambled over many a ridge line, and climbed a host of its passes and peaks. And even though I'm still an infant in this country, it's made its mark on me and I feel like I'm getting to know it a little bit. What's more, this peripatetic knowledge has sponsored and nurtured my deepest respect and love for this place and its inhabitants. For the Front is not just mountains and rocks. It's also the rivers, creeks, waterfalls, pools and riffles, the grizzlies and humans, goats and sheep, eagles and ouzels, bear grass and balsam root—the parts and sum total of this community, what I mean by a place, what Leopold means by "land." To know the land through the holy intercourse of dialogue is to know the land as warranting deep and abiding concern; I cannot help but care, and care deeply.

And yet, if my response to the manifold and aggregate voice of the Rocky Mountain Front were just a personal, private matter, there wouldn't be much point in my writing—or your reading—this essay. Who wants to read a stranger's love letters? And besides, maybe it's just me; maybe I'm just odd, prone to hearing voices in the woods and on mountaintops?

But it's not just me. Thousands of other people have similarly found themselves addressed by these evocative mountains, and when called on to do so, they have eloquently testified to the love, respect, and admiration engendered in their encounters with the Rocky Mountain Front. Here are a few brief examples of their testimony:

"I recently participated in the Rocky Mountain summer program
through San Francisco State in which I backpacked for six weeks all over
this area. This was my first time in Montana and I have just fallen in love
with this country. It is the most wild country I have ever been in and it is

my wish that it stay that way. There was such a special feeling emanating from this whole area. . . . This is a special place."

"I moved to Montana 4-1/2 years ago, drawn here equally by my work and its location—the proximity to the Rocky Mountains. . . . In all this time my most memorable hike, the day that stands out most vividly in my mind, was a September weekend two years ago when I climbed Mount Wright. It was one of those rare days when the sky was crystal clear and I could see vast distances from Mt. Wright's peak. The utter, stunning, undeveloped beauty I could see along the Front clear up to the Badger, across the Bob past the Chinese Wall to who knows how far was breathtaking. I delighted in the myriad possibilities of adventure and spiritual renewal that spread themselves before me. Completely immersed in the natural beauty surrounding me, I knew at that moment that it was the Front that I wanted to explore and get to know."

"My family homesteaded along the Front back in the 19th century and lived there until the 1950s. The root cellar still stands. The graves of my ancestors are here, and my father's ashes are scattered in the Bob Marshall Wilderness. The Rocky Mountain Front is sacred land to me and my family" (Public Comment 1996).

These three statements typify the various ways many people describe their feelings for, and relation to, the Front. They speak of contact and encounter—either for the first time, over the course of a lifetime, or even across generations. They speak of a certain way of knowing this particular place, a knowledge that, despite an uncanny, ineffable quality, conveys an indwelling sense of beauty, specialness, sacredness, and wildness.

For others, however, the sight of the Rocky Mountain Front has elicited a very different response. For the past 25 years or so, the oil and gas industry has had its eye on the Front, too, as well as on the protected lands of the Bob Marshall Wilderness extending to the west. And with good reason: According to the United States Forest Service, the area "has high potential for the occurrence of hydrocarbons," although they're quick to qualify this statement by adding that "there are differing opinions on specific estimates of the amount of hydrocarbon resources" (Lewis and Clark National Forest 1997, 5). The Forest Service has, in fact, offered some oil and gas leases on the Front—most infamously, within the Badger-Two Medicine, a highly disputed area of ceded land adjoining the Blackfeet Indian Reservation and of great cultural significance to many Pikuni tribal members. Some exploratory drilling and development have occurred. However, up until now, the vast majority of the Front has been spared the impacts and fragmentation of large scale oil and gas development.

In compliance with the National Forest Management Act, the Lewis and Clark National Forest (the forest charged with administering U.S. Forest Service lands on the Front) completed its National Forest Land and Resource Management Plan (Forest Plan) in 1986. This plan was developed to direct the management of forest lands and resources, including oil and gas, for the next 15–20 years.

However, the Forest Plan did not specify exactly which lands on the forest would be available for oil and gas leasing. To determine that, the Lewis and Clark Forest reinitiated the National Environmental Policy Act process to prepare an Environmental Impact Statement (EIS) that would examine the potential impacts of alternative oil and gas development scenarios on the forest. Beginning with an initial scoping period in 1994, the Environmental Impact Statement took over three years to complete, culminating (except for court challenges) in the Forest Supervisor's Final Record of Decision in September 1997.

As the decisive document in a very high-profile, extremely contentious issue, the oil and gas EIS drew a huge amount of public interest; over 1,400 written comments were submitted on the Draft EIS alone, as well as hundreds of statements made during six public hearings. According to the Forest Service, "The vast majority of those responding to the Draft EIS were strongly against *any* (emphasis mine) development for the purpose of oil and gas exploration in the Lewis and Clark National Forest, particularly on the Rocky Mountain Front" (Lewis and Clark National Forest 1997, 4–5).

Still, when the Final EIS came out, the authors recommended Alternative 7 as the preferred course of action, a compromise position that would allow for limited oil and gas leasing on the Front. Specifically, the Forest Service would offer leases along already-roaded corridors in Blackleaf Canyon, as well as Elk Creek, Cuniff Basin, and Falls Creek southwest of Augusta. In addition, Alternative 7 allowed for directional drilling leases along a one-mile wide strip of land on the forest's eastern boundary.

For the vast majority of people who opposed any oil and gas development on the Front, Alternative 7 was a major disappointment. So, once again, this very large and vocal segment of the population voiced its opposition to Alternative 7 and demanded stronger protection for the Front. And, in what should be remembered as a truly historic decision, the Forest Service listened to this public outcry. In her final decision, then-Supervisor of the Lewis and Clark Forest, Gloria Flora, selected, not Alternative 7, but Alternative 1—the "No Action" alternative that is included in all Environmental Impact Statements as a way of defining one extreme in the range of management options the various alternatives offer. In this instance, Alternative 1 meant *no lands* would be offered for oil and gas leasing along the Rocky Mountain Front during the entire management period for which the current Forest Plan remains in effect (another 10–15 years).

Why the switch? As Ms. Flora explains in her Final Record of Decision, she took three things into account when making her decision: the Lewis and Clark Forest Plan, the Final Environmental Impact Statement, and the public comment she received throughout the entire process. She writes, "I made my decision based on an evaluation of the alternatives to determine which best meets the project purpose and need, and resource objectives, while also responding to the public issues and concerns expressed throughout the project" (Lewis and Clark National Forest 1997, 3). Nothing unusual here—standard bureaucratic fare.

It's only when Ms. Flora begins to summarize "the public's issues and concerns" that things get interesting. Speaking about the comments she received opposing any oil and gas development along the Front (including the three testimonials I cited earlier in this essay), she says:

> A majority of the concerns . . . were expressed regarding the "value of place," speaking in particular to social and personal values attributed to the Front. It is clear that this is a very unique and special place to many people, both those who live here in Montana as well as those who have visited or only heard about the area. Many of those who commented during the process admitted they have not read the environmental analysis and many may not fully understand—or care to understand— the analysis. They simply want to express heartfelt emotions about a place they consider special. Many feel that development of any kind, particularly oil and gas development, would "ruin" the special feeling of the Front, regardless of whether they ever saw or experienced the results of development. Their perceptions about the value and spirituality of a place would be affected. (Lewis and Clark National Forest 1997, 5)

I applaud Ms. Flora's decision, and I especially appreciate her willingness to take these comments of the heart so seriously. As I'll soon suggest, these testimonies represent more than a simple flood of emotions and eco-sentimentalism; they bear witness to a deep concern, a concern born, in large part, of intimate contact with an overwhelmingly eloquent place. Of course, the oil and gas industry feels differently. They took the Lewis and Clark Forest to court (and lost) because they felt Ms. Flora's decision gave undue weight to public comment—too much public meddling in the management of public lands, democracy run amuck.

Earlier, when I presented my three samples of the public comment received on the Draft Environmental Impact Statement, I only offered fragments culled from larger, complete testimonies. These people were not just writing to express their affection for a place; they offered accounts of their encounters and experiences to provide the very basis for their opposition to oil and gas leasing on the Front. Each of the three testimonies cited earlier concludes with a heartfelt plea to prevent oil and gas leasing in the area. What follows is a composite of testimony gleaned from the public record that likewise speaks to the necessity of saying no to such development.

> "I am writing this letter because of my deep concern and great love for the wild lands that still remain on the Front" . . . "I am writing you because I care deeply about the wild country and wildlife of the Rocky Mountain Front area of Montana, and because I am greatly concerned about the draft oil and gas EIS that your agency has prepared." . . . "Scared and worried about this proposition, I felt impelled to write to you and urge you not to lease this land." . . . "I can't miss the opportunity to speak out in behalf of the Front that I have loved for so many years. . . . As I hold this area dearly in my heart, I was hoping for a strong NO decision and one with no compromises." . . . "It is with regret that I learned the beautiful wilderness I love is in jeopardy. . . . I urge all concerned to protect these lands. Do not make leasing available in Montana's Rocky Mountain Front." . . . "I can't imagine even considering opening this sacred area to development." . . . "To open the proposed area to oil and gas would be a sin." ... "I am a lover and a fighter and for the love of this land and this creation I will fight." . . . "[A]t certain moments in one's life, one must take a stand and be heard." . . . "In such times one needs to stop and listen to one's heart, to do what's right and take a stand for the protection and safeguard of what you have been given responsibility of. . . . There are great gifts in life deserving the highest reverence simply for what they are." . . . "With the help of a few good horses and a pair of extremely tattered hiking boots, I'm very proud to say I have encountered nearly every marked trail in the three wilderness areas bordering the Front, as well as the Forest Service land adjacent. I do not speak to you from afar—I know this land—its mountains, streams, wildlife—all of it. From this perspective I ask you— save it! ... Don't lease the Front." (Public Comment 1996)

So, let's rephrase Bugbee's original question in the context of this particular situation: How do the Rocky Mountain Front and its inhabitants (including its human inhabitants) speak to our concern? Clearly, the speech of this place communicates more than mere information, offers more than just an aggregate of objects to study and enjoy, or resources to manipulate and use. It's a speech that carries evocative power, eliciting our concern, calling forth our committed response, and informing our actions with a compelling sense of necessity.

It's not just that the Front is a special place *to me* or *to you*, or that I'll be sad if a drilling pad occupies a favorite hiking spot or mars my view from town.

Such a subjectivist twist is wholly unwarranted, nothing more than a deliberate attempt to dismiss our testimonies of concern as somehow self-interested and selfish. But, in truth, that dismissal is just as crass, and inaccurate, as saying that the reason I don't want my parents to be victimized by burglars is that it might reduce the amount of my inheritance. I readily admit that my concern for the Front is deeply personal and necessarily anthropogenic (after all, I'm only human); however, it need not be egocentric nor anthropocentric. Ethical responsibility means responding *to* the claims of our fellows (mountains, rivers, birds, trees, humans, flowers) *from* out of the respect and love they call forth from us and foster within us. It involves the enactment of *my* concern *for*—and commitment *to*—the other.

Along with the deep concern and commitment expressed by so many people in their testimonies on behalf of the Front, one also hears an unmistakable urgency in their words. "This is it"; "It's our last chance"; "Everything's on the line here." Oftentimes, this sense of urgency is framed in terms of the Front's uniqueness, which is usually pointed out through comparisons between the relatively undeveloped state of Montana's Rocky Mountain Front and the present state of the Colorado Front Range or Alberta's derrick-and-road-riddled Front. As members of a society that Loren Eiseley dubbed the "world eaters," such comparisons are worth considering (1970); indeed, places like the Front gain increasing value in a world where so little remains that hasn't been gobbled up and/or radically transformed by our society's "lust for overrunning reality" (Buber 1966, 65). And yet, the real ethical urgency is for *this* place, *these* grizzlies, *these* bighorn sheep, *these* creeks and rivers. The outcome of the oil and gas Environmental Impact Statement and Ms. Flora's subsequent decision is of vital import. People's words and actions reflect this recognition of "finality" (Bugbee 1958). Their loud and unified "NO" bespeaks a certain sense of necessity in action: I *must* respond in this way; it *must* not be otherwise.

So, it seems that in our decisive and meaningful encounters with the beings and things of the natural world, in this case the Rocky Mountain Front and its inhabitants, we come to know them in a way that speaks to our hearts. The tactile knowledge received in these moments of dialogical intercourse carries with it a sense of both the nature and meaning of our co-creaturely being-together. In dialogue, we come to know those whom we meet as both other and kin. To use Buber's famous relational typology for a moment, that which touches me—and which I touch—is neither "I," nor is it/she/he "It." It/She/He is not merely an object to be experienced, used, and manipulated according to my subjective interests and desires. It/She/He is not me; I cannot appropriate, acquire or possess it/her/him. Instead, as a being becomes present to me in the moment of encounter, I meet it/her/him as "Thou" ("You," the familiar *Du* in German)—one who is irreducibly and non-negotiably other, but whom I can nonetheless meet, touch, and therefore know as a partner in mutual dialogue, a fellow creature, a co-participant in the ongoing process of creation (Buber 1970). Needless to say, all of this requires a bit of unpacking.

In dialogue, we come to know the other as other. On these occasions, the voice of the other resonates within us in all of its singular and uncanny otherness. For me, the speech of Crown Mountain, Sawtooth Ridge, or the Scapegoat Massif proclaim, above all else, an awesome sense of otherness. And yet, it is precisely this resounding otherness that commands my attention, compels my response, and makes ethical claims on me. The beings and things of nature (including our fellow humans) are indeed other, but they are other in such a way that they can be met. And, as we come to meet them as independent partners in dialogue, we come to know them as fellow creatures—kin.

Recognized as other, we acknowledge beings and things as existing in their own right, fully independent of our purposes, desires, and intentions. So while we remain keenly attentive and intently interested in the particular others we meet, our interest is rendered, in a deeply moral sense, disinterested. For Bugbee, such disinterested interest is akin to respect (see Bugbee 1953 for details). We respect others to the degree that we acknowledge their otherness and take up with them in their own right and on their own terms—terms articulated in their self-speaking address as it comes to us in moments of dialogue. And so, as Bugbee points out, respect goes hand in hand with "leaving things be," where, "By 'leaving things be' I do not mean inaction; I mean respecting things, being still in the presence of things, letting them speak" (1958, 155). To let others present themselves (and to meet their presence with our full presence), to listen attentively to what they have to say, to allow them the space to flourish, and to actively encourage and promote their flourishing—these are all ways in which we show respect. Conversely, to ignore others, to fail to take them seriously or give them the consideration they deserve, to interrupt them, to silence them, or to hinder their growth—these are all terribly disrespectful ways to act. In addition, we show disrespect when we distort the self-speaking otherness of things by reducing them to mere objects, tools, or resources that we manipulate and use to gain our own ends, fulfill our own interests, and achieve our purposive agendas. Here, we simply twist their word to fit our needs, wants, and desires; our interest in them is not disinterested, but deeply self-interested.

So, what might it mean to show respect to a place like the Rocky Mountain Front? In general, it means following Bugbee's advice—"Be still in its presence": bracket our interests and listen to the eloquent speech of the place as it speaks of itself and in its own right; "Let it speak": don't translate its self-speaking address into the terms of our instrumentality, reducing it to one more resource to be exploited according to the language of humanly conferred values. It means fighting any attempts to compromise, distort, or silence its speech, and it means allowing it to continue speaking in the eloquent fullness of its integrity, stability, and beauty (to use the three primary criteria offered in Leopold's famous "key-log" statement or "preservation principle"; 1966, 262). Specifically, it means not opening it up to oil and gas (or hard rock mineral) development.

As kin, our fellow creatures call forth our respectful response. At the same time, this kinship conveys a sense of affinity, an intimacy that engenders and sustains our compassion and love. As we come into the self-speaking presence of our fellows, we meet someone/something who is, at root, like ourselves. In the intimacy of dialogue our fellows call forth our deepest affective response, and we hear God's injunction in Leviticus 19:18—"Love your neighbor as one like yourself"—with all the freshness and authority of that day on Mt. Sinai long ago. We re-discover the truth of another compelling ethical precept in and through our immediate encounters with our fellow beings. As Buber reminds us, "Genuine responsibility exists only where there is real responding" (1965, 16).

Each creature speaks in a voice wholly unique to itself and evokes in each of us a unique response. Crown Mountain, for example, speaks, above all else, of its radical, lithic otherness and calls forth from me a respect that grades into sheer awe. A similarly powerful otherness resounds in the flood-swollen waters of the South Fork of the Sun River in early summer, or in the crazed daytime stare of a great gray owl. Clearly, otherness holds sway here, but it's an otherness that calls out to me, touches me, meets me; in meeting, I come to know these beings as ones who command my respect and claim my concern. At the same time, other beings whom I meet speak more to our co-creaturely affinity, and their speech strikes the chords of my compassion. The *Calypso* orchids that bloom outside my cabin each May, the enduring limber pines standing watch along the windswept ridge line of Red Creek, or the water ouzels (dippers) bobbing, diving, and darting up and down Ford Creek—these and many kindred others come to mind here. And then there are the bears—whether seen barreling across a hillside or sitting back on haunches and sniffing the air to find me, or met as an enduring presence in fresh paw prints in the dust or berry-filled scat along the trail—for whom such terms as "respect" and "compassion" seem so woefully tame. Here, a wild, exuberant otherness speaks in tandem with a certain mammalian familiarity, a compelling bond of likeness-in-the-face-of-difference.

But really, all this talk of proportions seems like so much hair-splitting. Respect without love becomes arid, and love without respect runs the risk of becoming appropriative and consumptive. At some point, respect and love blend together. In fact, the particularities of my experiences among the mountains of the Rocky Mountain Front, while of utmost importance to me on a personal level are really incidental to the broader issue at hand. Which is this: The beings and things of nature do speak to us; they address us in ways that elicit our respect and love, and that cry out for the actualization of that respect and love in concrete instances of respectful and loving action. Through our participation in, and reflection on, mutual encounters with self-speaking creatures, we catch a glimpse of the experiential ground of our genuine concern for them and discover the animating and empowering source of our responsibility to them. As Leopold so clearly understood, this is the place where (land) ethics begins. In his essay, "The Land Ethic," he writes, "We can be ethical only in relation to something we can see, feel, understand, love, or otherwise have faith in" (1966, 251).

With a knowledge and certainty born of sustained contact with the being and things of the Rocky Mountain Front, I know that these mountains ought not—no, *must* not—be opened up to oil and gas (or mineral) development. Out of respect and love for the Front, we—I—must remain vigilant and active. As Ms. Flora's Final Record of Decision makes abundantly clear, the lands of the Rocky Mountain Front remain "administratively available for [oil and gas] leasing" (Lewis and Clark National Forest 1997); they're just not being offered for leasing *at this time*—the time remaining on the current Lewis and Clark National Forest Plan, about 15 years. This decision, for all its importance, is a temporary, stop-gap measure. It is only a moratorium, suspending oil and gas leasing *for now*. The issue will arise again, and we must be ready to answer the renewed challenges with conviction and enduring commitment. In a society driven by a fanatical obsession with growth and progress for their own sake (bigger is better; more is better), nothing requires more work than the ongoing struggle to respect things by leaving them be and letting them speak.

REFERENCES
Buber, M. *Good and Evil: Two Interpretations*. Trans. R.G. Smith and M. Bullock. New York: Charles Scribner's Sons, 1953.
Buber, M. *Between Man and Man*. Ed. and trans. M. Friedman. New York: Macmillan, 1965.
Buber, M. *The Origin and Meaning of Hasidism*. Trans. M. Friedman. New York: Harper & Row, 1966.
Buber, M. *I and Thou*. Trans. W. Kaufmann. New York: Charles Scribner's Sons, 1970.
Bugbee, H. "The Moment of Obligation in Experience." *Journal of Religion* 33 (1953): 1–15.
Bugbee, H. *The Inward Morning: A Philosophical Exploration in Journal Form*. State College, PA: Bald Eagle Press, 1958.
Bugbee, H. "On Starting with Love." Typescript V, 1–19. Orig. pub. in *Humanitas* 11 (2), 1966.
Eiseley, L. *The Invisible Pyramid: A Naturalist Analyses the Rocket Century*. New York: Charles Scribner's Sons, 1970.
Jones, A., ed., *The Jerusalem Bible*. Garden City, NY: Doubleday, 1968.
Leopold, A. *A Sand County Almanac: With Essays on Conservation from Round River*. New York: Ballantine Books, 1966.
Levinas, E. "Martin Buber and the Theory of Knowledge." In *The Philosophy of Martin Buber*, ed. P.A. Schilpp and M. Friedman. LaSalle, IL: Open Court Press, 1967.
Lewis and Clark National Forest Oil and Gas Leasing Final Environmental Impact Statement Record of Decision. Prepared by United States Department of Agriculture–Forest Service, Lewis and Clark National Forest. Great Falls, Montana, 1997.
Marcel, G. Introduction to Henry Bugbee, *The Inward Morning: A Philosophical Exploration in Journal Form* (1958): 25–39. State College, PA: Bald Eagle Press.
Public Comment on the Lewis and Clark National Forest Oil and Gas Leasing Draft Environmental Impact Statement. Compiled by United States Department of Agriculture—Forest Service, Lewis and Clark National Forest. Great Falls, Montana, 1996.

STUDY QUESTIONS
1. Have you experienced being "spoken to" by nature? How have you responded?
2. What does Friskics mean by "participatory" or "dialogical" knowing?
3. When is objective "knowing about" more appropriate than participatory knowing?

PART IV

Metaphysics: Glimpses Beyond Physical Reality

Introduction

BY DEFINITION, IT might at first seem that we cannot relate metaphysics to everyday experience. The term "metaphysics" refers to theories about what is beyond physical reality. Yet every once in a while, an ordinary experience leaves us with an intuition that there is more to life than what we can perceive with our five senses.

Some people say they experience God; some have an uncanny sense that a very different life is within their reach if they could just figure out how to choose it; others see something so unexpected that they begin to question their whole sense of reality. The authors of the essays in this section describe these sorts of experiences and the philosophical thoughts to which they lead.

In "Philosophy Out of the Cave," Christopher Miles Michaelson questions the need to go beyond our everyday experiences in order to find life's deepest meanings. For there is enough sensory stimulation, enough deep emotions, in everyday living to satisfy his soul. He juxtaposes an abstract philosophy lesson indoors with a glorious spring afternoon on the grass by a lake with a fellow student he admires, and raises the question: In which of these two settings would you find the meaning of life?

In "Confessions of a Recovering Rationalist," Judith Presler recalls her childhood days when she would not believe the words of others—unless she had experienced something herself and could give a rational explanation of it. Gradually, however, she came to see that some of her most profound experiences of passion or of moral commitment were not subject to rational explanation. Instead, these experiences made it possible for her to be rational because they made her care. They made it possible for her to identify ideals of goodness to live up to. She now finds herself a spiritual seeker, looking for life's ultimate meaning in the movement toward her ideals.

In "Body, Mind, and Breath: A Mystical Perspective," Laura Duhan Kaplan suggests that the births and deaths she has attended have given her a glimpse of God. Human lives, she notes, seem to begin and end as breathing begins and ends; human moods seem to change as breathing quickens or slows down. Several religious traditions identify the breath with the soul, and the soul as capable of unity with God. If the breath can become one with God, she wonders, can breath itself be a face of divinity? Conversations with her colleagues about her questions lead her to understand that using unusual metaphors for speaking about God can make mystical knowledge more accessible.

In "The Wrong Moment to Exit," James Adrian Marshall speaks of less profound, but possibly no less significant, events. A choice to run in a particular direction, a decision to exit the freeway to stop at a bathroom, an impulse to visit a friend on a particular weekend—each of these set off a chain of events that sent his life spinning in a new direction. In a reflective moment, he steps outside the reality of his life to consider a few nagging questions. "What if the choices had been different?" he wonders. "Is there an alternate path out there I could have taken?" He celebrates the power of small choices to have big impacts, tentatively wondering if it makes sense to speak of an "invisible hand of fate" pointing him toward one or another choice.

In "The Malice of Inanimates," Charles W. Harvey tells of the times his car, his keys, or his books were not where he left them. But instead of blaming his memory for making a mistake, he begins to wonder whether his mistake is much deeper. Perhaps his mistake lies in believing that inanimate objects are, in fact, inanimate. After all, the evidence points toward their ability to move, since inanimate objects so often are not where we left them. Although the essay is quite humorous, it legitimately asks us whether we might be too comfortable in some of our beliefs about reality, dismissing too quickly those experiences that challenge our beliefs.

QUESTIONS TO GET YOU STARTED

1. Where would you look to find the meaning of life?
2. What does it mean to you to be "spiritual"? Is "spirituality" connected with God?
3. How can you come to know the true essence of any individual's personality, life, or destiny?
4. How do we know things we cannot directly observe?

Suggested Readings

Augustine. *Confessions.* New York: Viking Press, 1979. Augustine (354–430) combines faith and reason in his Christian search for God.

Carse, James P. *Breakfast at the Victory: The Mysticism of Ordinary Experience.* San Francisco: Harper San Francisco, 1995. Drawing on Buddhist philosophy, Carse describes the mystical experiences hidden in ordinary life.

Dillard, Annie. *Pilgrim at Tinker Creek.* New York: Harperperennial, 1998. Dillard (1945– present) wonders at the mix of beauty and cruelty as she observes nature philosophically from her mountain cabin.

Frye, Marilyn. *The Politics of Reality.* Freedom, CA: Crossing Press, 1983. Frye identifies social assumptions about reality from the perspective of a radical lesbian feminist outsider.

James, William. *Varieties of Religious Experience.* New York: Random House, 1999. James (1842–1910) catalogues some of the many ways people describe their spiritual experiences.

Leibniz, Gottfried Wilhelm. *Discourse on Metaphysics and the Mondadology.* Trans. George R. Montgomery. New York: Prometheus, 1992. Leibniz (1646–1716) offers a theory of the structure of reality, including the determined nature of the world.

Lucretius. *On the Nature of Things.* Trans. Anthony Esolen. Baltimore: Johns Hopkins University Press, 1995. Lucretius (98–55 B.C.E.) describes the material basis of all reality.

Plato. *Symposium.* Trans. Alexander Nehamas and Paul Woodruff, Indianapolis: Hackett , Inc., 1989. Plato (c. 427–347 B.C.E.) suggests that all creatures seek love, beauty, and creative fulfillment.

Philosophy Out of the Cave

Christopher Miles Michaelson

Shortly after Christopher Miles Michaelson received his doctorate in philosophy, he took a job as a business ethics consultant, serving business, government, and nonprofit agencies. In his job, he has the opportunity to practice philosophy in the course of everyday life.

SCENE I: IN THE LECTURE HALL

I WAS A BOY—just a boy—and the man onstage professed to hold some sort of secret that I wanted to know, but initially it was a girl who kept me coming to philosophy lectures every Monday, Wednesday, and Friday in the spring of my sophomore year. I liked to think that I had something to do with her being there, too.

She was not just a girl, but seemed in her eyes, literally, to hold the secret to human happiness. Neither their size nor their shape was exceptional, and in fact their outlines seemed rather too laden with Long Island mascara for a Midwestern boy's tastes. Her face, moreover, was not all milky softness as had been my preference throughout my adolescence but was interrupted by freckles and a line or two on each cheek that I thought would someday become wrinkles. Beholding the great contrast in shade between the back of one of her cheeks to the space behind her ear, I could see she had spent too much time in the sun.

In profile, her nose was neither unusually long nor especially short, so that when confronted head on with it, one was presented no particular reason for looking, nor for looking away. Her hair extended beyond her shoulders, the way I liked it, though it was a rather unremarkable brunette without a notorious bounce or curl. When she entered a room there was never a clamor of libidinous college boys unabashedly making a bovine noise caused by a collective and simultaneous turn and creak in their seats.

There was only the clamor inside me. When she laughed, which was often, her reddish lips of medium thickness would curl into a crescent lying on its back, half of her little white teeth would mark the boundaries of the black void that emitted a giggle and, as for her eyes. . . . Well, her eyes of unexceptional shape and size had set within their glistening white backdrops two fabulous sapphires, so deeply blue as to suggest warm Mediterranean currents rather than Arctic ice, so dark that it took her laugh to light them. The lids of her eyes would clamp down on the bones of her upper cheeks so that there was nowhere her eyes could go, nothing her eyes could do but become little inverted crescents, almost impossible to make out were it not for the most extraordinary stars emerging from those sapphires as though something had suddenly illuminated within them and seared its way into my consciousness, no less than the secret to human happiness.

The effect was altogether brilliant when winter was giving way to spring. It was sunny and still cold enough that she looked comfortable in her blue winter coat but warm enough that the sun could turn the top layer of snow into a glistening crust of ice; and she laughed against such a background covering the campus lake shore as shrinking blocks of ice floated past on Lake Michigan.

Her squinting, laughing eyes made me philosophical.

I could scarcely indulge in that corporeal pleasure in class, however. Three times each week we performed the ritual of taking our seats in a cavernous basement lecture hall to hear progress being made through Plato's dialogues. The seats were of that immobile variety of auditoriums past, fired plywood molded into the approximate shape of a human rear, just approximate enough that the ridge in the center never hit you quite right and was consequently very uncomfortable. Once you were in that seat and you had lifted the ax-shaped writing surface (connected to the side of your seat by an unwieldy series of vertical and horizontal levers requiring a distinct patience to deploy) and once the writing surface was properly deployed, it completed a virtual circle around your midtorso. You were stuck, neither free to move nor to leave, facing forward, for the hour, like all of the other students on all of your sides.

The girl was always to my immediate right or left, but I could not see her sparkling eyes from where I was situated. Nor, moreover, could those eyes sparkle with their usual brilliance in the dim light that emanated faintly from the ceiling much higher up. With the assurance that there were sapphires beside me, I was resigned instead to watch the shadowy movements of a sinuous figure on stage, a figure with a beard, mustache, glasses, a voice too shrill for the beard, wearing an old brown suit and a Chicago Cubs cap, though he was not a Chicago Cub but rather our philosophy professor.

He appeared to be a man but was not entirely comprehensible to us. He occasionally let his wife and children intrude into the content of his lectures when he expressed his dream of bringing his children to Wrigley Field to see the Cubs in the World Series, and recounted his disappointments past. But when you would approach him after class he seemed to have lost all of his charisma; a much lower voice of almost indiscernible volume would emit a peculiar frost.

The man on the stage at the front of the room seemed a long distance away from those of us pinned to the floor, and our affairs. He had, it seemed, devoted a professional life to the study of philosophy and kept us there to hear about it. What I heard was competing with the girl at my side, with whom my relationship was, as we said, "Platonic," without understanding that in using the word we were in some sense perverting the doctrine that we were at the same time hearing from the stage above.

By mid-spring, as the professor approached that part of Plato's book, the *Republic*, in which Socrates designates the philosopher to be king of the perfect state, my attentions were divided between my attempts to glimpse the girl's spectacular knees (which were the most accessible of all of her inaccessible parts to my fettered self but which I could not see in their entirety because her desk was in the way, though their spectacularity was guaranteed by her special eyes), the breath in my ear as she ridiculed the professor for assigning such a long reading about a bunch of men hanging on the words of one Socrates, and the shrill and distant voice coming from the sinuous, shadowy, ridiculous figure in front.

Scene II: In the Cave

" 'Picture men dwelling in a sort of subterranean cavern,' " our professor said, is how the most famous portion of the most famous dialogue of the most famous philosopher begins. The dialogue itself, the *Republic*, begins as an exaltation of the just man over the unjust man but evolves into the construction of the perfect state in which the just man rules. The character of Socrates is choosing the rulers of his perfect state when he digresses into what is commonly known as the "cave allegory" (Book VII).

That is, the very character, who for 170 pages in our edition of the *Republic* had been the dominant conversant in a smooth dialogue about utopia, inexplicably retreated to the bowels of a dark, musty cave to tell a story. This sort of sudden change in direction is not uncommon for Socrates: in Plato's *Symposium*, for example, Socrates is on his way to a party when he literally stops in his tracks, leaves his companion to go to the party alone, and arrives himself, without apology, several hours later. Of this action, Socrates' friend Apollodorus says, "It's quite a habit of his, you know; off he goes and there he stands, no matter where he is" (175b).

"Do you realize what sort of superhuman qualities it would take, what sort of discipline would be necessary to be still for a period of hours without attending to the slightest urge, itch, bodily function?" asked the professor. There was a sense of incredulousness in this rhetorical question; we would see that the purpose of the cave allegory is to answer that very question by anointing the philosopher, bestowing upon him (or her?) the honor of ruling the Republic, because he is no ordinary human being.

The ordinary human beings, their "nature in respect to education and its lack," as Socrates' character says, are dwelling on the floor of the cave, their backs to a long entrance open to the light on its entire width. Conceive them as having their legs and necks fettered from childhood, so that they remain in the same spot, able to look forward only, and prevented by the fetters from turning their heads. Picture further the light from a fire burning higher up and at a distance behind them, and between the fire and the prisoners and above them a road along which a low wall has been built, as the exhibitors of puppet shows have partitions before the men themselves, above which they show the puppets.

Glaucon, who is one of the younger men with whom Socrates is having his conversation, assents—"All that I see"—but he does not seem to see what else is stirring. Socrates is calling Glaucon, and all the other nonphilosophers of Athens, "cavepeople," imprisoned in ignorance and in ignorance of their ignorance. "See also, then, men carrying past the wall implements of all kinds that rise above the wall, and human images and shapes of animals as well, wrought in stone and wood and every material, some of these bearers presumably speaking and others silent."

"A strange image you speak of . . . and strange prisoners," is Glaucon's reaction, because such a prisoner cannot remove himself from his fetters to see that it is of him that Socrates speaks: "In every way such prisoners would deem reality to be nothing else than the shadows of the artificial objects."

Socrates goes on to tell of one prisoner who "was freed from his fetters and compelled to stand up suddenly and turn his head around and walk and to lift up his eyes to the light." His freedom and passage toward the mouth of the cave are altogether passive; there is neither a description of how he came to be imprisoned, nor who has been deceiving him with shadowy objects, nor why his freedom was granted.

Of course the light frightens him, so he "turn[s] away and flee[s] [back] to those things [shadows] which he is able to discern." But then again, if the mysterious someone were to "drag him thence by force up the ascent which is rough and steep, and not let him go before he had drawn him out into the light of the sun," after a period of habituation, the former prisoner would eventually discern "things themselves."

"Well then," says Socrates, "if he recalled to mind his first habitation and what passed for wisdom there, and his fellow bondsmen, do you not think that he would count himself happy in the change and pity them?"

At this point in the lecture, the pretty prisoner beside me seemed to grow restless at the suggestion that she was missing out on the day's light, or perhaps she just needed to visit the bathroom. I sensed her repeated glances at her watch without my bothering to catch glimpses at her wrist. My eyes were fixed ahead of me at the shadowy figure onstage and the book on the surface that hid my own body from me.

I would learn that Socrates was not describing the passage to the giddy sort of exaltation that I might realize if the pretty prisoner and I ever were to kiss. Rather, he sought *eudaimonia*, an ancient Greek notion of happiness apart from hedonistic pleasure, which only the perfectly just person will ever realize.

"Do you think it at all strange . . . if a man returning from divine contemplations to the petty miseries of men cuts a sorry figure and appears most ridiculous, if, while still blinking through the gloom, and before he has become sufficiently accustomed to the environing darkness, he is compelled in courtrooms or elsewhere to contend about the shadows of justice or the images that cast the shadows and to wrangle in debate about the notions of these things in the minds of those who have never seen justice itself?"

So did Socrates and the professor appear most ridiculous to most of us. "Do not be surprised that those who have attained to this height are not willing to occupy themselves with the affairs of men, but their souls ever feel the upward urge and the yearning for that sojourn above."

SCENE III: ON TRIAL

Plato's *Apology* depicts Socrates on trial, facing the death penalty as the eventual result of his strangeness. Not only did Socrates appear ridiculous to his fellow citizens, but he appeared positively annoying, self-aggrandizing, and possibly even imperialistic. Like the teacher who assumes the pedestal of false dictatorship in the classroom, Socrates—who adopted the city street corners as his classroom—taught his brand of wisdom to anyone who would be engaged by his conversation, often making the other appear foolish.

The appearance of foolishness turned to the resentment of Socrates, especially after the oracle at Delphi proclaimed Socrates to be the wisest of all human beings. Socrates, however, in citing this proclamation at his own trial, was not doing so in self-exaltation but in self-defense. Rather than admit to accusations of wrongdoing—"he inquires into things below the earth and in the sky, and makes the weaker argument defeat the stronger, and teaches others to follow his example" (19b); "Socrates is guilty of corrupting the minds of the young, and of believing in deities of his own invention" (24b)—Socrates was engaged in a practical struggle: examining and defending his way of life.

It was not the god-like, self-exalting philosopher of the *Republic* who shaped my abiding sense of what philosophy, and living well, are about. It was Socrates on trial who did that, searching for answers to the most urgent question: "How should a human being live?" The answer in the *Republic*—that living well consisted in rising above one's humanity—was distinctly different from the humble answer that Socrates gave on trial. His earthy contention was that he was wiser than any other man in Athens because "neither of us has any knowledge to boast of, but he thinks that he knows something which he does not know, whereas I am quite conscious of my ignorance" (21d). The most famous Socratic quote was, therefore, appropriately expressed in negative terms—what not to do was the key to the way Socrates did live: "The unexamined life is not worth living" (38a).

However, when the time came to question the disparity between a philosophy about humans and philosophy above humans, we were interrupted. Somehow a bat had gotten into the lecture hall. Perched upside down among the rafters, it only produced giggles, so our professor tried to proceed. But then the bat swooped down menacingly, eliciting screams from the students at whom it aimed, and a bit of chaos erupted. This happened several times, causing papers to go flying and desk levers to slam as some students headed for the exits. The professor calmly tried to restore the attention of the class to himself, tapping on his lectern, and speaking softly into the microphone: "It's only a bat. . . . It will fly as near to you as it can without actually touching you if you stay still. . . . By moving you are confusing its radar. . . . We still have some material to get through. . . . " But he had lost us. There was sunlight outside and the bloom of mid-spring, and so after a futile few minutes of trying to create order, the professor set us free for the day. He unshackled us from our desks, and we moved from the dim light of the auditorium into the sun, but we did not imagine that we were on some sort of pilgrimage to transcendence. We were on our way to the lake.

SCENE IV: ON CAMPUS

The traditional American college campus is focused around an expanse of green, cast in the mornings and evenings beneath the shadows of buildings that house Physics and English and Mathematics and Philosophy departments, libraries, and Registrars. At midday, however, when the sun is high and the air is warm, one can hardly perceive the green. At such times, nearly every student on campus gravitates to the expanse, creating a field of skin, cotton, and paper. Nobody is studying, however: The students are looking at each other, at the sky, and at the treetops, and talking with each other.

No matter that the grass is not indigenous to the region. In the northern universities in the spring, after the snow has given way to a matted yellow and brown carpet, the green is rejuvenated and is for the rest of the outdoor season painstakingly manicured by the university's grounds crew under orders from the president. Inevitably, during the spring, too many students will have lain on the grass or else bypassed the sidewalks to cut a path across the field. By late summertime, when most students have gone to their hometowns and the sun's fury is not as furious, the expanse of green is roped off and reseeded so that the ritual can be repeated in spring.

To such an expanse did the girl and I ascend. The only thing natural about the green was its origins beneath the endless expanse of blue beside it, Lake Michigan, which might as well have been an ocean. The green actually grew out of earth that had been dredged from the lake bottom years before to make room for an addition to the library, student union, and playful students around a "lagoon." Rumor was that the library architect, in planning the foundation, had forgotten to factor in the weight of the books, and the library was sinking into the ground (which ought after all to have been a lake) at a rate of several inches each year.

A mysterious malady had its origins here. On the "Lakefill," as we called it, university administrators, for reasons unknown to but welcomed by students, permitted on one weekend day an annual late spring festival of hedonism. Even conservative students would dress in tie-dyed t-shirts—and liberal students would not dress at all—getting drunk, smoking pot, and singing to the rock-infused blues piped from John Lee Hooker's live guitar, which was as close as students at a largely upper-class private suburban university generally got to the real Chicago blues. But the defining drug of the day was the mushroom, the common name for an uncommon variety of a completely natural nonindigenous fungus, a variety that happened to produce vivid hallucinations that would allegedly turn tie-dyes into kaleidoscopes, quasi-blues into The Blues, Lake Michigan into the Mediterranean Sea (and, alternatively, a bathroom), and sex into better sex (but perhaps being outside had something to do with this).

The spirit of Armadillo Day haunted the Lakefill all year, and especially in the spring. It was the place to kiss late at night in defiance of campus police patrols, to succumb to deceptive, drug-induced realities, and in general to repudiate the reasoned judgments of authorities. It was also the place to examine one's life, to judge when such repudiation was warranted, and to regret or condone what one may have done there in the past. Thus, when I had been expecting to sit in philosophy class one Wednesday and was instead freed by a bat to go to the lake shore, I was not about study philosophy. Rather, if the girl and I were ever going to kiss, as I was wishing we were, the Lakefill would be the place to do it.

If the girl's eyes moved me to feelings of amnesty for all human beings living within a placid utopia, her Long Island mascara above imperfect cheeks atop a sinuous, soft, and curving figure moved me to anticipate happiness enough. I was ready to kiss her passionately, ignoring the public spectacle it would create and the school work that had to be done. But looking out onto the endless sea in a warm breeze that freed us from the musty, cavernous classroom, at that stage in our lives when neither of us knew where we were going, what kind of adults we would become, much less what our majors should be, we, as nonphilosophers like to say, "waxed philosophical."

"What is the meaning of life?" she asked.
"Do you think human beings are intrinsically good or evil?" I said.
"Are some people naturally smarter than others?"
"Do you suppose the sea gulls above our heads have souls?"
"Where did this lake come from?"
"Do you believe it ends, even though we can't see the other side?"
"Does the guy who sits near us in philosophy class like me?"

So we never kissed. I never discovered the secret of human happiness that I imagined lay within her eyes. I had by that time, however, made the mature Socratic admission that there was a secret that I did not know. But where was the secret that would make me a man: Would a girl lead me to it or did I need a professor, and philosophy, to lead me out of the cave?

NOTE

All quotes from Plato's dialogues are from the editions assigned by the professor in *The Collected Dialogues of Plato*, ed. Edith Hamilton and Huntington Cairns, Princeton, NJ: Princeton University Press, 1985. The translators are as follows: Hugh Tredennick (Socrates' Defense [*Apology*], *Crito*, *Phaedo*), Michael Joyce (*Symposium*), Paul Shorey (*Republic*). The trial in this article consists of the two dialogues that Plato wrote early in his career: the *Apology* and the *Crito*. This essay can also be found as "Into the Cave," the preface to my doctoral dissertation, *Philosophy Out of the Cave: An Expedition in Philosophical Style* (University of Minnesota, 1997).

STUDY QUESTIONS
1. Does Michaelson believe we can learn from teachers who point out the deeper meanings behind daily life?
2. In what sense might it be true that "living well consists in rising above one's humanity"?
3. What is the difference between a philosophy about humans and a philosophy above humans?

Confessions of a Recovering Rationalist

Judith Presler

Judith Presler teaches courses in Plato, Ethics, and Metaphysics at the University of North Carolina at Charlotte. She tries to integrate her philosophy with her spirituality and her ethics. She is writing a book about the search for the Good in ethics and society.

I WAS A RATIONALIST from a very early age. While I enjoyed an extensive and exciting imaginative life, I regarded that aspect of my inner life as pure entertainment. Truth and knowledge, I believed, must be guaranteed by certainty and deductive proof—not that, at the age of five, I thought of it in those words. I came by my rationalism honestly. My mother was a dyed-in-the-wool rationalist. Our rationalism was accompanied, as might be expected, by radical skepticism as well. For example, my mother's rationalistic inclination toward deductive proof led her to reject the Baptist religion of her childhood because, she reasoned, the nature of God was inconsistent with the sort of punishment for small sins that she was led to fear in her early years. The nature of God, she also reasoned, was far more consistent with various "occult" religious views that she embraced as she matured than with the Baptist conception of Christianity she learned as a child. But, because she did not have certainty about any of her initial propositions, she maintained a skeptical attitude about the views she embraced, or at least about many of the interpretations and manifestations of those views propounded by her fellow occultists.

One night when I was about five years old, my mother and a couple of her friends met at our house to participate in some sort of occult activity having to do with partial levitation of a table. They called on the spirits and said, "Rise, table, rise," which the table finally did. My mother, always the skeptic, suspected that one of her friends was actually manipulating the levitation; however, she played along—she was being entertained. As the evening wore on, a young man, a friend of my grown-up brother, came by for a visit. The young man, being young and all-knowing, derided the activity of the ladies and, being a Roman Catholic, also feared the activity going on in our house. His derision, seemingly, brought about fierce activity on the part of the table, which began to bang up and down on the floor in such a way as to maneuver out from under the hands of my mother and her friends and move menacingly toward the young man. He ran out of the house in fear. Three skeptics were convinced that night: the young man, my mother, and I. We were given the certain proof of immediate experience.

Ordinary humans are, by nature, rationalists in that we look for certainty. And, we tend to look for certainty in immediate experience. Skepticism arises for us when the certain proof of immediate experience is contradicted by other experiences. Philosophers refer to contradictions of this kind as the problems of perception. Descartes found these contradictions in his examination of perception in his First Meditation.[1] Ordinary humans do not usually fall into deep skepticism about perception, as some philosophers do—Descartes, for example, or Hume.[2] Rather, ordinary humans have a somewhat more relaxed attitude toward experience, making allowances for the common perceptual problems that might drive philosophers to extreme positions. Ordinary humans look at perceptual experience in general, or over the long haul, and explain away the anomalies that most ordinary folks explain away and in the manner most ordinary folks use to explain them away. Ordinary humans usually accept the evidence of immediate experience in general, as it commonly is interpreted, and in a way that is consistent with their worldviews.

Ordinary humans are also rationalists by nature in that we make deductions to increase our knowledge, or to explain or defend our positions. When I was young, for example, I reasoned that if, according to Jesus, whenever we sin in our hearts, we sin in the same way as if we had done the deed contemplated, then I was in deep trouble. I developed a large catalogue of sins of thought that would fall under that general rule. This rationally arrived at position caused me great pain for a long time during my adolescence. I also became horror-struck by the concept of infinite space, infinite time, infinite being. I could not comprehend it rationally. But thinking about a terminus led me to thinking about what was beyond it, so I was also unable to comprehend finite space, time, or being.

While humans are by nature rationalists, most of us tend also toward pragmatism when the rational-going gets tough. We become attached to our familiar and favorite first principles and do not question them. There is no time. We have to wash the dishes or the car, go to work or to the grocery store. Most humans exercise reason only so far or so long as it is possible to do so and maintain sanity and a desired lifestyle. And then reasoning stops. Some people, however, do not stop. Some people are radical rationalists. Some of these radical rationalists become philosophers, though not all philosophers are radical rationalists. I was stricken with an extreme case of rationalism. I came to the recognition that there were no first principles, there were no major premises that were self-evidently true, there were no starting places for knowledge that were unquestionable. Then I became stricken with a nearly paralyzing skepticism. I could avoid the paralysis only by ignoring the impasse to which my mind had taken me and involving myself in other things: daydreaming, reading novels, playing music, singing, and pursuing a career in theatre.

Ultimately I discovered that philosophy offered antidotes for this paralyzing skepticism. One antidote was Socrates. The antidote was his attitude toward the pursuit of truth and his method of inquiry. His attitude was that it was better to pursue truth, believing in its possibility, than to believe that there is no truth and to be idle, idle in the mind, idle in that activity (thinking) that belongs to us by nature and that furnishes with so much pleasure and fulfillment. His attitude, furthermore, was that the truth we must seek is the truth about ourselves. "Know thyself," he commanded.[3]

His methodology illuminates what we know when we know ourselves.[4] Since there are no first principles announcing themselves with complete clarity and certainty, when we reason, we must tentatively propose a starting point, a major premise, a position. (We have to start somewhere.) When we start in a Socratic way, we make deductions from the starting point, but we do not so often expand our knowledge, as we would like to think we can. Rather, we discover what is entailed in our position, what might lie behind it, what it means, what is consistent in it and with it, what is inconsistent in it and with it, what it adequately explains, what it fails to explain. We come to know something about ourselves—what we believe, what we put our trust in, what we accept blindly, what we expect, what we think we are. Inquiry also teaches us about what is entailed in the various options humans take in attempting to explain the moral life. And the very explication of these views often reveals, as well, the strengths and weaknesses of these options.

Plato adds another antidote to the paralyzing skepticism that results from radical rationalism. His antidote is "The Good." Look around the world, look at human lives. What do you see? "Eros," says Plato, love of, desire for something one does not have presently. One wants something, it is valuable to one, it entails some kind of fulfillment or completion or perfection for one. What one wants is a reality. Plato says that we can call it "Good" or call it "Beautiful." Now, of course, the fact that we desire something does not necessitate that it is real, or even if it is real, that it is good. And indeed there are, in life, things that we desire that we cannot have because they are not, in some sense, real. An infertile couple may desire a child generated out of them, but such a child is not and cannot be real. I could desire to travel on a spaceship to the earth's second moon, but could not do so. Such a moon is not real. We also desire things that are real but not good, usually believing, incorrectly, that they are good. But Plato is not claiming that because we desire something it therefore exists and is good. Nonetheless, he claims that the Good is real. What does he mean?

Let us look around at the world again, look at human lives. What do we see? Among other things we see disorder; we see unfulfilled hopes, dreams, and lives; we see torture, murder, pain, grief. These are things we would wish not to see, but they are there. The world abounds in incompleteness, unfulfillment, and imperfection. Yet, we look to and desire completeness, fulfillment, perfection. We think about these things, we form conceptions of them in our minds, we think about what we want. The conceptions we form when we think about what we want are not built up out of the experienced data of our disorderly and imperfect world, but are of something other than that world. The conceptions may be fuzzy and vague, or they may be clear, though incomplete. They are conceptions of a deep and complex object of aspiration, a perfection, a completion. The conception of the object of desire, which Plato usually calls "The Good," cannot be accounted for as a derivation from the imperfect world.

So what we are thinking about when we think about the Good is something real. Sometimes we make mistakes in our conceptions of the Good. We painfully discover these mistakes when we try to live our lives in respect of a mistaken concept of what is good and find that we are not fulfilled, completed, or made more perfect. It is less painful and more efficient and efficacious, both Socrates and Plato tell us, to uncover through inquiry as much as possible about the nature of the Good. It is less painful, obviously, to conceive of the mistakenness of a concept of the Good than to experience its badness in our lives. It is more efficient to pursue the Good conceptually because we can peruse in our minds many more interpretations and their consequences than we could live out in an experimental way. It is more efficacious because the very activity of inquiry develops one necessary element in the achievement of the Good, as it turns out, namely the intellect. This is why Socrates announced at the end of his trial that he had come to recognize that the unexamined life is not worth living.

All of this, and much more as well, I came to understand in my study of philosophy. I learned that while a radical rationalist position could not provide a starting point, one cannot stop thinking and acting, appealing to principles all the while. So one must pursue the principles in thought and live as best as one can on the basis of one's incomplete knowledge. But one must never stop the pursuit. One must be humble in the presence of truth. On the other hand, if, as a radical rationalist, one believes that one has discovered self-evidently true first principles that are rich enough to generate an account of reality, then one proceeds to the deduction of one's account of reality, as Descartes did. But, principles rich enough to generate an account of reality are complicated enough to need careful examination to discover what implications are entailed within them. If one examines them, one will discover that they are not clear and distinct self-evident truths. If the radical rationalist believes that those principles do not need to be examined, as Descartes did, or one pretends to a skepticism that cannot be consistently maintained, as Hume did, one is headed for trouble. In the first case, one's first principles are not self-evidently true, but import unexamined presuppositions into one's system. In the second case, one substitutes for knowledge of the nature of reality a surmise that one is not obliged to defend as knowledge but which one employs as though it were a known and true account of reality. In either case, assumptions are made and employed but not examined, supported, or evaluated. Such use of assumptions amounts to dogmatism.

Though I learned much from Plato and Socrates, I was still an unrecovered rationalist. All that I understood, I understood rationally, but not actually as a practice in which I myself was engaged. In some sense I rationally understood the arguments and reasons for Socrates' and Plato's positions, but I did not incorporate them into my life. I did not live a Socratic examined life, I did not pursue the Platonic Good. For many years I was bedeviled by my own rationalistic demands. I wanted to prove without a shadow of a doubt the existence of the Platonic Good. I wanted to defend rationally every aspect of Plato's theory, to explain away every doubt, to defeat every detracting remark and argument. I pretended to be a Platonist, but my ethics was a casuistry that produced rationally satisfying arguments that supported my actions—another trap into which radical rationalists fall. (What we call rationalization in other people we call reasonableness in ourselves.)

Further, I believed that for Plato, the preparation for apprehending the Good is dialectical inquiry, that dialectical inquiry can be described in respect of the mainly deductive operations used in its service, that its *reductio ad absurdum* arguments are deductive arguments, and that its method of hypothesis is deductive. It is true, I supposed, that some premises for these deductive arguments are prepared by analogy and generalization; but, I assured myself, these premises are then subjected to deductive testing, so the inquiry may be thought of as a deductively rational enterprise. I used to believe that apprehending the Good would just happen once I had gone through the dialectical examination of the virtues. But my experience indicates that is not the case. The actual attending to the Good is more than dialectical inquiry. It involves passion. We passionately want the good, want to understand it, want to instantiate it in our lives. Attending in this way to the Good in inquiry, both initially and finally, is what enables us to begin the inquiry, to continue the inquiry, and to apprehend, at the end of inquiry, the object of desire. We cannot get started on the path toward the Good, this real object of inquiry, this measure of truth and value, unless we first recognize that *it is a reality that affects our thought and action.*

Looking for it, attending to it, wanting it, desiring it, we attempt to comprehend it. Is it this? (For example, is it pleasure or is it something else? We examine thoroughly pleasure both for what it means conceptually and how it feels, what it does in life, what it would be like to be guided by pleasure. Is pleasure what we want exclusively in life? And we examine honor, perhaps, and virtue in the same way.)

And all through the inquiry we are driven by love, a powerful driving force. Love informs me of starting points of inquiry. Plato points out, in *Symposium*, that our erotic attractions are indications of the nature of love and the existence of Beauty. They are the first indications, but they are indications. Our artistic creations, our service to the community, our scientific enterprises: these are all indicators of our love of the Beautiful and indicators of the nature and existence of the Beautiful.

A cold, objective inquiry will not lead to the Good. A demand for clear and distinct starting points will not issue in the apprehension of the Good. That rationalistic demand either will not be satisfied, and thus lead to nothing, or will be infused with unexamined presuppositions and lead to a dogmatism. Human inquiry has a human interest, is driven by passion, and is informed by that passion. The attempt to engage in pure, objective inquiry, and the belief that one is engaging in pure, objective inquiry, mask the passion. The masked passion and its influence on the inquiry are left unexamined, and so the masked passion dogmatizes the results of the inquiry. Plato attempted to understand the integrated human soul, and he recognized that human activities, even intellectual inquiries, are activities of the whole human being, are functions of passion and reason working together. But I missed that point of Plato. I was being purely rational.

My conversion to living an examined life and pursuing the Good came about, eventually, or more properly, is coming about, slowly. The principal determinative causes are writings that are very little about Plato but which turn my attention to God. While the Church Fathers used Platonic thought to explain religion, I am finally able to comprehend Platonic thought through religion.

I begin with a statement of Dame Julian of Norwich:

> To know the goodness of God is the highest prayer of all, and it is a
> prayer that accommodates itself to our most lowly needs. It quickens our
> soul, and vitalizes it, developing it in grace and virtue. Here is the grace
> most appropriate to our need, and most ready to help. Here is the grace
> which our soul is seeking now, and which it will ever seek until that day
> when we know for a fact that he has wholly united us to himself.[5]

Loving the Good, too, quickens the soul, vitalizes it, and develops it. According to another thinker, Simone Weil, prayer as knowing the goodness of God is an activity of focusing one's attention on the goodness of God and waiting to receive the presence of God, the love of God, God's truth.[6] For Plato, too, a relationship with the Good is not merely intellectual. For him, arriving outside the cave and looking at the sun is an analogy for attending to the Good. One cannot merely understand the arguments about why it is important to pursue and apprehend the Good, one must do it. But, it is a lifelong project. We must never stop inquiring about the Good and attempting to understand it or to understand it better that we did previously. But we must go on with our lives. How do we carry on without complete knowledge of the Good? How do we incorporate what we do understand about the Good into our lives? How do we guide our actions so that we are just in our treatment of others and in our nurturing of ourselves?

Again, my answer comes from religion, though the writer I cite is skeptical about the religion she explicates so clearly. Iris Murdoch, in *The Sovereignty of Good*, describes moral activity as lovingly and justly attending to an individual. This activity takes place over a long period of time, is a progressive attempt to see an individual clearly, and is infinitely perfectible.[7] Love, says Murdoch, is knowledge of the individual. Moral tasks are characteristically endless because our efforts are imperfect and our conception of perfection is developing and deepening as we approach the always receding ideal limit of love or knowledge.[8] Murdoch says,

> In suggesting that the central concept of morality is 'the individual' thought of as knowable by love, thought of in the light of the command, 'Be ye therefore perfect,' I am not, in spite of the philosophical backing which I might here resort to, suggesting anything in the least esoteric. In fact this would, to the ordinary person, be a very much more familiar image than the existentialist one. We ordinarily conceive of and apprehend goodness in terms of virtues which belong to a continuous fabric of being. . . . There exists a moral reality, a real though infinitely distant standard: the difficulties of understanding and imitating remain. . . . Where virtue is concerned we often apprehend more than we clearly understand and *grow by looking.*[9]

Murdoch's notion of moral activity is that it is a twofold attention. It is loving attention to an individual and love of or attention to the Good. Both of these forms of attention are long-term, progressive activities that lead to greater clarity about the Good and increasingly just treatment of the individual. According to Murdoch, through attending to the Good, I understand to some extent what is good, how I should be, what I should expect and cultivate in others. Through my knowledge of the Good, which is also an object of loving attention, I am capable of apprehending what is truly good in another person, of attending lovingly and justly to another. Murdoch's idea is that the cultivation of a loving regard for another person is something that can be done deliberately. One can decide to attend lovingly to another, and with practice over time, one will so regard that other person. Out of this sort of love of another issues morally right actions and responses toward that person.

Murdoch's conception of moral activity—namely, cultivating a loving attention to another person and lovingly attending to the Good—seems to me to be an enlightening explanation of the concept of Christian love commanded in the New Testament: "Love God and love thy neighbor." Simone Weil expresses a similar notion of moral activity. She says,

> At the bottom of the heart of every human being, from earliest infancy until the tomb, there is something that goes on indomitably expecting, in the teeth of all experience of crimes committed, suffered, and witnessed, that good and not evil will be done to him. It is this above all that is sacred in every human being.[10]

This sacred something expects the Good, loves the Good. This sacred something is what can recognize the same sacredness in another and love the other. This love is the foundation for moral activity. Weil writes, "If you say to someone who has ears to hear: 'What you are doing to me is not just,' you may touch and awaken at its source the spirit of attention and love."[11] This love is the source of just treatment of the other. "Because affliction and truth need the same kind of attention before they can be heard, the spirit of justice and the spirit of truth is nothing else but a certain kind of attention, which is pure love."[12]

The perfect Good, according to Weil, is the source of all that is just, beautiful, and good in our world. "Supernatural good," she suggests, "is not a sort of supplement to natural good. . . . In all the crucial problems of human existence the only choice is between supernatural good on the one hand and evil on the other."[13]

Murdoch's and Weil's notion of love—love of the Good and love of other persons as the central source for moral activity—offers moral instruction that relates to the reality of human experience. We are emotive, we are related to others by passions of love and hate, our actions toward others often do arise from how we regard those others. While Murdoch and Weil defend a Platonic conception of the Good and a conception of moral action as being the natural outcome of what one is, that is, one's character, they also have been able to instruct me in *how* I can apprehend and learn what is good and be aware of the good in others, a practice.

When I first received the antidotes of Socrates and Plato, I was still in the throes of rationalism. My approach to reality, while instructed by Plato, was tainted by my radical rationalism. Though Plato does indicate in the divided line and the cave that the apprehension of the Good is synthetic and intuitive and that its result is a transformation of the soul, I only intellectually apprehended what he said. I did not experience the Good. I was still expecting something logical, neat, and tidy, something I could intellectually dominate. While Plato does indicate the role of passion in learning and becoming just, I only conceived of it. I did not give myself over to it. Being guided by Dame Julian, Weil, and Murdoch to attend to God or Good and to the God or Good reflected in other persons, I have experienced—as a result of paying attention—what I was never able to experience as a result of mere rational conviction. It took the humility that I experienced when approaching God to instruct me about the reality and nature of the Good.

NOTES

1. René Descartes, *Meditations on First Philosophy*, trans. Donald A. Cress (Indianapolis: Hackett, 1993).
2. David Hume, *A Treatise of Human Nature*, ed. L.A. Selby-Bigge (Oxford: Clarendon Press, 1985).
3. Plato, "Apology," in *The Trial and Death of Socrates*, trans. G.M.A. Grube (Indianapolis: Hackett, 1980).
4. Plato, *The Collected Dialogues of Plato*, ed. Edith Hamilton and Huntington Cairns (Princeton: Princeton University Press, 1961).
5. Dame Julian of Norwich, "Revelations of Divine Love," Revelation I, chapter 6, in *Readings for the Daily Office from the Early Church*, ed. J. Robert Wright (New York: The Church Hymnal Corporation, 1991), 55.
6. Simone Weil, "Reflections on the Right Use of School Studies," in *The Simone Weil Reader*, ed. George A. Panichas (New York: David McKay Company, Inc., 1977), 44–51.
7. Iris Murdoch, *The Sovereignty of Good and Other Essays* (New York: Routledge, 1990), 23.
8. Ibid., 28.
9. Ibid., 30, 31.
10. Simone Weil, "Human Personality," in Panichas, 315.
11. Ibid., 325.
12. Ibid., 333.
13. Ibid., 327.

STUDY QUESTIONS

1. According to Presler, what is rationalism? What are the advantages and pitfalls of this way of thinking?
2. What are the sources of our motivations to be rational and moral?
3. Would you agree that the "Good" as defined by Presler is the same thing as God?

Body, Mind, and Breath:
A Mystical Perspective

Laura Duhan Kaplan

Laura Duhan Kaplan teaches philosophy, along with many other humanities courses, at the University of North Carolina at Charlotte. She has studied yoga, Jewish mysticism, and phenomenology. In her book *Family Pictures: A Philosopher Explores the Familiar* (1998), she wrote about the way issues of life and death affect her sense of self. Here she writes about the way these issues affect her religious beliefs.

WHY THIS TOPIC?

FOR WEEKS, I HAD been making false starts on writing a conference paper. My scattered thoughts would not coalesce around a topic. Exasperated, frustrated, I threw myself face down on the den floor. I grabbed my husband's leg as he walked by. "Chas!" I begged, "What have I been thinking about lately?"

"The breath," he said, for he had been listening carefully to the words I had been breathing out to him. The breath gives shape to language and ideas, making it possible for people to communicate, for us to gain philosophically elusive knowledge of other minds. Spoken language is breath passed through chambers of various shapes. Laughter is breath given out to the world in short bursts. Surprise is a breath interrupted.

LIFE, DEATH, AND BREATH

I begin with everyday observations. As a sort of sideline while engaged in the business of life—attending births and deaths, and everything in between—I have made an informal and chaotic study of the rules of the world. If my honesty disturbs you, I can say the same thing borrowing the jargon of philosopher Edmund Husserl: In the phenomenological reduction in which I bracket the scientific standpoint, I return to the pre-theoretical stance of pre-classical Greece, where I am immersed in the life-world.[1] Cynicism is a quick snort of breath out the nose.

Twice I have observed the death of bodies I care about, both after prolonged illnesses. Each time a version of pneumonia, fluid-filled lungs, took over the body's last hours. Pneumonia arrived as a sort of angel of death, saying, I will begin the process of releasing you now. (Releasing what from what, I do not know.) Each time, as the breath became shallower, the body seemed to die from the feet up. With less oxygen, and poorer circulation, of course the extremities starve first. But that scientific knowledge does not quell the uncanniness of watching life withdraw from the body to the rhythm of a thickening breath. Each time, I sorrowed and I wondered, and I held the image in my mind. Compassion, your sympathy with me, is a long, slow, sighing breath out.

I have given birth after sharing my breath with a fetus through a tube connected to its belly button (go figure). I never did see my babies' first breaths; I was always too busy catching my own. My second baby almost didn't breathe. What would that have been like, death at the moment of birth? A body fully prepared, a vessel perfectly formed, waiting to receive the gift of breath—yet somehow not kissed, the wind blowing past it instead of into it. We have only a few short moments, only a short window of opportunity, before the vessel would lie useless and discarded. Hold your breath, thinking of a birthparent's sorrow.

The Hebrew Bible borrows from the reality of birth the metaphor of a vessel receiving the gift of breath. This metaphor forms the centerpiece of the Bible's second description of the creation of human beings. (Surely, as many scholars say, the author of the second creation story was a woman!) Here are the words of Genesis 2:7: "And God formed the man of dirt from the ground, and He blew into his nostrils the soul of life and man became a living being."[2] In this story, God formed a man from the most ordinary of materials: from dirt, the unnoticed background to the business of life; from the earth, an unsung source of support. But the prosaic came to life when God breathed into it. Pause and take a deep breath, the kind that makes possible a heartfelt "Wow!" of reverence and awe.

EMOTION, INTELLECT, AND BREATH

Clearly, breath is connected with the emotions. We have already played with six different rhythms and shapes of breath connected with six different emotions. As with the breath, so it is with music. Singing, chanting, dancing, playing instruments, are all done in rhythm with the breath. Different rhythms express different emotions. And different rhythms evoke different emotions. My musical expressions, if effective, spark your emotional expressions, maybe even your musical ones. And your own musical activities alter your emotional tone. Have you not cheered yourself up by making music or become sorrowful singing along with a mournful crooner?

Perhaps your thoughts and emotions are wandering now as you make your own associations or begin to formulate your objections or agreements with my argument. Take a deep breath and focus your mind. Prepare for a moment of serious philosophy.

Traditional yoga philosophy connects the practice of disciplined breathing with the focused intellect. As B.K.S. Iyengar writes,

> the mind can go in many directions in a split section. But the breath cannot go in many directions at once. It has only one path: inhalation and exhalation. Controlling the breath and observing its rhythm bring the consciousness to stillness.[3]

Iyengar points out that the classic yoga text *Hatha Yoga Pradipika* defines yoga as "stilling the fluctuations of the breath," while another classic text, the *Yoga Sutras* of Patanjali, defines yoga as "stilling the fluctuations of the mind." There is no difference between these definitions, says Iyengar. The two practices "meet at a certain point."[4] If you intentionally practice one, you end up practicing the other. Focused intellectual study goes hand in hand with focused breathing.

According to traditional philosophical stereotypes of the psyche, emotion is playful, easily swayed by external events. Intellect is disciplined, directed, its focus sustained through a highly developed will. Both intellect and emotion are reflected in states of the breath: one in quick changes of depth and tempo, the other in a fixed and focused pattern. Both can be shaped through equally premeditated manipulations of the breath.

BREATH AND THE ESSENCE OF CONSCIOUSNESS

Intellect, emotion, and bodily awareness make up a trio that could be seen as a map of human consciousness. This is not an ad hoc generalization that I make in order to advance my argument. Rather, it is a very old and well-respected theory of consciousness that finds expression in Plato's map of the psyche as composed of reason (or thought), spirit (emotion), and appetite (sensation).[5] Some philosophers define essence as the *sine qua non*, that without which a thing would not be itself. In the simplest sense, humans cannot exist without the breath. A human being can exist for weeks without food, for days without water, but only for minutes without breath. In a more philosophically sophisticated sense, the particular states of all three faculties—thought, emotion, and sensation—the combination of which makes us distinctively human, are brought into being by the breath. Could I say, then, that breath is the essence of human consciousness? For centuries, the philosophical debate about human nature has pitted a view of mind as essential against a view of body as essential.[6] But both depend on the breath.

In positing breath as essence, I may be confusing what I might call the "fuel" of human consciousness with its essence. The word fuel suggests to me a machine, perhaps a car, so I shall think analogically for a moment, comparing the parts of a human being with the parts of a car. The essence of a car is its engine; the engine needs gas to run. On this analogy, breath would merely be the fuel for human consciousness. But perhaps my separation of an engine from its fuel is overly simplistic, for an engine is essentially designed to process fuel. Its essence is its ability to transform fuel into motion. On this version of the analogy, a human being appears as a breath processing machine. Our function is to take in oxygen and transform it into states of consciousness.

We could take this image of a breath processing machine even farther. Looking from the perspective of deep ecology, perhaps our main function is to support plant life. We take in raw material (oxygen) and transform it into nutrition for plants (carbon dioxide). A waste product generated by plants (oxygen) keeps us alive so that we can continue to sustain them. Our own consciousness is merely a wondrous by-product of the process, a gratuitous gift to be savored.

HUMAN ESSENCE AND THE ESSENCE OF REALITY

The description of breath as a gift takes me back to the image presented in Genesis 2:7, the second account of the creation of human beings presented in the Hebrew Bible. There God creates a body and breathes something divine into it, animating human consciousness. (Does this ever happen when you blow on a lump of dirt? No.) In the first account of the creation, God creates human beings, male and female, in the image of God. No details of the technology of this act are given. If the second account is read as an elaboration on the first, perhaps the breath is the image of God. The book of Genesis is a Hebrew text. Not surprisingly, Jewish mysticism has made much of this metaphor of God as breath. According to mainstream Jewish tradition, we know how to spell the name of God, but we do not know how to pronounce it. The letters are all open aspirants, yod, hey, vav, hey—Y, H, W, H. These are not consonants, but they are not vowels either. They direct us to open our mouths and breathe, but they do not tell us much about how to shape the breath into determinate sounds. Some Jewish mystics, however, depart from the traditional interpretation of our ignorance. Nothing is missing from this representation of God's name, they say. All the information on how to pronounce it is given. Take a deep breath in, and a slow breath out. *That* is the name of God.[7]

The root of the word "YHWH" means "being." Without knowing the Hebrew vowels that guide pronunciation, we do not know which tense of "being" is represented. So we assume that the name encompasses past, present, and future being simultaneously. The name of God is *Pure Being*. Choose your metaphor for giving this definition of God a more concrete application: everything that exists was created by God; everything that exists is a manifestation of God; everything that exists is a face of God. The mystical Hebrew understanding of God offers the most extreme vision of monotheism: a thoroughgoing pantheism. In yoga philosophy, breath is called "*prana*," the life force that animates all beings.[8] If I wed Hebrew mysticism with yogic practice, it turns out that God is the play of organic chemicals exchanged in the breath, and perhaps through other processes as well.

This image of God offered by a mystical monotheism is eerily similar to the image of a Godless universe presented by Hellenistic philosopher Lucretius. For Lucretius, the universe is an endless play of atoms taking different forms.[9] For Jewish mystics, and Hindu mystics who practice yoga, God is also an endless play of atoms taking different forms. Here the most extreme image of a God-permeated universe is identical with the most extreme image of a Godless universe. The debate about whether human beings are essentially mind or essentially body—the idealism/materialism debate—disappears, absorbed into the breath, if you will. The metaphysics of both coincide. Perhaps the question at the heart of the idealism-materialism debate, or at the heart of the mind-body problem is not really a metaphysical one. Perhaps the question raises an issue in what we might, for lack of a better word in the philosophical vocabulary, call "ethics." With what emotional attitude and behavioral choices shall we respond to reality? Shall we treat human beings as sacred reflections of an awesome divinity or as complex objects that help us achieve our material objectives?

MYSTICISM AND KNOWLEDGE

I began with a discussion about the essence of human consciousness and wandered off into a discussion about the essential nature of reality. This wandering, although pleasurable, makes the analytic part of my mind uncomfortable. For I may have said nothing enlightening at all about the essence of human consciousness by concluding that it is essentially the same as everything else. Or perhaps I have said something significant about the essential connectedness between human consciousness and the world, a connection forged at least partly through the breath. When I first read this essay to a small group of colleagues and fellow-travelers, I was not shy about my uncertainty. I asked them to help me understand what, if anything, I had accomplished philosophically. At first glance, their responses did not help me at all, but as I reflected on them later, I gained some insight.

Bill Gay, a phenomenologist and peace activist, immediately made connections between my words and his experiences. Hiking down to the floor of the Grand Canyon, he said, was an experience of altered consciousness. The air passing through his lungs changed drastically in composition from many feet above sea level to many feet below sea level; perhaps that was responsible for the experience. I replied by describing my experience up on the windy tundra, 10,000 feet above sea level. There meditation is effortless—the world seems to reach out and meditate you. Perhaps as the thin air fills your lungs, the atmosphere there literally does reach into you and change your consciousness. Bill added the fact that monasteries, centers for meditative retreat, are often built on mountaintops.

Marvin Croy, a specialist in logic and information technology, asked about the implications of my view for machine consciousness. He referred back to my analogy between human consciousness and a car. As an engine transforms gasoline and electrical sparks into motion, it relies on the mixing of gasoline with air. Can we then say, Marvin asked with some excitement, that machines breathe? And thus that they share a feature of human consciousness?

Dick Toenjes, an ethicist with a strong background in scholastic Catholic philosophy, was concerned that I had jumped too quickly to the conclusion that breath is the essence of human consciousness. How would I argue against an alternative hypothesis? Why not say, for example, that food is the essence of human consciousness? After all, we cannot live without it. I told Dick that I respected his question, and that I did not have a completely satisfactory answer for it. After all, food intake does change our consciousness, although not always as quickly as breathing does; and we cannot live without food, although we can live longer without eating than without breathing. Perhaps, I said, I am simply falling back on a long tradition in philosophy and theology of identifying breath with life.

At this point in the discussion, Judith Presler, a scholar of ancient philosophy, reinforced my appeal to tradition. She recalled my reference to Plato's theory of the psyche, informing us that the Attic Greek word *psyche* translates literally as "breath." So, for Plato, reason, emotion, and sensation are all aspects of the breath. Plato's word, of course, is always the first and last word in philosophy, so discussion ended here.

Bill's, Marvin's, and Judith's responses seem to have moved along one track, and Dick's response seems to have moved along another track. The two tracks are parallel, and can run without touching one another. Bill, Marvin, and Judith did not need the logical clarity Dick sought in order to take hold of my conclusion and extend its reach. Dick did not need an experiential grasp of my theory in order to question it logically. Each track lays down a different road to knowledge, perhaps even aims toward a different definition of knowledge.

Normally, we think we know something when we get it right. Truth is the agreement of knowledge with its object, we say. Knowing is the result of processing information from the external world and connecting it logically with other, reliable information from the external world. We trust that a person knows something when they can point to their concrete evidence and lay out its connections to their conclusion. This is a classic philosophical theory of knowledge. The most famous philosophers of the early modern era, Descartes and Leibniz, clearly wrote that experience plus logic, if both are applied correctly, yield knowledge.[10]

This conception of knowledge seemed to animate Dick's question about food as essence. Dick did not doubt the accuracy of my reports on my personal experiences. He did not question whether I had represented my sources correctly. His only concern was that I had not adequately articulated the logical connections between my experiences and my conclusion. By his standards, I had leapt far too quickly from the premises "breath is indispensable to human life" and "breath affects our consciousness" to the conclusion "breath is the essence of human consciousness." And he is right. From a traditional philosophical perspective, I have not adequately demonstrated knowledge of my thesis.

Bill, Marvin, and Judith, however, did not care if I had demonstrated a proper logical connection between my experiences and my thesis. Instead, they saw other kinds of connections. They grasped whatever strands looked interesting to them, wove their own thoughts around them, and emerged with their own ideas seeming larger and more far-reaching. To borrow words again from Husserl, less pejoratively this time, perhaps they sought "fulfillment" rather than knowledge.

In his own work, Husserl is careful to explain that he is studying consciousness, not knowledge. So when he tries to understand the way we think, he does not look for connections between the contents of consciousness and the external world. He does not bring a preconceived notion of how logical connections between the various contents of consciousness must be structured. Instead he studies the many different ways that our conscious experiences connect with one another. He calls these connections "fulfillments." For example, a memory that pops up when one wonders about the past can seem to fulfill a vague notion; a sensation that evokes a dream can seem to fulfill the dream; an experience of the external world can seem to fulfill a theory.[11]

I understand the word *fulfillment* literally—making the contents of our consciousness fuller, filling experiences with other experiences. All four of my colleagues were pursuing different ways of "fulfilling" their own consciousness with my thoughts about the breath. Bill fulfilled his memory of hiking the Grand Canyon, adding to the experience of changed consciousness a theory about its physiological cause. Marvin fulfilled his theories about machine consciousness, adding another analogy to the many he sees between human and computer information processing. Judith fulfilled her interpretation of Plato, gaining additional support that her nuanced translation was correct. Dick may have been moved to wonder about the role of the body in human consciousness, but he did not add the dimension of breath to any of his memories or theories. Perhaps I could say he fulfilled his views about logical process, particularly when

I acknowledged that he had applied them correctly in assessing my lack of a good argument.

In retrospect, I was not offering an argument, really, but an opportunity for fulfillment. Your reflection on the breath itself, your willingness to observe its role in your own consciousness, are indispensable to the successful fulfillment of my ideas. Your ability to plant in your imagination the seeds of the metaphor of breath as divine spirit, and your willingness to watch it bear fruit, are the kinds of participation that bring about the fulfillment of my ideas. No wonder I call my presentation a mystical one rather than a philosophical one. Mystics often say their understanding defies conventional knowledge, that it cannot be grasped using the usual categories of logic. They communicate mystical experience through metaphor. They speak of the willingness to change one's consciousness. In terms of knowledge, I believe they are speaking of fulfillment, of watching ideas blossom within other lived experiences, of breathing life into metaphors—so to speak.

NOTES

1. Edmund Husserl, *The Crisis of European Science and Transcendental Phenomenology*, trans. David Carr (Evanston, IL: Northwestern University Press, 1970).
2. Rabbi Nosson Scherman, *The Chumash: The Torah with a Commentary Anthologized from the Rabbinic Writings* (New York: Mesorah, 1994).
3. B.K.S. Iyengar, *The Tree of Yoga* (Boston: Shambhala Press, 1989).
4. Ibid.
5. Plato, *Republic*, trans. Allan Bloom. (New York: Basic Books, 1991).
6. Paul Churchland, *Matter and Consciousness* (Cambridge, MA: MIT Press, 1988).
7. Marcia Prager, *The Path of Blessing* (New York: Bell Tower, 1998).
8. Iyengar, 178.
9. Lucretius, *On the Nature of Things*, trans. Anthony Esolen (Baltimore: Johns Hopkins University Press, 1995).
10. Stephen M. Cahn, Classics of Western Philosophy (Indianapolis: Hackett, 1990).
11. Edmund Husserl, *Ideas. A General Introduction to Pure Phenomenology*, trans. W.R. Boyce Gibson (London: Allen and Unwin, 1931).

STUDY QUESTIONS

1. Why does Kaplan believe that "breath" is a better description of human essence than the traditional concepts of body, mind, and soul?
2. Are you comfortable with a description of God as a universal life force?
3. What does it mean to say that fulfillment is a type of knowledge? How do you fulfill the ideas in this essay?

The Wrong Moment to Exit

James Adrian Marshall

James Adrian Marshall, the son of a philosophy professor, works as a statistical analyst for a large bank. He is still not sure where life's many twists and turns will lead him.

I AM HAVING much trouble with this paper about philosophy and ordinary life that I am supposed to write for class. Writer's block, I guess; but true writers should be offended by my use of the term. The only useful piece of learning that came out of Freshmen English was: "when stuck . . . just write." So here I am, just writing.

I complained out loud to my girlfriend, Frances, that the paper's topic is flawed. I think that the topic possesses an error of assumption: possibly no ordinary life situation led me to think of philosophical ideas. But rude pride in my philosophical nature interrupted that line of reasoning.

Nonetheless, for over a week I have been kicking this idea around in my head; and yet, I have nothing about which to write. I am also quick to blame my memory, or lack thereof. On more than one occasion, I have been involved in conversations about personal memory. I take from those conversations that my memory is weak. One theory—my stepfather's—is that because I lived in the same room of the same house for eighteen years, I was never presented with a need to remember anything; since my immediate environment never changed, my "skills" were never strongly developed. Neat theory, though I don't buy into it. Moreover, discussion of how memory works is hardly philosophic.

I feel technically justified to argue that by definition, "ordinary life situation" lends itself to being not remembered. I guess I need someone to blame besides myself for not having an inspired story to tell.

Still, how can I present the ideas that subsequently flowed from an event if I am not currently aware that the ideas ever existed? Even if I do remember the general occasion, I will doubtfully remember the details of my thoughts.

I could blame my years of statistical training for overshadowing my self-reflecting side. I can say with a straight face that my general thinking these days does come from a very numerical foundation. But, as my graduate statistics class is proving with little doubt, I never really studied statistics very much. I guess that is a commentary on the current status of a college education, but I always did very well in statistics without doing any real work. By no stretch of the imagination can I blame anything on "my years of statistical training." But the declining quality of a college education doesn't fit this assignment either.

I thought enough to dig out an old edition of *Coastal Plains Poetry,* which contains two of my father's poems. I hoped that this poetry might trigger a memory of mine. At the very least, I expected to be put in an autobiographical, reflective mood. But all I found were poems. The were about my family, and I still didn't understand them. Poetry . . . ugh.

I read James Carse's essay "Shadows in the Eyes of God," in which his son frees a fish instead of eating it. Naturally I thought about my own fish story. I reread an essay that my best friend Randall wrote while in grad school that was published in a college journal. The essay was about the time four of us from the neighborhood caught a fish, blew it up with firecrackers, and were subsequently chastised by the police.

I guess we were not as humane as Carse's family.

Regardless, the short story was pretty much fiction. (Although he submitted under the category of nonfiction, Randall has confessed that he had to spice up the story to give it some life.) In the published version, I was central to the events. My memory is that I was a bystander. I know for certain that I had nothing to do with the actual catching of the fish. I hated fishing—boring, dirty, smelly, gross. I much prefer not to know from where my meals come. I do remember being in the parking lot when the police came to break up our little party.

The Greenville police had little better to do than chase the dreaded fish murderers. I mean, citizens could not sleep peacefully at night knowing that our rogue band of fourteen-year-olds were terrorizing parking lots with dead, mutilated fish. Sorry, I digress.

I do remember that I got away and the other three didn't. They knowingly ran into a dead end. I never understood that move. I also remember feeling the need to go back outside to check on my friends. I had made it safely to my house (only across the street from their capture), so I decided to change shirts just in case the police only saw my clothes. At the time I thought that was a very crafty move on my part.

Anyway, I came upon the three of them talking to an officer and calmly gave myself up. What I remember most is having to vouch for their honesty. You see, their last names were Kasperik, Martoccia, and Tschetter, too much for a small-town Greenville police officer to believe. But considering we were fourteen, I always thought that the peculiarity of the names reeked of honesty. Smith, Jones, and Williams sound fake. But, again, these were Greenville police officers.

Nothing too philosophical came from that encounter. Or, if it did, I have since forgotten the revelations.

The story did begin a stroll down the "trouble with the law" section of memory lane. I was in trouble with the law quite often. The irony of my misspent youth is that there is a very weak, if not negative, correlation between my behavior and being in trouble. The time I was taken downtown for the destroyed vending machine, I was guilty only by association; the time of the paper machine larceny, I volunteered as the headman because I knew my parents would handle "the phone call" the best; the time I spent a weekend in Duvall County Prison for reckless driving, I was driving as legally as I ever had in my life. These are just a few examples. The countless times I behaved regrettably, I rarely faced the consequences.

That last bit spins my brain off in a "what if" direction. Maybe if I had more reason to understand the connection between my actions and my lot in life, I would have accomplished more. Being thirty years old and an undergraduate student does make me wonder occasionally how much potential I wasted. But that type of an analysis is more fitting in a psychology class.

Yet, the "I wonder how different life would be if . . ." line of thought reminds me of something. There was one time that I got caught when actually doing something wrong, which does begin a new fork of thinking that could be considered philosophic.

While in high school, I committed several vehicular moving violations. The three least of these were noticed by the police. Within one month, I was issued three citations. The result was an automatic loss of my license for thirty days. After that period expired, I could hardly afford to insure myself, so I went without a license. I thought little of it because I had no shot at getting a car anyway. As for dates, I would borrow Randall's car, playing the percentages that if I had already been pulled over three times, chances were that I would not be pulled over during my rare dates. Life clicked along without police intervention for the rest of high school.

The summer after graduation, my mom made a stunning offer. She had a colleague who wanted to sell his car. She knew him well, he had taken great care of the car, and since he was getting a company car, he was willing to sell it to her for very little. The car was also a Volkswagen Scirocco, one of my absolute favorites. As a reward for "earning" a Teaching Fellows scholarship at Elon College—room, board, books, tuition, pocket money, the whole nine yards—my mom offered to buy me the car and pay for the insurance. The only catch was that I had to maintain good grades.

I was as excited as I could get. The offer came on Thursday. That Friday, I was to leave for Hendersonville to spend a week with Randall at his family's mountain house. On returning, I would then buy the car.

Well, before this deal came along, I had convinced Randall to ride to the mountains with his parents in their car. I would drive his car up after I finished my week of work (I think I was working at an ice-cream parlor at the time).

As planned, I left Friday for Hendersonville in Randall's car. Somewhere in Catawba County I was pulled over for speeding. I had no license, no way of proving who I was, and no way to explain possession of the car since I couldn't rat out Randall for giving his car to someone without a license. Rightly, the officer should have arrested me. Instead, he gave me a citation for 98 in a 45. (The speed limit was really a 65, but I was in no position to argue. He claimed that the area was a work zone.)

I could forget getting my license back.

I had to call my mom and make up some excuse for why I didn't want to buy the car. I lost my license for another year and spent both years at Elon College without a car.

I blame much of my failure at Elon on feeling trapped in a horribly small town. I had no way to escape the walls of the campus. I truly believe that if I had a car I would have been acceptably happy. Then, possibly, I would not have flunked all my classes my fourth semester there and would have gone to Europe my fifth semester as planned. A semester in Europe had been the original enticement to attend Elon. Though the school chose not to drop me from the Teaching Fellows program, they did decide that I needed another year to settle down and get back on track before going abroad. If Europe had still been an option, I probably would never have transferred to a large university and who knows where I would be now. Probably teaching somewhere.

My point, which gets lost in the story, is that very small decisions, ones seemingly inconsequential, can have major life altering impacts.

To make my point more clearly, let me explain the details of the ticket itself. I got the ticket because I exited an off ramp and hit the gas pedal before checking my surroundings. The state trooper just happened to be a quarter mile behind me when I exited. If I had simply merged at a different moment (say I took longer at the gas station where I had stopped to use the restroom or had taken a different exit) or if the cop had made any decisions differently than he did—hell, if I had simply waited two miles before flooring the pedal—my life could have been significantly different. To my thinking, whether or not to use the bathroom at a gas station is a minor decision. Yet, the outcomes of the two possible choices are conceivably quite divergent.

What struck me about the incident was not "poor me, why is my life so ill fated"; instead I was stunned how such small, unrelated events can, without warning or announcement, greatly alter one's life.

I will quickly grant you that some decisions are obviously very important. Others seem run-of-the mill, yet are very defining. A simple example is accidental deaths. In those instances, think of all the things that could have changed the outcome. The decision whether to push through a yellow light or to stop at it changes your location on this earth by two seconds. If anything tragic happens during the remainder of the drive, that decision becomes crucial.

Who knows what different events could take place if you do stop for a donut before work? Maybe you meet someone new, who becomes the contact for a new job. Maybe playing golf at three instead of three-thirty causes you to meet your future spouse. Or maybe you just miss an encounter with someone who would alter your life because you decided to change your outfit one last time before leaving the house.

Just think about your life being a path of constant forks! And the only result we are aware of is the one chosen. The "what if" game becomes mind-blowing.

Last semester I did a lot of research into the philosophy of the sublime, mostly as connected to art. I liked the idea of the mind expanding until it cannot expand anymore, yet still be unable to completely comprehend a work of art. The closest I come to relating to this concept of expanding but still not comprehending is thinking about a nonpredestined life and the exponential possible outcomes. Though I typically enjoy badgering myself with what is basically inconceivable for me, I usually end up with the same conclusion. Since these decisions do not have knowable outcomes, there is no point in fretting over them.

Nonetheless, Frances and I stayed up late one night, drinking wine and discussing all the crazy instances of "fate" that allowed us to be together. I still do not believe in an invisible hand guiding our fate. Yet, I do marvel at all the little things that had to fall just the way they did in order for me to be here and now. She and I came up with dozens of petty instances that were probable and would have made our getting together very unlikely. And since I am equally astonished at how happy I have become, I view these quirks of fate as wondrous.

Funny, six months ago I thought that the very same quirks proved that I was a cursed individual. My, how the tide has changed.

STUDY QUESTIONS
1. What is Marshall's understanding of the relationship between actions and their consequences?
2. Do human beings live a life with no predestined events and an infinity of possible outcomes?
3. How do you understand moral responsibility if human beings are completely free? If they are completely determined?

The Malice of Inanimates

Charles W. Harvey

Charles Harvey, professor of philosophy at the University of Central Arkansas, is the author of two books and many articles on phenomenology, the self, and social criticism. His book *Conundrums: A Book of Philosophical Questions* (1995) is an idiosyncratic introduction to the great problems of philosophy in the form of a coffee-table book.

> *Human being has been delivered over to beings which it needs in order to be as it is.*
>
> —Martin Heidegger

I LOST MY car twice. And though I was drunk both times that it vanished, it wasn't my fault. The first time, when I walked out of the bar, it just wasn't there. It wasn't where I parked it, nor was it anywhere near where I had been. So I walked home. Then, I was like you. I blamed myself. I'd find it tomorrow. I'd walk over to campus, stroll through the halo of bars that fringed the university, and I'd find the car where I left it. When I did, I'd remember leaving it wherever I found it. "Stupid me." I'd say, "what a drunk fool."

But I didn't find it. I looked all around. I checked the lots of the pubs philosophers frequented, I checked the campus spots where I usually parked, I

Reprinted with permission from Charles W. Harvey, "The Malice of Inanimates," *Phenomenological Inquiry* 19 (October 1995).

asked friends who had been with me that day. They didn't know. I had appeared at "Bullwinkles" alone. I'd said nothing about how I'd gotten there.

After two days of searching, reluctantly, I called the police. They found it, of course, after a couple more days. It was in uptown Tallahassee, near some jazz bars I patronized. The keys were in the ignition, the car was undamaged. It was locked, with no sign of having been vandalized. My girlfriend hadn't been happy about the car disappearing (it was really her car). And she never believed (doesn't today, even as my wife), that *I* didn't lose it. The police thought the same way. "Nobody stole it," they said. "No evidence of that."

For weeks, however, I had not been in that section of town. I had had the car yesterday. So while I acquiesced in the common view of these things— "blame the person, not the thing"—I sheltered my suspicions. One more bit of evidence for a conclusion I subconsciously held but could not admit consciously: the inanimates were going away.

The second time there could be little doubt. When I awoke in the morning and walked out to my car, it just wasn't there. I was late already. I had my class to teach shortly. So I walked fast to campus. My subject that day was David Hume's argument concerning "skepticism with regard to the senses." I had a ready example of his thesis that there is *no evidence* and *there cannot be any* to show that inanimates persist when we don't perceive them.

Lecture over, I called the police. They were skeptical with regard to my senses. They listened, however. A few hours later, Dot, the philosophy secretary, sent a message. "The police say that your car is in front of your house. I don't ask questions anymore, Harvey; I only take messages."

They blamed me, of course. I had even made the mistake of calling Jeanne to see if she had taken the car. "I didn't take it," she said. "You'd better find it."

I went home. There it was. Not *exactly* where I usually parked it. One house down, to the right of my front door. But there's *no way* I could have missed it when I walked out of my door, and *no reason* I would have parked it there. The two houses were part of a foursome arranged in a square. Each of us parked right in front of our respective doors. The cars couldn't be missed when we stepped outside.

Once again, I swallowed the common view as if it were fact—"blame the person, not the thing"—but now I knew in my heart that the car had *popped-out, gone right out of being*. And it had done so deliberately—to get me. Once the inanimates get you on the ropes—and what better candidate than a drunken philosopher?—they show you no mercy. I had to be cautious. These were bold moves on the part of my enemies. Until now only small entities had popped-out. In that way they had kept me blaming myself. The fact that a large being such as a car had twice popped-out on me gave me reason to worry—and to think. Here is my story, my evidence, and my thesis about our reluctant war with inanimates.

DAVID HUME WAS, to my knowledge, the first to provide philosophical grounds for what we have always known but have been afraid to admit: inanimates are not to be trusted, they are unpredictable, they are obstinate, they are ornery and sometimes downright malicious—and, they are out to get us. Hume didn't say *exactly* this, but he provided the reasons to believe it just might be so. He was the first to admit that it is mere animal prejudice to believe that inanimates persist when no one perceives them. But even he didn't conceive just how malicious inanimates are.

In an anxious episode in *The Centaur*, John Updike shows us: George Caldwell and son, Peter, are returning from school, late. Foolishly, stubbornly, in an automobile unfit for the task, Caldwell has decided to get home before the Pennsylvania blizzard bars access. Their automobile fails in its attempt to climb an icy hill. At the bottom of the hill—snow on the ground already deep, snow in the air still swirling—Caldwell and son must put chains on their tires; if they cannot, they will die.

They must jack up the car. First try: the automobile spits the jack from under itself. "Jesus," says Caldwell, "this is a way to get killed." They try again, but it is too dark for their eyes to see, too cold for their numb fingers to feel. The father tries. The son watches the father fail. "With a sob or curse blurred by the sound of the storm Caldwell stands erect and with both hands hurls the tangled web of iron links into the soft snow. The hole it makes suggests a fallen bird." Peter tries next. But "as he drapes the cumbersome jacket of links around the tire, the tire lazily turns and shucks its coat of mail like a girl undressing." He tries again. A little catch is the secret to life. "Only a tiny gap remains to close. . . . He prays, and is appalled to discover that, *even when a microscopic concession would involve no apparent sacrifice of principle, matter is obdurate.* [My emphasis.] The catch does not close. He squeals in agony, *'No!'*"

Updike's insight: One mistake from minded-beings and unminded ones take charge of their destiny. Not only do inanimates refuse human request, they scorn human endeavor. The image of the fallen bird in the snow mocks Caldwell's overly-reflective, other-world values; it submerges that which would fly (a bird, the winged horse, Caldwell himself) into that which has fallen and stuck fast to Earth. And Peter, who, along with most of the male species, will have his share of difficulties undressing girls, can't, to save his life and that of his father, keep this rubber maiden dressed in her chain-mail belt.

One time or another, though usually in circumstances less dire than these, we have all had this kind of experience. A catch, a latch, a microscopic concession of matter, and our problems are solved. But does matter consent? Virtually never. And when it does, it is usually too late. The pants are bepissed when the zipper unlocks, the TV mystery solved when electricity returns, the human being is *dead* when, all by itself, the catch drops into place.

Again and again, great literature recounts this experience. Think only of the inanimate snow that kills the fire whose absence kills the man in Jack London's "To Build a Fire." A person dies because of the malice of matter. And here, too, the author gives an "objectivistic" explanation of the event. He blames the man. Or think of Ivan Illich's horrified disbelief when he looks at the window knob that ruptured his liver that ruptured his life. "Is it really so!" Illich says to himself. "I lost my life over that curtain as I might have done when storming a fort. Is that possible? How terrible and how stupid. It can't be true! It can't but it is."

Literature has, in these cases, described a region of being where metaphysics has not dared to tread; a region in which philosophical metaphysics has followed daily belief and fled true explanation. But in spite of its many heart-rending accounts, literature, too, has failed to save the phenomena; it has chosen to explain it away—quite *in spite of* the evidence of each minded-being.

Are inanimate objects *merely* stupid and obdurate, as these writers suggest? Merely blind non-actors, automatons of cause? Or perhaps, are even the great authors to whom I've referred afraid of a deeper, darker, more sinister truth? A truth so sinister, in fact, that neither artists nor philosophers have been able to mouth it, perhaps not even to *think* it? Might it not be that inanimates are *inimical* towards human aspirations and hopes? As we will see, it wasn't merely "an imperceptible agitation to the tree," that brought from the boughs a load of snow that doused the man's fire. Nor should Ivan Illich have felt unheroic and stupid about the cause of his death. He died a warrior in a guerrilla war that has paralleled, moment by moment, the history of humankind.

UPDIKE'S PREFERRED WORD, "obdurate," is really too passive for the phenomena we want to describe. *Webster* defines "obdurate" as "hardened, not giving in to persuasion, unyielding." It defines "obstinacy" as "stubbornness, the quality or state of being difficult to remedy, relieve, or subdue." Certainly, these are characteristics of the inanimates. But these are their quiet, less aggressive features—the ones we can bear to acknowledge. "Orneriness" gets closer to the phenomena. It is described as "tending towards an irritable disposition, cantankerousness." "Malice" is the best word of all: "the desire to harm others, or to see others suffer; ill will; spite." And add "inimical" to this: "having the disposition of an enemy; hostile; being adverse by reason of hostility or malevolence." These last, I think, reveal the essence of inanimates. Consider examples.

The most common experience with the inimical ways of inanimates occurs with socks and with underwear. These inanimates are malicious most often because they *can be*. They can be because they are small and usually mixed with other inanimates. They can pop-out without giving away the plot of inanimates to make miserable the lives of the animates. Repeatedly I (and you) have placed socks or underwear into the wash, and they've been gone when the washing was done. I am well aware of the common hypotheses here: "Oh, you must have forgotten to put them in the wash in the first place," says my wife. "Well, where

THE MALICE OF INANIMATES 249

are they *now*?!" I ask. "If I didn't put them in the wash, they should at least be somewhere!" Of course, they are usually nowhere, until a day or two later—most likely, the day *after* I buy a new set of socks or of underwear.

"They were stuck to some other clothes," you are probably thinking. Well, I, at least, haven't been accused by students or colleagues of having underwear stuck to my shirt or my trousers. Nor do I know of anyone who has been so accused. Indeed, knowing how common this explanation is, I have kept a vigilant eye on colleagues, students, and strangers, in cities the world over. Not once have I seen underwear or socks clinging to trousers, shirts, dresses, blouses, hats, or even to sweaters. The reason is clear if you'll only admit it: the socks or underwear simply *popped-out of Being*.

Similar experiences often occur with pencils, pens, shoes and glasses. How many times have you placed one of these objects beside or directly in front of yourself, turned away for a moment, looked back, reached for the object and found it was gone? And what did you do? Blamed yourself! But *why* blame yourself? Again, the answer is clear. The slight embarrassment of seeming stupid is psychologically and metaphysically less disturbing than is the gnawing fear that arises with the truth about inanimates.

Inanimates are ornery, malicious, inimical towards the life-plans of animates. And really, you already knew this. Recall only how many times you have retaliated against malicious inanimates. How many times have you smashed a door after it slammed on your face? How often have you kicked hell out of an end-table after it gouged one of your shins? Don't college students even today burn their math books after a semester of one-way harassment? Don't be ashamed or embarrassed about the revenge that you've taken. In the war of ontological kinds, pay-back is always fair game.

THE FUNDAMENTAL VIRTUE required to acknowledge the malice of inanimates is *courage*. Courage, because understanding the metaphysics of malice requires that we acknowledge the sinister intents of the seemingly benign material webwork that girds our lives—and quite often *ends* them as well.

Inanimates s[d]eek revenge.

(Take note of this very sentence as an example! I'm leaving the "d" here because I wrote this word correctly a half-dozen times. Each time I printed the document it said "deek" instead of "seek." The inanimates don't want my case intelligibly made. I'll compromise. We'll have it both ways.)

For two full years a former colleague and friend—a theologian mind you—had a lower case "m" that appeared in the margin of everything he wrote. He never knew why. Could it have stood for "malice," or "mischief," or even "Mephistopheles"? He finally printed his essays with the "m" in them and whited-out the little sucker once the papers were printed. And for years, too, whenever I have written the word "sold"—sorry, "soul" (damn!)—in philosophical essays, it has appeared as "sold" when I printed the essay. I accept this. The battle goes on.[1]

As I was saying, there is a passive but persistent ferocity at the heart of inanimate Being. This ferocity, perhaps generated from resentment at the animation of animates, is aimed at all and any unsuspecting animates—*just because they are animate.* And the more the animate creature refuses to acknowledge the evil workings of the inanimates, the more the poor creature is victimized. So let this essay serve as an edifying guide, as well as an ontological and metaphysical one—let it serve as warning and guide.

Here are two general rules about what *not* to do when encountering malice in objects. *Do not blame yourself and do not blame other animates.* Note how even fellows as courageous as Freud and Jack London still felt the need to blame humans for all of their mishaps. Here is how London blamed the man for his own death: "Each time he had pulled a twig he had communicated a slight agitation to the tree—*an imperceptible agitation,* so far as he was concerned, but an agitation sufficient to bring about the disaster." (My emphasis.) Why "imperceptible"? Because there was really no "agitation"! The snow dumped, plain and simple, because the opportunity arose. No other humans around, no explanation required. Written from the proper metaphysical perspective the story could be called "To Kill an Animate" rather than "To Build a Fire." But even London hesitated before this intolerable truth.

So, do not say "I didn't see it," when you have spent hours searching for a key that you finally find in a place you have looked a dozen or more times. *Don't blame yourself, because it wasn't there when you looked.* Inanimates can hide; they work together so the table somehow covers the key, makes it blend in, so that no animate being can see it. Sometimes, I suspect, an inanimate entity pops-out, de-ontologizes, only to re-ontologize just when the animate will look and feel the most idiotic. Or, even worse, it re-ontologizes at the very moment its usefulness has passed—useless by a few seconds, and there, suddenly, *it is.*

Don't blame other animates when inanimates befool you. Inanimates like nothing better than causing strife between animates. When your daughter says, "I put your keys right there when I was done playing with them!" believe her. Don't punish her when she is merely a victim. Stay calm, pretend you don't need the keys, say so aloud. The keys will reappear that much more quickly.[2]

The clinching experience in my life, the one that finally forced to conscious awareness the gruesome truth about things, occurred in relation to a copy of Nietzsche's *Antichrist* and a pair of nun's underwear. Jim Garrison, my graduate school buddy, had found in a back-street bookstore in Baltimore, an old, rare, hard-covered edition of Nietzsche's *The Antichrist*; a reward and a bracer, we figured, for our first Eastern Division American Philosophical Association trauma. Purchasing it, he drawered it with his clothes in the room of our big Baltimore hotel. When we returned from our day of sparse job interviews, he decided to page through it before we went off to drink and to dine. I was in bed.

A pair of women's underwear hovered above my face, landed there. I jumped up ready to wrestle. "Okay, Harvey, where the hell is my book! And why'd you put a pair of Jeanne's underwear in my drawer! Damned pervert!"

"What?!", I exclaimed. "What are you talking about?!"

"There's a woman's underwear in my drawer and no *Antichrist*!" he shouted.

I looked at the underwear. They were too big to be Jeanne's. "Look at this," I said, stretching the underwear as is done in the Hanes' underwear ads. "These can't be Jeanne's, these are size 60 or there'bouts."

"They are pretty big," he grudgingly admitted. "I don't care where you got 'em from Harvey. I don't care what kind of kinky tricks you're into these days. Just give me *The Antichrist*!"

"I don't have your damned *Antichrist*! Maybe the devil took it!"

"Well, where the hell is it?" he asked of the room. "Damn! I know I put it here." And I knew so too. I had seen him.

We tore through everything, my stuff and his (little that he had), but there was no sign of *The Antichrist*. It was gone, the fat lady's underwear mocking us both. It was time for some drinking. For reasons like these the long love affair between Philosophy and Bacchus hasn't proved fungible. Perhaps Bacchus would speak to us; tell us the truth. We'd by-pass the dining.

As we walked from the room, a group of nuns was exiting the elevator. They cackled like an electric storm, voices big with revealed metaphysical truth. Jim and I walked past them, then stopped in the corridor, stunned. The nun at the center of the astonished discourse held Jim's copy of *The Antichrist*. Why were they so excited? Why were they all focused on the book held by the stout nun in the center? Jim and I boarded the elevator, metaphysically punch drunk.

If we had not both had lives and beliefs that made us uncomfortable in the presence of nuns, we might have done something. But what could we have done? If the nuns had said the book appeared to them suddenly, out of the blue, what would we have responded? That Jim's copy had vanished, and we had the nun's underwear? What might this have done to the old nun's career? And *where* did the book appear when it appeared to the nun? Did it simply shift in space-time with the abode of her underwear? What would it have been like to be a nun, feel something sharp and bulky between your thighs, reach down and pull out an old battered copy of *The Antichrist*? And then what about us? Two young, jobless philosophers, away from big-treed Tallahassee, in the big city, looking for philosophical futures anywhere, gifted suddenly with a hefty nun's underwear in exchange for *The Antichrist*?! What omen was this? What *could* we possibly say?

Instinctively, each of us knew it was best not to talk. We couldn't have if we had wanted. Inanimates had de-animated our voices. Made us like them.

THAT NIGHT WE formulated the basics of the thesis I'm here putting forth. On a few technical points I remain stymied,[3] but the phenomenology of the whole thing is clear. Hume had been right when he argued that there is no evidence of "real" or "necessary" connection in any causal relation. It was mere animal prejudice—desire, fear, expectation—that made us posit causal consistency, object persistency. No more than Bertrand Russell's chicken, who waits for the farmer to feed it each morning, until one morning the farmer wrings its neck, do we know what morning will bring. The sun might be a fried egg tomorrow, your mustache a twitching caterpillar stuck to your face. Bread might no longer nourish us, rain might sizzle our flesh and burn to our bones. But here there is nought we can do. We are nourished at the bosom of inanimates; birth unto death. They are always around us, we need them for our animation. But lest you wish to end up like old Bertie's chicken, note well my concluding advice.

HERE ARE EIGHT tactics concerning what you *should do* to foil inanimates before they foil you. First, whenever moving an inanimate from one place to another, *take conscious note of it*. Say to yourself, "I am placing the pen on the desk," "I am putting my shoes in the closet," "these green socks are going into the wash," "into the drawer," and so on. Better, *write these things down*. Make notes to yourself about the slightest things possible. If you write the word "soul" and see it there on your monitor, write a note to yourself: "I wrote the word 'soul' and it said 'soul'—s-o-u-l—on page 10 of the essay on inanimates." At least in this way, if it comes out as "sold," you'll maintain confidence in yourself, know that you did it right. Third, and perhaps best of all, if there are others about, *say these things aloud* so the others can hear you and can later publicly confirm your behavior; you don't want them to think it is *you* who are crazy when things go astray. Fourth, *put numbers to use*: whenever you can, count things, say "there are five apples in the refrigerator," when you eat one, say "there are now four apples there." Do this with big things and small. If you own a car lot, number the cars just as you number the cans in your cupboard at home, as you number the eggs in your 'fridge, or the socks in your drawers. A fifth tactic is to *surprise the inanimates whenever you can*. Yank open the drawer just after you've closed it, double-check to see that nothing is changing or has already changed; pull open the dryer as soon as it's started, see if some particularly significant sock is still there. Or, like a close friend of mine, *buy socks all of the same color and brand*. (After reading my essay he collected them all and counted them. Naturally, there was an odd number. But in practical terms, he had outflanked the inanimates. The vanishing sock caused him no problem.) Some activities deserve special precautions—presenting a paper at a conference, for instance. Whenever I leave to give a paper I make what Jeanne calls the "paranoid check." As soon as I pull from the driveway, I stop the car and go through all of my luggage to see that everything, especially the paper I'll read, is still there. Of course, the paper *could* pop-out as soon as I close my briefcase, but this would provide too much evidence in support of my thesis and that is why, I think, it has not happened yet. The inanimates lose much of their sadistic reward once we get wise to their workings.

Here is a seventh strategy: *be prepared to out-wait the vanished inanimates*— they usually return. To this day, for instance, Jim Garrison keeps the nun's underwear right in his bookcase, among his Nietzsche books, where *The Antichrist* would have been placed. We are convinced that someday it will return—suddenly, there it will be, and the underwear will have returned to its rightful abode.

Take my word on these methods. They have worked well for me. I haven't lost an automobile in many years now. And my children, whom I've schooled, avoid much of the trouble into which others kids get. (They do, I admit, have a few special problems of their own, but that has much more to do with other human beings and their resistance to the truth than it has to do with non-animate beings. After repeated refusal to take responsibility for vanishing objects, for instance, their teachers make rash remarks concerning their characters. But I have taught my children well. They haven't yet succumbed to these popular pressures. Perhaps I might someday be forced to make a legal issue of all this, given the separation of church and state, and given that the fully rational behavior of my children is grounded in life-guiding metaphysical beliefs.)

Eighth, and finally, *do not relax your guard when things start going well*. This is precisely the opportunity for which inanimates wait. As soon as your guard goes down, you will once more blame yourself. You will say, "how did I miss those shoes in the middle of the floor!?" "How embarrassing that I did not know my glasses were right on my face! I must be going insane." Don't be deceived. And don't be embarrassed. Such occasions are inevitable in a guerrilla war, where one party tries to hide from its very existence, while the other party is constantly vigilant. Should Ivan Illich have thought his death from a knob ignoble and stupid? Much less so than dying while storming a fort? Not at all! His death was heroic, as have been so many others. He died in a war which neither he nor Tolstoy could admit exists. Knobbed down by sniper fire to the liver in the prime of his life, killed dead on life's ontological battlefield. And is it any surprise that precisely *Ivan Illich* died in this way? Not in the least. Was he not constantly vigilant that things remained where he put them? Was he not inordinately upset when things went astray? *He noticed*—that is the secret to his untimely demise. Without knowing it, Ivan's behavior spawned powerful enemies. All things in his home were against him. I can almost hear it now. The curtain rod says to the knob, "With such vigilant powers of observation, Ivan Illich might soon comprehend. Finish him off before he does." The knob did the deed.

And what about me? Shall I soon go the way of Illich, or Jack London's man in the snow? Possibly so. Indeed, I have fretted continually since I started this essay about when the garage door might suddenly fall (a curtain wouldn't be heavy enough), when the knob might lash out at my kidneys, or when the lawn-mower might roar into action. But perhaps it has been precisely my precautions based on my cognizance that have protected me. And now that I have made my thoughts public, I will, if I must, take my place next to Giodorno Bruno on history's torched stake of truth. I'll take my position next to the many seekers-of-truth who have sacrificed themselves for the good of the many. And I'll take strength from Pascal's magnificent words: "Through space the universe grasps me and swallows me up like a speck; through thought I [the thinking reed] grasp it." I, at least, have, and *will always have had*, the *gift* of an animate's awareness. You have it too. *Be(a)ware* of those beings without it.

NOTES

1. I need not be reminded of the Freudian explanation of such events. Freud's doctrine of parapraxes—slips of the tongue, and so forth—is a prime example of the extremes to which we will go in order not to recognize the truth about inanimates. Freud, too, it seems, was afraid to admit what was obvious. Hence, he conjured a fantastic theory about our tricking ourselves, albeit unconsciously, of course. For all of his courage, he too displayed what Nietzsche called the "aescetic's need": the need to maintain security by denying the brutal truths of the universe and by blaming ourselves for all that goes wrong. It is precisely the ontology that grounds this metaphysics of self-blame that I would like most to overcome with this essay.

2. In addition to the revolutionary implications of my thesis for psychology (n. 1, above) and physics (n. 3, below), it is deeply significant for ethics as well. While we have become increasingly aware of our ethical inconsistencies in relation to gender and species differences, we still operate with the most unreflective prejudices in relation to the ethics of inanimates. If an inanimate pops out on you, for instance, and your spouse accuses you of carelessness and neglect, you immediately plead innocent and (rightly) feel victimized and falsely accused. Yet when your spouse is in the same situation, you express neither sympathy nor understanding, and accuse him or her of carelessness and neglect! Think, just for a moment, how many divorces, broken homes, suicides and perhaps even murders would have been averted if only people had sooner admitted the truth about inanimates. (In a future work I hope to pursue the implications of my thesis for ethics, religion, art, and the various sciences.)

3. For instance, while my ontological paradigm is the first to show that Heisenberg's uncertainty principle holds for macro as well as microscopic objects, the full physics of malicious inanimates is still undetermined. Do the objects pop out of being entirely? Or do they simply change locations in space-time? While the later hypothesis preserves the law of the conservation of energy, it would have to function as a regulative ideal (as does Galileo's doctrine of free fall in a vacuum), because it could never be verified; there are simply too many places inanimates might pop to—to Venus, to Peoria, on the roof, or under the bed. But I will leave the physics of the thing to others. I will be satisfied in this work if I establish the research paradigm—the sweep-up work can be left to puzzle-solvers who come after me.

STUDY QUESTIONS

1. Harvey thinks philosopher David Hume is wrong to say "there can be no evidence that inanimate objects persist when we don't see them." What does Hume mean, and why does Harvey disagree?
2. How does this essay play with our usual methods of explaining our perceptions?
3. Why do we sometimes believe in realities we cannot see, and theories we cannot verify?